Conceptual Framework of
EDUCATIONAL PSYCHOLOGY

Conceptual Framework of EDUCATIONAL PSYCHOLOGY

Kamaleswar Talwar

ADHYAYAN PUBLISHERS & DISTRIBUTORS
NEW DELHI (INDIA)

Published by
ADHYAYAN PUBLISHERS & DISTRIBUTORS
4378/4B, 105, J.M.D. House, Murari Lal Street
Ansari Road Darya Ganj, New Delhi - 110002
Ph.: 011-23263018, 011-23277156, Fax: 011-23280028
Email: adhyayanpublishers@yahoo.com

Conceptual Framework of EDUCATIONAL PSYCHOLOGY

Edition 2011
ISBN 978-81-8435-228-3

Printed in India

Published by Harish Chandra Yadav for Adhyayan Publishers & Distributors, Laser Typeseting at A.V. Rao and Printed at Tarun Offset Printers, Delhi

Preface

Educational psychology is a distinct scientific discipline within psychology that includes both methods of study and a resulting knowledge base. It is concerned primarily with understanding the processes of teaching and learning that take place within formal environments and developing ways of improving the affiliated operations and procedures. Educational psychologists are interested in a wide variety of topics such as learning theories; teaching methods; motivation; cognitive, emotional, and moral development; and parent/child relationships.

Educational psychology can in part be understood through its relationship with other disciplines. It is informed primarily by psychology, bearing a relationship to that discipline analogous to the relationship between medicine and biology. Educational psychology in turn informs a wide range of specialities within educational studies, including instructional design, educational technology, curriculum development, organisational learning, special education and classroom management. Educational psychology both draws from and contributes to cognitive science and the learning sciences.

The text provides solid, up-to-date coverage of the foundational areas within educational psychology: learning, development, motivation, teaching, and assessment, combined with intelligent examination of emerging trends in the field and society that affect student learning, such as student diversity, inclusion of students with special learning needs, technology, etc. The book concentrates on core concepts and principles and gives readers an in-depth understanding of the central ideas of educational psychology. Its unique approach helps readers understand concepts by encouraging them to examine their own learning and then showing them how to apply these concepts as teachers.

Kamaleswar Talwar

Contents

1

Introduction to Educational Psychology

Educational psychology is the study of how humans learn in educational settings, the effectiveness of educational interventions, the psychology of teaching, and the social psychology of schools as organisations. The terms "educational psychology" and "school psychology" are often used interchangeably. In the US researchers and theorists are likely to be identified as educational psychologists, whereas practitioners in schools or school-related settings are identified as school psychologists. In the UK, however, this distinction is not made and the generic term for practitioners is "Educational Psychologist". Educational psychology is concerned with how students learn and develop, often focusing on subgroups, such as gifted children and those subject to specific disabilities.

Educational psychology can in part be understood through its relationship with other disciplines. It is informed primarily by psychology, bearing a relationship to that discipline analogous to the relationship between medicine and biology and also between Engineering and Physics. Educational psychology in turn informs a wide range of specialities within educational studies, including instructional design, educational technology, curriculum development, organisational learning, special education and classroom management. Educational psychology both draws from and contributes to cognitive science and the learning sciences. In universities, departments of educational psychology are usually housed within faculties of education, possibly accounting for the lack of representation of educational psychology content in introductory psychology textbooks.

1.1. Social, Moral and Cognitive Development

To understand the characteristics of learners in childhood, adolescence, adulthood and old age, educational psychology develops and applies theories of human development. Often cast as stages through which people pass as they mature, developmental theories describe changes in mental abilities, social roles, moral reasoning, and beliefs about the nature of knowledge. For example, educational psychologists have researched the instructional applicability of Jean Piaget's theory of development, according to which children mature through four stages of cognitive capability. Piaget hypothesised that children are not capable of abstract logical thought until they are older than about 11 years, and therefore younger children need to be taught using concrete objects and examples. Researchers have found that transitions, such as from concrete to abstract logical thought, do not occur at the same time in all domains. A child may be able to think abstractly about mathematics, but remain limited to concrete thought when reasoning about human relationships.

Piaget proposed a developmental theory of moral reasoning in which children progress from a naive understanding of morality based on behaviour and outcomes to a more advanced understanding based on intentions. There is evidence that the moral reasoning described in stage theories is not sufficient to account for moral behaviour.

Developmental theories are sometimes presented not as shifts between qualitatively different stages, but as gradual increments on separate dimensions. Development of epistemological beliefs have been described in terms of gradual changes in people's belief in: certainty and permanence of knowledge, fixedness of ability, and credibility of authorities such as teachers and experts. People develop more sophisticated beliefs about knowledge as they gain in education and maturity.

1.2. Individual Difference and Disabilities

Each person has an individual profile of characteristics, abilities and challenges that result from learning and development. These manifest as individual differences in intelligence, creativity, cognitive style, motivation, and the capacity to process information, communicate, and relate to others. The most prevalent disabilities found among schoolage children are attention-deficit hyperactivity disorder (ADHD), learning disability, dyslexia, and speech disorder. Less common disabilities include mental retardation, hearing impairment, cerebral palsy, epilepsy and blindness.

Although theories of intelligence have been discussed by philosophers since Plato, intelligence testing is an invention of educational psychology, and is coincident with the development of that discipline. Continuing debates about the nature of intelligence revolve on whether intelligence can be characterised by a single, scalar factor, multiple factors, or whether it can be measured at all. In practice, standardised instruments such as the Stanford-Binet IQ test and the WISC are widely used in economically developed countries to identify children in need of individualised educational treatment. Children classified as gifted are often provided with accelerated or enriched programmes. Children with identified deficits may be provided with enhanced education in specific skills such as phonological awareness.

1.3. Learning and Cognition

Two fundamental assumptions that underlie formal education systems are that students (a) retain knowledge and skills they acquire in school, and (b) can apply them in situations outside the classroom. Research has found that, even when students report not using the knowledge acquired in school, a considerable portion is retained for many years and longterm retention is strongly dependent on the initial level of mastery. There is much less consensus on the crucial question of how much knowledge acquired in school transfers to tasks encountered outside formal educational settings, and how such transfer occurs. Several perspectives have been established within which the theories of learning used in educational psychology are formed and contested. These include behaviourism, cognitivism, social cognitive theory, and constructivism.

1.3.1. Behaviour Perspective

Applied behaviour analysis, a set of techniques based on the behavioural principles of operant conditioning, is effective in a range of educational settings. For example, teachers can improve student behaviour by systematically rewarding students who follow classroom rules with praise, stars or tokens exchangeable for sundry items. Despite the demonstrated efficacy of awards in changing behaviour, their use in education has been criticised by proponents of self-determination theory, who claim that praise and other rewards undermine intrinsic motivation. There is evidence that tangible rewards decrease intrinsic motivation in specific situations, such as when the student already has a high level of intrinsic motivation to perform the goal behaviour. But the results showing detrimental effects are counterbalanced by evidence that, in other situations, such as when rewards are given for attaining a gradually increasing standard of performance, rewards enhance intrinsic motivation.

1.3.2. Cognitive Perspective

Among current educational psychologists, the cognitive perspective is more widely held than the behavioural perspective perhaps because it admits causally related mental constructs such as traits, beliefs, memories, motivations and emotions. Cognitive theories claim that memory structures determine how information is perceived, processed, stored, retrieved and forgotten. Among the memory structures theorised by cognitive psychologists are separate but linked visual and verbal systems described by Allan Paivio's dual coding theory. Educational psychologists have used dual coding theory and cognitive load theory to explain how people learn from multimedia presentations.

The spaced learning effect, a cognitive phenomenon strongly supported by psychological research, has broad applicability within education. For example, students have been found to perform better on a test of knowledge about a text passage when a second reading of the passage is delayed rather than immediate. Educational psychology research has confirmed the applicability to education of other findings from cognitive psychology, such as the benefits of using mnemonics for immediate and delayed retention of information.

Problem solving, regarded by many cognitive psychologists as fundamental to learning, is an important research topic in educational psychology. A student is thought to interpret a problem by assigning it to a schema retrieved from long term memory. When the problem is assigned to the wrong schema, the student's attention is subsequently directed away from features of the problem that are inconsistent with the assigned schema. The critical step of finding a mapping between the problem and a pre-existing schema is often cited as supporting the centrality of analogical thinking to problem solving.

1.3.3. Social Cognitive Perspective

Social cognitive theory is a highly influential fusion of behavioural, cognitive and social elements. The theory identifies several factors that determine whether observing a model will affect behavioural or cognitive change. These factors include the learner's developmental status, the perceived prestige and competence of the model, the consequences received by the model, the relevance of the model's behaviours and consequences to the learner's goals, and the learner's self-efficacy. The concept of self-efficacy, which played an important role in later developments of the theory, refers to the learner's belief in his or her ability to perform the modeled behaviour.

An experiment was conducted to study grade 2 students who had previously experienced difficulty in learning subtraction. One group of students observed a subtraction demonstration by a teacher and then participated in an instructional programme on subtraction. A second group observed other grade 2 students performing the same subtraction procedures and then participated in the same instructional programme. The students who observed peer models scored higher on a subtraction post-test and also reported greater confidence in their subtraction ability. The results were interpreted as supporting the hypothesis that perceived similarity of the model to the learner increases self-efficacy, leading to more effective learning of modelled behaviour. It is supposed that peer modeling is particularly effective for students who have low self-efficacy.

Over the last decade, much research activity in educational psychology has focused on developing theories of self-regulated learning (SRL) and metacognition. These theories work from the central premise that effective learners are active agents who construct knowledge by setting goals, analysing tasks, planning strategies and monitoring their understanding. Research has indicated that learners who are better at goal setting and self-monitoring tend to have greater intrinsic task interest and self-efficacy; and that teaching learning strategies can increase academic achievement.

1.3.4. Constructivist Perspective

Constructivism is a category of learning theories in which emphasis is placed on the agency and prior knowledge of the learner, and often on the social and cultural determinants of the learning process. Educational psychologists distinguish individual constructivism, identified with Piaget's learning theory, from social constructivism.

One view is that behaviour, skills, attitudes and beliefs are inherently situated, that is, bound to a specific sociocultural setting. According to this view, the learner is enculturated through social interactions within a community of practice. The social constructivist view of learning has spawned approaches to teaching and learning such as cognitive apprenticeship, in which the tacit components of a complex skill are made explicit through conversational interactions occurring between expert and novice in the setting in which the skill is embedded.

1.4. Motivation

Motivation is an internal state that activates, guides and sustains behaviour. Educational psychology research on motivation is concerned with the volition or will that students bring to a task, their level of interest and intrinsic motivation, the personally held goals that guide their behaviour, and their belief about the causes of their success or failure.

A form of attribution theory describes how students' beliefs about the causes of academic success or failure affect their emotions and motivations. For example, when students attribute failure to lack of ability, and ability is perceived as uncontrollable, they experience the emotions of shame and embarrassment and consequently decrease effort and show poorer performance. In contrast, when students attribute failure to lack of effort, and effort is perceived as controllable, they experience the emotion of guilt and consequently increase effort and show improved performance.

Motivational theories also explain how learners' goals affect the way that they engage with academic tasks. Those who have mastery goals strive to increase their ability and knowledge. Those who have performance approach goals strive for high grades and seek opportunities to demonstrate their abilities. Those who have performance avoidance goals are driven by fear of failure and avoid situations where their abilities are exposed. Research has found that mastery goals are associated with many positive outcomes such as persistence in the face of failure, preference for challenging tasks, creativity and intrinsic motivation. Performance avoidance goals are associated with negative outcomes such as poor concentration while studying, disorganised studying, less self-regulation, shallow information processing and test anxiety. Performance approach goals are associated with positive outcomes, and some negative outcomes such as an unwillingness to seek help and shallow information processing.

1.5. Psychology of Teaching and Learning

In the past two decades teaching has changed significantly, so much in fact that schools are not what some of us may remember from our own childhoods. The changes have affected both the opportunities and the challenges of teaching, as well as the attitudes, knowledge and skills that it takes to prepare for a teaching career. There are four new trends in education, at how the trends have changed what teachers do, and at how you will therefore need to prepare yourself to teach.

— *The first trend is toward diversity*: students today are more diverse in many ways. The diversity has made teaching more fulfilling as a career, but also made instructional planning more challenging in certain respects.

— *The second trend is toward instructional technology*: classrooms, schools, and students use computers today than in the past for research, writing, communicating, and keeping records. The use of technology has created new ways for students to learn, but in the process has altered how teachers can teach most effectively, and even raised issues about what constitutes "true" teaching and learning.

— *The third trend is toward accountability in education*: both the public and educators themselves are paying much more attention than in the past to how to assess (or provide evidence for) learning and good quality teaching. The attention has increased the importance of education to the public (a good thing) and also improved educational choices for some students. But it also may be creating new constraints on what teachers teach on what students learn.

— The fourth trend is toward increased the professionalism of teachers. Now more than ever, teachers are in positions to assess the quality of their own work as well as that of colleagues, and to take steps to improve it when or if it is necessary. This change gives teachers more opportunity to use their professional expertise, but it also creates higher standards of commitment and of practice and therefore greater worries about teaching "well enough."

1.5.1. Diversity in Students

Students have, of course, always been diverse in the sense that each student learns at his or her special pace and special way, each has a one-of-a-kind personality, and each shows a unique pattern of motives to learn.

1.5.1.1. Using technology to support learning

For most teachers and classrooms, "technology" means using computers and the Internet as resources for teaching and learning. In principle, these tools have greatly increased the amount and range of information available.

1.5.1.2. Accountability in education

In recent years, the general public and public leaders have begun expecting schools, teachers, and students to be more accountable for their work, meaning that schools and teachers are held responsible for their educational activities, and that students are held responsible for learning particular amounts or types of knowledge.

1.5.1.3. Increased professionalism of teachers

Whether you consider the first three educational trends worrisome, exicitng, or a mixture of the two, they have all contributed to a fourth trend in education, the increase in *professionalism* of teachers.

1.5.2. Teachers' Perspectives on Learning

For teachers, learning usually refers to things that happen in schools or classrooms, even though every teacher can of course describe examples of learning that happen outside of these places. In particular, teachers' perspectives on learning often emphasize three ideas, and sometimes even take them for granted:

— curriculum content and academic achievement,

— sequencing and readiness, and

— the importance of transferring learning to new or future situations.

1.5.3. Learning on Curriculum and Academic Achievement

When teachers speak of learning, they tend to emphasize whatever is taught in schools deliberately, including both the official curriculum and the various behaviours and routines that make classrooms run smoothly. In practice, defining learning in this way often means that teachers equate learning with the major forms of academic achievement—especially language and mathematics—and to a lesser extent musical skill, physical coordination, or social sensitivity.

The imbalance occurs not because the goals of public education make teachers responsible for certain content and activities (like books and reading) and the skills which these activities require (like answering teachers' questions and writing essays). It does happen not because teachers are biased, insensitive, or unaware that students often learn a lot outside of school.

A side effect of focusing learning on curriculum and academics is that classroom social interactions and behaviours become issues for teachers—become something that they need to manage. In the small space of a classroom, no other viewpoint about social interaction makes sense. Yet in the wider world outside of school, learning often does happen incidentally, "accidentally" and without conscious interference or input from others: I "learn" what a friend's personality is like, for example, without either of us deliberately trying to make this happen.

As teachers, we sometimes see incidental learning in classrooms as well, and often welcome it; but our responsibility for curriculum goals more often focuses our efforts on what students can learn through conscious, deliberate effort. In a classroom, unlike in many other human settings, it is always necessary to ask whether classmates are helping or hindering individual students' learning.

1.5.4. Dependence of Learning on Teaching

Focusing learning on changes in classrooms has several other effects. One, for example, is that it can tempt teachers to think that what is taught is equivalent to what is learned—even though most teachers know that doing so is a mistake, and that teaching and learning can be quite different.

1.5.4.1. Sequencing and readiness

The distinction between teaching and learning creates a secondary issue for teachers, that of educational readiness. Traditionally the concept referred to students' preparedness to cope with or profit from the activities and expectations of school. A kindergarten child was "ready" to start school, for example, if he or she was in good health, showed moderately good social skills, could take care of personal physical needs, could use a pencil to make simple drawings, and so on. At older ages (such as in high school or university), the term readiness is often replaced by a more specific term, prerequisites. To take a course in physics, for example, a student must first have certain prerequisite experiences, such as studying advanced algebra or calculus. To begin work as a public school teacher, a person must first engage in practice teaching for a period of time.

1.5.4.2. Transfer as a crucial part of learning

Still another result of focusing the concept of learning on classrooms is that it raises issues of usefulness or transfer, which is the ability to use knowledge or skill in situations beyond the ones in which they are acquired. Learning to read and learning to solve arithmetic problems, for example, are major goals of the elementary-school curriculum because those skills are meant to be used not only inside the classroom, but outside as well. We teachers intend, that is, for reading and arithmetic skills to "transfer"—even though we also do out best to make the skills enjoyable while they are still being learned.

In the world inhabited by teachers, even more than in other worlds, making learning fun is certainly a good thing to do, but making learning useful as well as fun is even better. Combining enjoyment and usefulness, in fact, is a "gold standard" of teaching: we generally seek it for students, and even though we may not succeed at providing it all of the time.

1.5.5. Theories and Models of Learning

Several ideas and priorities, then, affect how teachers think about learning, including the curriculum, the difference between teaching and learning, sequencing, readiness, and transfer. The ideas form a "screen" through which to understand and evaluate whatever psychology has to offer education. As it turns out, many theories, concepts, and ideas from educational psychology do make it through the "screen" of education, meaning that they are consistent with the professional priorities of teachers and helpful in solving important problems of classroom teaching. In the case of issues about classroom learning, for example, educational psychologists have developed a number of theories and concepts that are relevant to classrooms, in that they describe at least some of what usually happens there and offer guidance for assisting learning.

It is helpful to group the theories according to whether they focus on changes in behaviour or in thinking. The distinction is rough and inexact, but a good place to begin. For starters, therefore, consider two perspectives about learning, called behaviourism (learning as changes in overt behaviour) and constructivism, (learning as changes in thinking). The second category can be further divided into *psychological constructivism* (changes in thinking resulting from individual experiences, and *social constructivism,* (changes in thinking due to assistance from others).

1.5.5.1. Behaviourism

Behaviourism is a perspective on learning that focuses on changes in individuals' observable behaviours—changes in what people say or do.

— *Respondent Conditioning*: Learning New Associations with Prior Behaviours

— *Operant Conditioning*: New Behaviours Because of New Consequences

1.5.5.2. Constructivism

Behaviourist models of learning may be helpful in understanding and influencing what students do, but teachers usually also want to know what students are thinking, and want to enrich what they are thinking. For this aspect of teaching, some of the best help comes from constructivism, which is a perspective on learning focused on how students actively create (or construct) knowledge out of experiences.

1.6. Instructional Strategies

There are two broad categories of instruction, sometimes called direct instruction and student-centered instruction. Each of these approaches to teaching is useful for certain purposes. Although instructional strategies differ in their details, they all function to encourage certain major forms of learning and thinking, each with distinctive educational purposes. The forms sometimes overlap, in the sense that one form of thinking may contribute to a student's success with another form. There are three complex forms of thinking that are common goals of classroom learning:

— critical thinking,

— creative thinking, and

— problem-solving.

1.6.1. Critical Thinking

Critical thinking is the mental skill for analysing the reliability and validity of information, as well as an attitude or disposition to do so. The skill and attitude may be expressed or displayed with regard to a particular subject matter or topic, but in principle it can occur in any realm of knowledge or living. A critical thinker does not necessarily have a negative attitude in the everyday sense of being critical of someone or something. Instead he or she can simply be thought of as astute: the critical thinker asks key questions, evaluates the evidence for ideas accurately, reasons about problems logically and objectively, and expresses ideas and conclusions clearly and precisely. Last, the critical thinker can apply these habits of mind in more than one realm of life or knowledge, though he or she may not always do so in fact.

With such a broad definition, it is not surprising that educators have nominated a wide variety of specific cognitive skills as contributors to critical thinking. In one study, for example, the researcher found that critical thinking about a published article was stimulated by annotation—writing questions and comments in the margins of the article. In this study students who were initially instructed in ways of annotating reading materials. Later, when the students completed additional readings for assignments, it was found that some students in fact used their annotation skills much more than others—some simply underlined passages, for example, with a highlighting pen. When essays written about the readings were later analysed, the ones written by the annotators were found to be more well-reasoned—more critically astute—than the essays written by the other students.

But the skills comprising critical thinking are not just written ones. In another study, for example, a researcher found that critical thinking can also involve oral discussion with classmates of personal issues or dilemmas. In this study, students were asked to describe to classmates a recent personal incident that disturbed them. Classmates then discussed the incident together in order to identify the precise reasons why the incident was disturbing to the individual, as well as the assumptions that the student had made in thinking about the incident.

The original student—the one who had first told the story—then used the results of the group discussion to frame a topic for a research essay. In one story of a troubling incident, for example, a student told of a time when a store clerk has snubbed or rejected the student during a recent shopping errand. Through discussion, classmates decided that an assumption underlying the student's disturbance was her suspicion that she had been a victim of racial profiling based on her skin color.

The student then used this idea as the basis for a research essay on the topic of "racial profiling in retail stores." The group discussion thus stimulated critical thinking in the student and the classmates, but it also relied on their prior critical thinking skills at the same time.

Notice that in both of these research studies, as in others like them, what made the thinking "critical" was students' use of metacognition—strategies for thinking about thinking and for monitoring the success and quality of one's own thinking. There we pointed out that when students acquire experience in building their own knowledge, they also become skilled both at knowing how they learn, and at knowing whether they have learned something well. These two defining qualities of metacognition are part of critical thinking as well. In fostering critical thinking, then, a teacher is really fostering a student's ability to construct or control his or her own thinking and to avoid being controlled by ideas unreflectively.

How best to teach the skills of critical thinking, however, remains a matter of debate. One issue is whether to infuse critical skills into existing courses or to teach them through separate, freestanding units or courses. The first approach has the potential advantage of demonstrating how critical thinking relates to students' entire educations. But it does so at the risk of diluting students' understanding and use of critical thinking simply because critical thinking takes on so in many different forms—its details and appearance varying among courses and teachers. The freestanding approach has the opposite qualities: it stands a better chance of being understood clearly and coherently, but by the same token its connections to other courses, tasks, and activities may not be as clear to students. Unfortunately, research to compare the infusion versus freestanding strategies for teaching critical teaching does not settle the matter; it suggests that either approach can work as long as it is implemented thoroughly and the teachers are committed to the value of critical thinking.

A related issue about teaching critical thinking is about who needs or should learn critical thinking skills the most. Should it in fact be all students? This goal seems the most democratic and therefore appropriate for educators. Surveys of teachers have found, however, that teachers sometimes favour teaching of critical thinking to high-advantage students—the ones who already achieve well, who come from relatively high-income families, or (for high school students) who take courses intended for university entrance. Presumably the rationale for this bias is that high-advantage students can benefit and/or understand and use critical thinking better than other students. There is little evidence to support this idea, however, even if it were not ethically questionable.

1.6.2. Creative Thinking

Creativity is the ability to make something new that is also useful or valued by others. The "something" can be an object (like an essay or painting), a skill (like playing an instrument), or an action.

1.6.3. Problem-solving

Somewhere between open-ended, creative thinking and the focused learning of content lies problem solving, the analysis and solution of tasks and situations that are somewhat complex or ambiguous and that pose difficulties, inconsistencies, or obstacles of some kind.

1.6.4. Relationships of Major Instructional Strategies

Because the forms of thinking just described—critical thinking, creativity, and problem solving—are broad and educationally important, it is not surprising that educators have identified a lot of strategies to encourage their development. There are so many possibilities, in fact, that just keeping them all in mind—let alone choosing among them—can be difficult.

1.6.4.1. Lectures and readings

Lectures and readings are traditional staples of educators, particularly when teaching older students. At their best, they are the good examples of pre-organised information, so that the student only has to remember what was said in the lecture or written in the text in order to begin understanding it.

1.6.4.2. Mastery learning

This term refers to an instructional approach in which all students learn material to an identical, high level, even if some students require more time than others to do so. In mastery learning the teacher directs learning, though sometimes only in the indirect sense of finding, writing, and orchestrating.

1.6.4.3. Direct instruction

Sometimes this term serves as a synonym for teacher-directed instruction, but more often direct instruction refers to a relatively scripted version of mastery learning, meaning that it not only organises the curriculum into small modules or units, but it also dictates how teachers should teach, including.

1.6.4.4. Madeline Hunter's effective teaching model

Many teacher-directed strategies have been combined by Madeline Hunter into a single, relatively comprehensive approach that she calls mastery teaching (not to be confused with the related term mastery learning) or the effective teaching model.

1.6.4.5. Student-centered models of learning

Student-centered models of learning shift some of the responsibility for directing and organising learning from the teacher to the student. Being student-centered does not mean, however, that a teacher gives up organisational and leadership responsibilities completely. It only means.

You can see that choices among instructional strategies are numerous indeed, and that deciding among them depends on the forms of thinking that you want to encourage, the extent to which ideas or skills need to be organised by you to be understood by students, and the extent to which students need to take responsibility for directing their own learning. Although you may have personal preferences among possible instructional strategies, the choice will also be guided by the uniqueness of each situation of teaching—with its particular students, grade-level, content, and purposes.

1.6.5. Instructional Planning

Casey Stengel, a much-admired baseball coach, was talking about baseball when he made this remark. But he could easily have been speaking of teaching as well. Almost by definition, education has purposes, goals, and objectives, and a central task of teaching is to know these are and to transform the most general goals into specific objectives and tasks for students. Otherwise, as Casey Stengel said, students may end up "someplace else" that neither they, nor the teacher, nor anyone else intends. A lot of the clarification and specification of goals needs to happen before a cycle of instruction actually begins, but the benefits of planning happen throughout all phases of teaching.

If students know precisely what they are supposed to learn, they can focus their attention and effort more effectively. If the teacher knows precisely what students are supposed to learn, then the teacher can make better use of class time and choose and design assessments of their learning that are more fair and valid.

At the most general or abstract level, the goals of education include important philosophical ideas like "developing individuals to their fullest potential" and "preparing students to be productive members of society." Few teachers would disagree with these ideas in principle, though they might disagree about their wording or about their relative importance. As a practical matter, however, teachers might have trouble translating such generalities into specific lesson plans or activities for the next day's class.

What does it mean, concretely, to "develop an individual to his or her fullest potential"? Does it mean, for example, that a language arts teacher should ask students to write an essay about their personal interests, or does it mean that the teacher should help students learn to write as well as possible on any topic, even ones that are not of immediate interest? And what exactly should a teacher do, from day to day, to "prepare students to be productive members of society" as well? Answers to questions like these are needed to plan instruction effectively. But the answers are not obvious simply by examining statements of general educational goals.

1.6.5.1. National and state learning standards

Some (but not all) of the work of transforming such general purposes into more precise teaching goals and even more precise objectives has been performed by broad national organisations that represent educators and other experts about particular subjects or types of teaching. The groups have proposed national standards, which are summaries of what students can reasonably be expected to learn at particular grade levels and in particular subjects areas. In the United States, in addition, all state governments create state standards that serve much the same purpose: they express what students in the state should (and hopefully can) learn at all grade levels and in all subjects.

Because they focus on grade levels and subject areas, general statements of educational standards tend to be a bit more specific than the broader philosophical goals. As a rule of thumb, too, state standards tend to be more comprehensive than national standards, both in coverage of grade levels and of subjects. The difference reflects the broad responsibility of states in the United States for all aspects of public education; national organisations, in contrast, usually assume responsible only for a particular subject area or particular group of students.

Either type of standards provides a first step, however, toward transforming the grandest purposes of schooling (like developing the individual or preparing for society) into practical classroom activities. But they provide a first step only. Most statements of standards do not make numerous or detailed suggestions of actual activities or tasks for students, though some might include brief classroom examples—enough to clarify the meaning of a standard, but not enough to plan an actual classroom programme for extended periods of time. For these latter purposes, teachers rely on more the detailed documents, the ones often called curriculum frameworks and curriculum guides.

1.6.6. Curriculum Frameworks and Curriculum Guides

The terms curriculum framework and curriculum guide sometimes are used almost interchangeably, but for convenience we will use them to refer to two distinct kinds of documents. The more general of the two is curriculum framework, which is a document that explains how content standards can or should be organised for a particular subject and at various grade levels. Sometimes this information is referred to as the scope and sequence for a curriculum. A curriculum framework document is like a standards statement in that it does not usually provide a lot of detailed suggestions for daily teaching. It differs from a standards statement, though, in that it analyses each general standard in a curriculum into more specific skills that students need to learn, often a dozen or more per standard. The language or terminology of a framework statement also tends to be somewhat more concrete than a standards statement, in the sense that it is more likely to name behaviours of students—things that a teacher might see them do or hear them say. Sometimes, but not always, it may suggest ways for assessing whether students have in fact acquired each skill listed in the document. Teachers' need for detailed activity suggestions is more likely to be met by a curriculum guide, a document devoted to graphic descriptions of activities that foster or encourage the specific skills explained in a curriculum framework document. The descriptions may mention or list curriculum goals served by an activity, but they are also likely to specify materials that a teacher need, time requirements, for grouping students, drawings or diagrams of key equipment or materials, and sometimes even suggestions for what to say to students at different points during the activity. In these ways the descriptions may resemble lesson plans.

1.6.6.1. Formulating learning objectives

Given curriculum frameworks and guides like the ones just described, how do you choose and formulate actual learning objectives? Basically there are two approaches: either start by selecting content or topics that what you want students to know (the cognitive approach) or start with what you want students to do (the behavioural approach).

1.6.6.2. Taxonomies of educational objectives

When educators have proposed taxonomies of educational objectives, they have tended to focus on one of three areas or domains of psychological functioning: either students' cognition (thought), students' feelings and emotions (affect), or students' physical skills (psychomotor abilities). Of these three areas, they have tended to focus the most attention on cognition. The taxonomy originated by Benjamin Bloom, for example, deals entirely with cognitive outcomes of instruction.

1.6.6.3. Students as a source of instructional goals

The instructional planning has described goals and objectives as if they are selected primarily by educators and teachers, and not by students themselves. The assumption may be correct in many cases, but there are problems with it. One problem is that choosing goals and objectives for students, rather than by students, places a major burden on everyone involved in education—curriculum writers, teachers, and.

1.6.6.4. Enhancing student learning through a variety of resources

Whether instructional goals originate from curriculum documents, students' expressed interests, or a mixture of both, students are more likely to achieve the goals if teachers draw on a wide variety of resources. As a practical matter, this means looking for materials and experiences that supplement—or occasionally even replace—the most traditional forms of information, such as textbooks.

1.6.6.5. Creating bridges among curriculum goals and students' Experiences

To succeed, then, instructional plans do require a variety of resources. But they also require more: they need to connect with students' prior experiences and knowledge. Sometimes the connections can develop as a result of.

1.6.6.6. Planning for Instruction as well as for Learning

It started with the idea that teachers need to locate curriculum goals, usually from a state department of education or a publisher of a curriculum document. These authorities provide for individual classroom teachers, and how their documents can be clarified and rendered specific enough for classroom use. Instructional planning, in other words, has to be not just for students, but also by students, at least to some extent.

1.6.7. Assessment of Student Learning

Best practices in assessing student learning have undergone dramatic changes in the last 20 years. The tests varied little format and students always did them individually with pencil and paper. Now, however, many teachers—including mathematics teachers—use a wide variety of methods to determine what their students have learned and also use this assessment information to modify their instruction.

Assessment is an integrated process of gaining information about students' learning and making value judgments about their progress. Information about students' progress can be obtained from a variety of sources including projects, portfolios, performances, observations, and tests. The information about students' learning is often assigned specific numbers or grades and this involves measurement. Measurement answers the question, "How much?" and is used most commonly when the teacher scores a test or product and assigns numbers. Evaluation is the process of making judgments about the assessment information. These judgments may be about individual students, the assessment method used, or one's own teaching.

Assessment for learning is often called formative assessment, i.e., it takes place during the course of instruction and provides information that teachers can use to revise their teaching and students can use to improve their learning. Formative assessment includes both informal assessment involving spontaneous unsystematic observations of students' behaviours and formal assessment involving preplanned, systematic gathering of data.

Assessment *of* learning involves assessing students in order to certify their competence and to fulfill accountability mandates, which is primarily about standardized tests. Assessment of learning is typically summative, that is, administered after the instruction is completed. Summative assessments provide information about how well students mastered the material, whether students are ready for the next unit, and what grades should be given.

Using assessment to advance students' learning not just check on learning requires viewing assessment as a process that is integral to the all phases of teaching including planning, classroom interactions and instruction, communication with parents, and self-reflection. Essential steps in assessment for learning include:

1.6.7.1. Step 1: Having Clear Instructional Goals and Communicating them to Students

This may be hard for beginning teachers. For example, Vanessa, a middle school social studies teacher, might say that the goal of her next unit is, "Students will learn about the civil war." Clearer goals require that Vanessa decides what it is about the civil wear she wants her students to learn, e.g. the dates and names of battles, the causes of the civil war, the differing perspectives of those living in the North and the South, or the day-to-day experiences of soldiers fighting in the war. Vanessa cannot devise appropriate assessments of her students' learning about the civil war until she is clear about her own purposes. For effective teaching Vanessa also needs to communicate clearly the goals and objectives to her students so they know what is important for them to learn. No matter how thorough a teacher's planning has been, if students do not know what they are supposed to learn they will not learn as much.

1.6.7.2. Step 2: Selecting Appropriate Assessment Techniques

Selecting and administrating assessment techniques that are appropriate for the goals of instruction as well as the developmental level of the students are crucial components of effective assessment for learning. Teachers need to know the characteristics of a wide variety of classroom assessment techniques and how these techniques can be adapted for various content, skills, and student characteristics. They also should understand the role reliability, validity, and the absence of bias should play is choosing and using assessment techniques.

1.6.7.3. Step 3. Using Assessment to Enhance Motivation and Confidence

Students' motivation and confidence is influenced by the type of assessment used as well as the feedback given about the assessment results. Consider, Samantha a college student who takes a history class in which the professor's lectures and text book focus on really interesting major themes. However, the assessments are all multiple choice tests that ask about facts and Samantha, who initially enjoys the classes and readings, becomes angry, loses confidence she can do well, and begins to spend less time on the class material. In contrast, some instructors have has observed that that many students in educational psychology classes like the one you are now taking will work harder on assessments that are case studies rather than more traditional exams or essays.

1.6.7.4. Step 4: Adjusting Instruction Based on Information

An essential component of assessment for learning is that the teacher uses the information gained from assessment to adjust instruction. These adjustments occur in the middle of a lesson when a teacher may decide that students' responses to questions indicate sufficient understanding to introduce a new topic, or that her observations of students' behaviour indicates that they do not understand the assignment and so need further explanation. Adjustments also occur when the teacher reflects on the instruction after the lesson is over and is planning for the next day.

1.6.7.5. Step 5: Communicating with Parents and Guardians

Students' learning and development is enhanced when teachers communicate with parents regularly about their children's performance. Teachers communicate with parents in a variety of ways including newsletters, telephone conversations, email, school district websites and parent-teachers conferences. Effective communication requires that teachers can clearly explain the purpose and characteristics of the assessment as well as the meaning of students' performance. This requires a thorough knowledge of the types and purposes of teacher made and standardized assessments and well as clear communication skills.

1.7. Research Methods in Educational Psychology

The history of scientific educational psychology started in 1860, with Stanley Hall as the founder and William James, J.M. Cattell and E.L. Thorndike as prominent contributors to the rapid growth of the field. In 1866, the first department of educational psychology was established at Indian University and later a second at the University of North Carolina, both in the USA. The year 1890 marked the beginning of research on the development of an intelligence test by Alfred Binet in France. Thorndike appeared on the educational psychology scene in the beginning of the 20th century. By 1910, learning, motivation, emotion, heredity, personality, and individual difference were being studied as the subject matter of educational psychology. Even though John Dewey was not an educational psychologist, his contribution to the progressive education movement was of prime importance for the development of educational psychology, which was very much in the air by 1940.

After the first and second World Wars, three factors contributed to the development of educational psychology: psychoanalysis, Gestalt psychology, and educational measurement. Early experience and its contribution to the educability of children was emphasized by psychoanalysts. Insight and understanding were stressed by Gestalt psychologists, and the use of Intelligence tests became quite prominent. Individual differences came to light. Around 1950, educational psychological principles were applied to classroom situations.

Research activities increased both in number and quality. By 1963, teaching-learning models had been devised. After 1965, educational psychologists received wide recognition in the western world and after 1970, they have played decisive roles in educational planning. Planning for the education of children has been extensively done in the USA, the UK, Europe and Japan on the basis of measurement of intelligence, personality, interest, etc. School psychologists have been appointed in each school or for a cluster of schools in these countries. Compensatory education and enrichment programmemes have given educational psychologists a special status in the educational system. Educational technology, programmemed instruction, computerised instruction, instructional designs, and elucidation of the nature of cognitive development, as outlined by Piaget, Bruner and other developmental psychologists, have revolutionised the field of education and all these contributed squarely to progress in educational psychology.

In India, educational psychology had a late beginning. In 1915, the Calcutta University started a psychology department, the first in India. Even though educational psychology was included in the curriculum, it did not have a special status either in Calcutta or in Madras University, which had also set up a department. Since 1961, educational psychology is being taught as a compulsory subject in the Calcutta and Lucknow Universities. It is being taught now in various universities and 'Centres of Advanced Studies in Education and Psychology', but it has not yet become a separate department anywhere in our country. The reasons are many and varied. The NCERT has a full-fledged department of educational psychology, the largest in the country. Since 1973, it has been a specialised centre for instruction at the master's degree level in psychology.

The research methods used in educational psychology tend to be drawn from psychology and other social sciences. Research methods address problems in both research design and data analysis. Research design informs the planning of experiments and observational studies to ensure that their results have internal, external and ecological validity. Data analysis encompasses methods for processing both quantitive and qualitative research data.

1.7.1. Quantitative Methods

Because educational assessment is fundamental to most quantitative research in the field, educational psychologists have made significant contributions to the field of psychometrics. The reliability of assessments are routinely reported in quantitative educational research. Although, originally, educational measurement methods were built on classical test theory, item response theory and Rasch models are now used extensively in educational measurement worldwide. These models afford advantages over classical test theory, including the capacity to produce standard errors of measurement for each score or pattern of scores on assessments and the capacity to handle missing responses.

Meta-analysis, the combination of individual research results to produce a quantitative literature review, is another methodological innovation with a close association to educational psychology. In a meta-analysis, effect sizes that represent, for example, the differences between treatment groups in a set of similar experiments, are averaged to obtain a single aggregate value representing the best estimate of the effect of treatment. Today, meta-analysis is among the most common types of literature review found in educational psychology research.Other quantitative research issues associated with educational psychology include the use of nested research designs and the use of longitudinal statistical models to measure change.

1.7.2. Qualitative Methods

Qualitative methods are used in educational studies whose purpose is to describe events, processes and situations of theoretical significance. The qualitative methods used in educational psychology often derive from anthropology, sociology or sociolinguistics. For example, the anthropological method of ethnography has been used to describe teaching and learning in classrooms. In studies of this type, the researcher may gather detailed field notes as a participant observer or passive observer. Later, the notes and other data may be categorised and interpreted by methods such as grounded theory. Triangulation, the practice of cross-checking findings with multiple data sources, is highly valued in qualitative research.

Case studies are forms of qualitative research focusing on a single person, organisation, event, or other entity. Qualitative analysis is most often applied to verbal data from sources such as conversations, interviews, focus groups, and personal journals. Qualitative methods are thus, typically, approaches to gathering, processing and reporting verbal data. One of the most commonly used methods for qualitative research in educational psychology is protocol analysis.

In this method the research participant is asked to think aloud while performing a task, such as solving a math problem. In protocol analysis the verbal data is thought to indicate which information the subject is attending to, but is explicitly not interpreted as an explanation or justification for behaviour. In contrast, the method of verbal analysis does admit learners' explanations as a way to reveal their mental model or misconceptions. The most fundamental operations in both protocol and verbal analysis are segmenting and categorising sections of verbal data.

References

Lave, J. and Wenger, E. *Situated Learning, Legitimate peripheral participation*, Cambridge: University of Cambridge Press, 1991.

Mezirow, J., *Transformative Dimensions of Learning,* San Francisco: Jossey-Bass, 1991.

Newman, F. and Holzman, L., "*The End of Knowing", A new developmental way of learning*, London: Routledge, 1997.

Retallick, J., Cocklin, B. and Coombe, K., *Learning Communities in Education, London: Cassell,* 1998.

Wenger, E., "Communities of Practice", *Learning, meaning and identity*, Cambridge: Cambridge University Press, 1999.

2

Process of Learning

Learning can be defined as the process leading to relatively permanent behavioural change or potential behavioural change. In other words, as we learn, we alter the way we perceive our environment, the way we interpret the incoming stimuli, and therefore the way we interact, or behave. John B. Watson was the first to study how the process of learning affects our behaviour, and he formed the school of thought known as Behaviourism. The central idea behind behaviourism is that only observable behaviours are worthy of research since other abstraction such as a person's mood or thoughts are too subjective.

Perhaps the most well known Behaviourist is B. F. Skinner. Skinner followed much of Watson's research and findings, but believed that internal states could influence behaviour just as external stimuli. He is considered to be a Radical Behaviourist because of this belief, although nowadays it is believed that both internal and external stimuli influence our behaviour.

Behavioural psychology is basically interested in how our behaviour results from the stimuli both in the environment and within ourselves. They study, often in minute detail, the behaviours we exhibit while controlling for as many other variables as possible. Often a grueling process, but results have helped us learn a great deal about our behaviours, the effect our environment has on us, how we learn new behaviours, and what motivates us to change or remain the same.

2.1. Teacher Perspective on Learning

For teachers, learning usually refers to things that happen in schools or classrooms, even though every teacher can of course describe examples of learning that happen outside of these places. In particular, teachers' perspectives on learning often emphasise three ideas, and sometimes even take them for granted: (1) curriculum content and academic achievement, (2) sequencing and readiness, and (3) the importance of transferring learning to new or future situations.

2.1.1. Dependence of Learning on Curriculum

When teachers speak of learning, they tend to emphasize whatever is taught in schools deliberately, including both the official curriculum and the various behaviours and routines that make classrooms run smoothly. In practice, defining learning in this way often means that teachers equate learning with the major forms of academic achievement-especially language and mathematics-and to a lesser extent musical skill, physical coordination, or social sensitivity. The imbalance occurs not because the goals of public education make teachers responsible for certain content and activities and the skills which these activities require. It does happen not because teachers are biased, insensitive, or unaware that students often learn a lot outside of school.

A sideeffect of focusing learning on curriculum and academics is that classroom social interactions and behaviours become issues for teachers-become something that they need to manage. In particular, having dozens of students in one room makes it more likely that a teacher thinks of "learning" as something that either takes concentration or that benefits from collaboration. In the small space of a classroom, no other viewpoint about social interaction makes sense. Yet in the wider world outside of school, learning often does happen incidentally, "accidentally" and without conscious interference or input from others. Teachers, we sometimes see incidental learning in classrooms as well, and often welcome it; but their responsibility for curriculum goals more often focuses their efforts on what students can learn through conscious, deliberate effort. In a classroom, unlike in many other human settings, it is always necessary to ask whether classmates are helping or hindering individual students' learning.

2.1.2. Dependence of Learning on Teaching

Focusing learning on changes in classrooms has several other effects.

One, for example, is that it can tempt teachers to think that what is taught is equivalent to what is learned-even though most teachers know that doing so is a mistake, and that teaching and learning can be quite different. If a teacher assigns a reading to his students about the Russian Revolution, it would be nice to assume not only that they have read the same words, but also learned the same content. But that assumption is not usually the reality. Some students may have read and learned all of what he assigned; others may have read everything but misunderstood the material or remembered only some of it; and still others, unfortunately, may have neither read nor learned much of anything. Chances are that his students would confirm this picture, if asked confidentially.

2.1.3. Sequencing and Readiness

The distinction between teaching and learning creates a secondary issue for teachers, that of educational readiness. Traditionally the concept referred to students' preparedness to cope with or profit from the activities and expectations of school. A kindergarten child was "ready" to start school, for example, if he or she was in good health, showed moderately good social skills, could take care of personal physical needs, could use a pencil to make simple drawings, and so on. At older ages, the term readiness is often replaced by a more specific term, prerequisites. To take a course in physics, for example, a student must first have certain prerequisite experiences, such as studying advanced algebra or calculus. To begin work as a public school teacher, a person must first engage in practice teaching for a period of time.

Note that this traditional meaning, of readiness as preparedness, focuses attention on students' adjustment to school and away from the reverse: the possibility that schools and teachers also have responsibility for adjusting to students. But the latter idea is in fact a legitimate, second meaning for readiness: If five-year-old children normally need to play a lot and keep active, then it is fair to say that their kindergarten teacher needs to be "ready" for this behaviour by planning a programme that allows a lot of play and physical activity. If she cannot do so, then in a very real sense this failure is not the children's responsibility. Among older students, the second, teacher-oriented meaning of readiness makes sense as well. If a teacher has a student with a disability, then the teacher has to adjust her approach in appropriate ways-not simply expect a visually impaired child to "sink or swim."

2.1.4. Transfer as a Crucial Part of Learning

Still another result of focusing the concept of learning on classrooms is that it raises issues of usefulness or transfer, which is the ability to use knowledge or skill in situations beyond the ones in which they are acquired. Learning to read and learning to solve arithmetic problems, for example, are major goals of the elementaryschool curriculum because those skills are meant to be used not only inside the classroom, but outside as well. Teachers intend, that is, for reading and arithmetic skills to "transfer" — even though also do they/their best to make the skills enjoyable while they are still being learned. In the world inhabited by teachers, even more than in other worlds, making learning fun is certainly a good thing to do, but making learning useful as well as fun is even better. Combining enjoyment and usefulness, in fact, is a "gold standard" of teaching: we generally seek it for students, and even though we may not succeed at providing it all of the time.

2.2. Theories and Models of Learning

Several ideas and priorities, then, affect how we teachers think about learning, including the curriculum, the difference between teaching and learning, sequencing, readiness, and transfer. The ideas form a "screen" through which to understand and evaluate whatever psychology has to offer education. As it turns out, many theories, concepts, and ideas from educational psychology do make it through the "screen" of education, meaning that they are consistent with the professional priorities of teachers and helpful in solving important problems of classroom teaching. In the case of issues about classroom learning, for example, educational psychologists have developed a number of theories and concepts that are relevant to classrooms, in that they describe at least some of what usually happens there and offer guidance for assisting learning. It is helpful to group the theories according to whether they focus on changes in behaviour or in thinking. The distinction is rough and inexact, but a good place to begin. For starters, therefore, consider two perspectives about learning, called behaviourism and constructivism. The second category can be further divided into psychological constructivism (changes in thinking resulting from individual experiences), and social constructivism. The rest of this chapter describes key ideas from each of these viewpoints. Each describes some aspects of learning not just in general, but as it happens in classrooms in particular. So each perspective suggests things that you might do in your classroom to make students' learning more productive.

2.3. Learning Tactics and Strategies

A learning strategy is a general plan that a learner formulates for achieving a somewhat distant academic goal. Like all strategies, it specifies what will be done to achieve the goal, where it will be done, and when it will be done.

A learning tactic is a specific technique that a learner uses to accomplish an immediate objective. As you can see, tactics have an integral connection to strategies. They are the learning tools that move you closer to your goal. Thus, they have to be chosen so as to be consistent with the goals of a strategy.

If you had to recall verbatim the preamble to the Indian Constitution, for example, would you use a learning tactic that would help you understand the gist of each stanza or one that would allow for accurate and complete recall? It is surprising how often students fail to consider this point.

2.3.1. Types of Tactics

Most learning tactics can be placed in one of two categories based on each tactic's intended primary purpose.

One category, called memory-directed tactics, contains techniques that help produce accurate storage and retrieval of information.

The second category, called comprehension-directed tactics, contains techniques that aid in understanding the meaning of ideas and their interrelationships.

Within each category there are specific tactics from which one can choose.

The first two, rehearsal and mnemonic devices, are memory-directed tactics. Both can take several forms and are used by students of almost every age.

The last two, notetaking and self-questioning, are comprehension-directed tactics and are used frequently by students from the upper elementary grades through college.

2.3.1.1. Rehearsal

The simplest form of rehearsal, rote rehearsal, is one of the earliest tactics to appear during childhood and is used by most everyone on occasion. It is not a particularly effective tactic for long-term storage and recall because it does not produce distinct encoding or good retrieval cues.

Most five- and six-year-olds do not rehearse at all. Seven-year-olds sometimes use the simplest form of rehearsal. By eight years of age, instead of rehearsing single pieces of information one at a time, youngsters start to rehearse several items together as a set.

A slightly more advanced version, called cumulative rehearsal, involves rehearsing a small set of items for several repetitions, dropping the item at the top of the list and adding a new one, giving the set several repetitions, dropping the item at the head of the set and adding a new one, rehearsing the set, and so on.

By early adolescence rehearsal reflects the learner's growing awareness of the organisational properties of information. When given a list of randomly arranged words from familiar categories, 13-year-olds will group items by category to form rehearsal sets.

2.3.1.2. Mnemonic Devices

A mnemonic device is a memory-directed tactic that helps a learner transform or organise information to enhance its retrievability.

Such devices can be used to learn and remember individual items of information, sets of information, and ideas expressed in text.

These devices range from simple, easy-to-learn techniques to somewhat complex systems that require a fair amount of practice.

Since they incorporate visual and verbal forms of elaborative encoding, their effectiveness is due to the same factors that make imagery and category clustering successful—organisation and meaningfulness.

2.3.1.3. Self-questioning

Since students are expected to demonstrate much of what they know by answering written test questions, self-questioning can be a valuable learning tactic.

The key to using questions profitably is to recognise that different types of questions make different cognitive demands. Some questions require little more than verbatim recall or recognition of simple facts and details.

If an exam is to stress factual recall, then it may be helpful for a student to generate such questions while studying. Other questions, however, assess comprehension, application, or synthesis of main ideas or other high level information.

Since many teachers favour higher-level test questions, we will focus on self-questioning as an aid to comprehension. Much of the research on self-questioning addresses two basic questions:

1) Can students as young as those in fourth grade be trained to write comprehension questions about the content of a reading passage?
2) And does writing such questions lead to better comprehension of the passage in comparison to students who do not write questions?

The answer to both questions is yes, if certain conditions are present. Research on teaching students how to generate questions as they read suggests that the following conditions play a major role in self-questioning's effectiveness as a comprehension-directed learning tactic:

1) The amount of prior knowledge the questioner has about the topic of the passage.
2) The amount of metacognitive knowledge the questioner has compiled.
3) The clarity of instructions.

4) The instructional format.
5) The amount of practice allowed the student.
6) The length of each practice session.

2.3.1.4. Notetaking

As a learning tactic, notetaking comes with good news and bad.

The good news is that notetaking can benefit a student in two ways. First, the process of taking notes while listening to a lecture or reading a text leads to better retention and comprehension of the noted information than just listening or reading does.

Second, the process of reviewing notes produces additional chances to recall and comprehend the noted material. The bad news is that we know very little at the present time about the specific conditions that make notetaking an effective tactic.

2.3.2. Components of a Learning Strategy

As noted, a learning strategy is a plan for accomplishing a learning goal. It consists of six components: metacognition, analysis, planning, implementation of the plan, monitoring of progress, and modification.

2.3.2.1. Metacognition

In the absence of some minimal awareness of how we think and how our thought processes affect our academic performance, a strategic approach to learning is simply not possible.

We need to know, at the very least, that effective learning requires an analysis of the learning situation, formulation of a learning plan, skilful implementation of appropriate tactics, periodic monitoring of our progress, and modification of things that go wrong.

In addition, we need to know why each of these steps is necessary, when each step should be carried out, and how well prepared we are to perform each step.

Without this knowledge, students who are taught one or more of the learning tactics mentioned earlier do not keep up their use for very long, nor do they apply the tactics to relevant tasks.

2.3.2.2. Analysis

Any workable plan must be based on relevant information. By thinking about the type of task that one must confront, the type of material that one has to learn, the personal characteristics that one possesses, and the way in which one's competence will be tested, the strategic learner can generate this information by playing the role of an investigative journalist and asking questions that pertain to what, when, where, why, who, and how.

In this way the learner can identify important aspects of the material to be learned (what, when, where), understand the nature of the test that will be given (why), recognise relevant personal learner characteristics (who), and identify potentially useful learning activities or tactics (how).

2.3.2.3. Planning

Once satisfactory answers have been gained from the analysis phase, the strategic learner then formulates a learning plan by hypothesizing.

2.3.2.4. Implementation of the plan

Once the learner has formulated a plan, each of its elements must be implemented skilfully.

A careful analysis and a well-conceived plan will not work if tactics are carried out badly. Of course, a poorly executed plan may not be entirely attributable to a learner's tactical skill deficiencies.

Part of the problem may be a general lack of knowledge about what conditions make for effective use of tactics (as is the case with notetaking).

2.3.2.5. Monitoring of progress

Once the learning process is under way, the strategic learner assesses how well the chosen tactics are working.

Possible monitoring techniques include writing out a summary, giving an oral presentation, working practice problems, and answering questions.

2.3.2.6. Modification

If the monitoring assessment is positive, the learner may decide that no changes are needed.

If, however, attempts to memorise or understand the learning material seem to be producing unsatisfactory results, the learner will need to reevaluate and modify the analysis. This, in turn, will cause changes in both the plan and the implementation.

There are two points we would like to emphasize about the nature of a learning strategy.

The first is that learning conditions constantly change. Subject matters have different types of information and structures, teachers use different instructional methods and have different styles, exams differ in the kinds of demands they make, and the interests, motives, and capabilities of students change over time.

Accordingly, strategies must be formulated or constructed anew as one moves from task to task rather than selected from a bank of previously formulated strategies. The true strategist, in other words, is very mentally active.

The second point is that the concept of a learning strategy is obviously complex and requires a certain level of intellectual maturity.

Thus, you may be tempted to conclude that, although you could do it, learning to be strategic is beyond the reach of most elementary and high school students. Research evidence suggests otherwise, however. A study of high school students in Scotland, for example, found that some students are sensitive to contextual differences among school tasks and vary their approach to studying accordingly.

2.3.3. Reciprocal Teaching

A study of strategy training aimed at improving reading comprehension is the reciprocal teaching (RT) programme.

Students learn certain comprehension skills by demonstrating them to each other. A small group of seventh graders, whose reading comprehension scores were at least two years below grade level, were trained to use the techniques of summarising, self-questioning, clarifying, and predicting to improve their reading comprehension.

These four methods were chosen because they can be used by students to improve and monitor comprehension.

During the early training sessions, the teacher explained and demonstrated the four methods while reading various passages. The students were then given gradually increasing responsibility for demonstrating these techniques to their peers, with the teacher supplying prompts and corrective feedback as needed.

Eventually, each student was expected to offer a good summary of a passage, pose questions about important ideas, clarify ambiguous words or phrases, and predict upcoming events, all to be done with little or no intervention by the teacher.

This produced two general beneficial effects. First, the quality of students' summaries, questions, clarifications, and predictions improved. Early in the programme students produced overly detailed summaries and many unclear questions. But in later sessions concise summaries and questions dealing explicitly with main ideas were the rule. For example, questions on main ideas increased from 54 percent to 70 percent. In addition, the questions were increasingly stated in paraphrase form rather than as verbatim statements from the passage.

Second, RT-trained students scored as well as a group of average readers on tests of comprehension and much better than a group taught how to locate information that might show up in a test question.

Most impressively, these levels of performance held up for at least eight weeks after the study ended and generalised to tests of social studies and science.

2.4. Information Processing Approach to Cognition

Cognitive psychology represents the dominant approach in psychology today. A primary focus of this approach is on memory, a subject that has been of interest for thousands of years. The most widely accepted theory is labelled the "stage theory," based on the work of Atkinson and Shriffin. The focus of this model is on how information is stored in memory; the model proposes that information is processed and stored in three stages. In this theory, information is thought to be processed in a serial, discontinuous manner as it moves from one stage to the next.

In addition to the stage theory model of information processing, there are three more that are widely accepted. The first is labelled the "levels-of-processing" theory. The major proposition is that learners utilise different levels of elaboration as they process information. This is done on a continuum from perception, through attention, to labeling, and finally, meaning. The key point is that all stimuli that activate a sensory receptor cell are permanently stored in memory, but that different levels of processing contribute to an ability to access, or retrieve, that memory. Evidence from hypnosis and forensic psychology provide some interesting support for this hypothesis. It is not only how the information is processed, but how the information is accessed. When the demands for accessing information more closely match the methods used to elaborate or learn the information, more is remembered.

Two other models have been proposed as alternatives to the Atkinson-Shiffrin model: parallel-distributed processing and connectionistic. The parallel-distributed processing model states that information is processed simultaneously by several different parts of the memory system, rather than sequentially as hypothesized by Atkinson-Shiffrin. Work done on how we process emotional data somewhat supports this contention. The stage-theory model shown below differs slightly from the original Atkinson-Shriffin model in order to incorporate this feature.

The connectionistic model extends the parallel-distributed processing model. It is one of the dominant forms of current research in cognitive psychology and is consistent with the most recent brain research. This model emphasizes the fact that information is stored in multiple locations throughout the brain in the form of networks of connections. It is consistent with the levels-of-processing approach in that the more connections to a single idea or concept, the more likely it is to be remembered.

2.4.1. General Principles

Even though there are widely varying views within cognitive psychology, there are a few basic principles that most cognitive psychologists agree with.The first is the assumption of a limited capacity of the mental system. This means that the amount of information that can be processed by the system is constrained in some very important ways. Bottlenecks, or restrictions in the flow and processing of information, occur at very specific points.

A second principle is that a control mechanism is required to oversee the encoding, transformation, processing, storage, retrieval and utilisation of information. That is, not all of the processing capacity of the system is available; an executive function that oversees this process will use up some of this capability. When one is learning a new task or is confronted with a new environment, the executive function requires more processing power than when one is doing a routine task or is in a familiar environment.

A third principle is that there is a two-way flow of information as we try to make sense of the world around us. We constantly use information that we gather through the senses and information we have stored in memory in a dynamic process as we construct meaning about our environment and our relations to it. This is somewhat analogous to the difference between inductive reasoning and deductive reasoning. A similar distinction can be made between using information we derive from the senses and that generated by our imaginations.

A fourth principle generally accepted by cognitive psychologists is that the human organism has been genetically prepared to process and organise information in specific ways. For example, a human infant is more likely to look at a human face than any other stimulus. Given that the field of focus of a human infant is 12 to 18 inches, one can surmise that this is an important aspect of the infant's survival. Other research has discovered additional biological predispositions to process information.

For example, language development is similar in all human infants regardless of language spoken by adults or the area in which they live. All human infants with normal hearing babble and coo, generate first words, begin the use of telegraphic speech, and overgeneralise at approximately the same ages. The issue of language development is an area where cognitive and behavioural psychologists as well as cognitive psychologists with different viewpoints have fought many battles regarding the processes underlying human behaviour. Needless to say the disussion continues.

2.4.2. Stage Model of Information Processing

One of the major issues in cognitive psychology is the study of memory. The dominant view is labelled the "stage theory" and is based on the work of Atkinson and Shiffrin.

Sensory memory (STSS). Sensory memory is affiliated with the transduction of energy. The environment makes available a variety of sources of information, but the brain only understands electrical energy. The body has special sensory receptor cells that transduce this external energy to something the brain can understand. In the process of transduction, a memory is created. This memory is very short.

It is absolutely critical that the learner attend to the information at this initial stage in order to transfer it to the next one. There are two major concepts for getting information into STM:

1) Individuals are more likely to pay attention to a stimulus if it has an interesting feature. We are more likely to get an orienting response if this is present.
2) Individuals are more likely to pay attention if the stimulus activates a known pattern. To the extent we have students call to mind relevant prior learning before we begin our presentations, we can take advantage of this principle.

Short-term memory (STM). Short-term memory is also called working memory and relates to what we are thinking about at any given moment in time. In Freudian terms, this is conscious memory. It is created by our paying attention to an external stimulus, an internal thought, or both. It will initially last somewhere around 15 to 20 seconds unless it is repeated at which point it may be available for up to 20 minutes. The hypothalamus is a brain structure thought to be involved in this shallow processing of information. The frontal lobes of the cerebral cortex is the structure associated with working memory. For example, you are processing the words you read on the screen in your frontal lobes. However, if I ask, "What is your telephone number?" your brain immediately calls that from long-term memory and replaces what was previously there.

Another major limit on information processing in STM is in terms of the number of units that can be processed an any one time. Because of the variability in how much individuals can work with it is necessary to point out important information. If some students can only process three units of information at a time, let us make certain it is the most important three.

There are two major concepts for retaining information in STM: organisation and repetition. There are four major types of organisation that are most often used in instructional design:

1) *Component (part/whole)*—classification by category or concept (e.g., the components of the teaching/learning model);
2) *Sequential* — chronological; cause/effect; building to climax (e.g., baking a cake, reporting on a research study);
3) *Relevance* — central unifying idea or criteria (e.g., most important principles of learning for boys and girls, appropriate management strategies for middle school and high school students);
4) *Transitional (connective)* — relational words or phrases used to indicate qualitative change over time (e.g., stages in Piaget's theory of cognitive development)

A related issue to organisation is the concept of chunking or grouping pieces of data into units. For example, the letters "b d e" constitute three units of information while the word "bed" represents one unit even though it is composed of the same number of letters. Chunking is a major technique for getting and keeping information in short-term memory; it is also a type of elaboration that will help get information into long-term memory.

Repetition or rote rehearsal is a technique we all use to try to "learn" something. However, in order to be effective this must be done after forgetting begins. Researchers advise that the learner should not repeat immediately the content, but wait a few minutes and then repeat. For the most part, simply memorising something does not lead to learning. We all have anecdotal evidence that we can remember something we memorised, but just think about all the material we tried to learn this way and the little we are able to remember after six months or a year.

Long-term memory (LTM). Long-term memory is also called preconscious and unconscious memory in Freudian terms. Preconscious means that the information is relatively easily recalled (although it may take several minutes or even hours) while unconscious refers to data that is not available during normal consciousness. It is preconscious memory that is the focus of cognitive psychology as it relates to long-term memory. The levels-of-processing theory, however, has provided some research that attests to the fact that we "know" more than we can easily recall. The two processes most likely to move information into long-term memory are elaboration and distributed practice.

There are several examples of elaboration that are commonly used in the teaching/learning process:

a) imaging — creating a mental picture;
b) method of loci (locations)—ideas or things to be remembered are connected to objects located in a familiar location;
c) pegword method (number, rhyming schemes)—ideas or things to be remembered are connected to specific words (e.g., one-bun, two-shoe, three-tree, etc.)
d) Rhyming (songs, phrases)—information to be remembered is arranged in a rhyme (e.g., 30 days hath September, April, June, and November, etc.)
e) Initial letter—the first letter of each word in a list is used to make a sentence (the sillier, the better).

2.4.3. Organisation (types) of Knowledge

As information is stored in long-term memory, it is organised using one or more structures: declarative, procedural, and/or imagery.

2.4.3.1. Declarative memory

a) *Semantic memory*— facts and generalised information (concepts, principles, rules; problem-solving strategies; learning strategies).
b) *Schema / Schemata* — networks of connected ideas or relationships; data structures or procedures for organising the parts of a specific experience into a meaningful system.
c) *Proposition* — interconnected set of concepts and relationships; if/then statements.

d) *Script* — "declarative knowledge structure that captures general information about a routine series of events or a recurrent type of social event, such as eating in a restaurant or visiting the doctor".

e) *Frame* — complex organisation including concepts and visualisations that provide a reference within which stimuli and actions are judged.

f) *Scheme* — an organisation of concepts, principles, rules, etc. that define a perspective and presents specific action patterns to follow.

g) *Program* — set of rules that define what to do in a particular situation.

h) *Paradigm* — the basic way of perceiving, thinking, valuing, and doing associated with a particular vision of reality.

i) *Model* — a set of propositions or equations describing in simplified form some aspects of our experience. Every model is based upon a theory or paradigm, but the theory or paradigm may not be stated in concise form.

j) *Episodic memory*— personal experience.

k) *Procedural memory* — how to

l) Imagery — pictures

2.4.4. Concept Formation

One of the most important issues in cognitive psychology is the development or formation of concepts. A concept is the set of rules used to define the categories by which we group similar events, ideas or objects. There are several principles that lend themselves to concept development:

1) Name and define concept to be learned (advance organiser)
    a) reference to larger category
    b) define attributes
2) Identify relevant and irrelevant attributes (guided discovery)
3) Give examples and nonexamples (tie to what is already known — elaboration)
4) Use both inductive (example/experience —> definition) and deductive reasoning (definition —> examples)

5) Name distinctive attributes (guided discovery)

2.4.5. Learning Styles

Learning styles are, simply put, various approaches or ways of learning. They involve educating methods, particular to an individual, that are presumed to allow that individual to learn best. It is commonly believed that most people favour some particular method of interacting with, taking in, and processing stimuli or information. Based on this concept, the idea of individualised "learning styles" originated in the 1970s, and has gained popularity in recent years. It has been proposed that teachers should assess the learning styles of their students and adapt their classroom methods to best fit each student's learning style. The alleged basis for these proposals has been extensively criticised.

2.4.6. Models

2.4.6.1. David Kolb's model

The David Kolb styles model is based on the Experiential Learning Theory (ELT), as explained in David A. Kolb's book *Experiential Learning: Experience as the source of learning and development*. The ELT model outlines two related approaches toward grasping experience: Concrete Experience and Abstract Conceptualisation, as well as two related approaches toward transforming experience: Reflective Observation and Active Experimentation. According to Kolb's model, the ideal learning process engages all four of these modes in response to situational demands. In order for learning to be effective, all four of these approaches must be incorporated. As individuals attempt to use all four approaches, however, they tend to develop strengths in one experience-grasping approach and one experience-transforming approach. The resulting learning styles are combinations of the individual's preferred approaches. These learning styles are as follows:

1) Converger
2) Diverger
3) Assimilator
4) Accomodator

Convergers are characterised by abstract conceptualisation and active experimentation. They are good at making practical applications of ideas and using deductive reasoning to solve problems.

Divergers tend toward concrete experience and reflective observation. They are imaginative and are good at coming up with ideas and seeing things from different perspectives.

Assimilators are characterised by abstract conceptualisation and reflective observation. They are capable of creating theoretical models by means of inductive reasoning.

Accommodators use concrete experience and active experimentation. They are good at actively engaging with the world and actually doing things instead of merely reading about and studying them.

2.4.6.2. Anthony Gregorc's model

Gregorc and Butler worked to organise a model describing how the mind works. This model is based on the existence of perceptions-our evaluation of the world by means of an approach that makes sense to us. These perceptions in turn are the foundation of our specific learning strengths, or learning styles.

In this model there are two perceptual qualities: concrete and abstract; and two ordering abilities: random and sequential.

Concrete perceptions involve registering information through the five senses, while abstract perceptions involve the understanding of ideas, qualities, and concepts which cannot be seen.

In regard to the two ordering abilities, sequential involves the organisation of information in a linear, logical way and random involves the organisation of information in chunks and in no specific order.

Both of the perceptual qualities and both of the ordering abilities are present in each individual, but some qualities and ordering abilities are more dominant within certain individuals.

2.4.6.3. Sudbury model

Some critics of today's schools, of the concept of learning disabilities, of special education, and of response to intervention, take the position that every child has a different learning style and pace, and that each child is unique, not only capable of learning but also capable of succeeding.

Sudbury Model democratic schools assert that there are many ways to study and learn. They argue that learning is a process you do, not a process that is done to you; That is true of everyone. It's basic.

The experience of Sudbury model democratic schools shows that there are many ways to learn without the intervention of teaching, to say, without the intervention of a teacher being imperative. In the case of reading, for instance in the Sudbury model democratic schools, some children learn from being read to, memorising the stories and then ultimately reading them. Others learn from cereal boxes, others from games instructions, others from street signs.

Some teach themselves letter sounds, others syllables, others whole words. Sudbury model democratic schools adduce that in their schools no one child has ever been forced, pushed, urged, cajoled, or bribed into learning how to read or write, and they have had no dyslexia. None of their graduates are real or functional illiterates, and no one who meets their older students could ever guess the age at which they first learned to read or write. In a similar form students learn all the subjects, techniques and skills in these schools.

Describing current instructional methods as homogenisation and lockstep standardisation, alternative approaches are proposed, such as the Sudbury Model of Democratic Education schools, an alternative approach in which children, by enjoying personal freedom thus encouraged to exercise personal responsibility for their actions, learn at their own pace and style rather than following a compulsory and chronologically-based curriculum. Proponents of unschooling have also claimed that children raised in this method learn at their own pace and style, and do not suffer from learning disabilities.

2.4.7. Assessment Methods: Learning Style Inventory

The Learning Style Inventory (LSI) is connected with Kolb's model and is used to determine a student's learning style. The LSI diagnoses an individual's preferences and needs regarding the learning process. It does the following: (1) allows students to designate how they like to learn and indicates how consistent their responses are; (2) provides computerised results which show the student's preferred learning style; (3) provides a foundation upon which teachers can build in interacting with students; (4) provides possible strategies for accommodating learning styles; (5) provides for student involvement in the learning process; (6) provides a class summary so students with similar learning styles can be grouped together.

2.4.8. Evidence or Lack of Evidence

Learning-style theories have been criticised by many. Some psychologists and neuroscientists have questioned the scientific basis for these models and the theories on which they are based. Many educational psychologists believe that there is little evidence for the efficacy of most learning style models, and furthermore, that the models often rest on dubious theoretical grounds.

2.4.8.1. Applications: Learning Styles in the Classroom

Various researchers have attempted to provide ways in which learning style theory can take effect in the classroom. Learners are affected by their: (1) immediate environment (sound, light, temperature, and design); (2) own emotionality (motivation, persistence, responsibility, and need for structure or flexibility); (3) sociological needs (self, pair, peers, team, adult, or varied); and (4) physical needs (perceptual strengths, intake, time, and mobility). Not only can students identify their preferred learning styles, but that students also score higher on tests, have better attitudes, and are more efficient if they are taught in ways to which they can more easily relate. Therefore, it is to the educator's advantage to teach and test students in their preferred styles.

Although learning styles will inevitably differ among students in the classroom, teachers should try to make changes in their classroom that will be beneficial to every learning style. Some of these changes include room redesign, the development of small-group techniques, and the development of Contract Activity Packages. Redesigning the classroom involves locating dividers that can be used to arrange the room creativel, clearing the floor area, and incorporating student thoughts and ideas into the design of the classroom.

Small-group techniques often include a "circle of knowledge" in which students sit in a circle and discuss a subject collaboratively as well as other techniques such as team learning and brainstorming. Contract Activity Packages are educational plans that facilitate learning by using the following elements: (1) clear statement of what the students needs to learn; (2) multisensory resources (auditory, visual, tactile, kinesthetic) that teach the required information; (3) activities through which the newly-mastered information can be used creatively; (4) the sharing of creative projects within small groups of classmates; (5) at least three small-group techniques; 6) a pre-test, a self-test, and a post-test.

Methods for visual learners include ensuring that students can see words written down, using pictures when describing things, drawing time lines for events in history, writing assignments on the board, using overhead transparencies/handouts, and writing down instructions.

Methods for auditory learners include repeating difficult words and concepts aloud, incorporating small-group discussion, organising debates, listening to books on tape, writing oral reports, and encouraging oral interpretation.

Methods for tactile/kinesthetic learners include providing hands-on activities, assigning projects, having frequent breaks to allow movement, using visual aids and objects in the lesson, using role play, and having field trips. By using a variety of teaching methods from each of these categories, teachers are able to accommodate different learning styles.

References

Ames, C., & Archer, J., "Achievement goals in the classroom: Students' learning strategies and motivation processes", *Journal of Educational Psychology,* 1988.

Condry, J., and J. Chambers, "Intrinsic Motivation and the Process of Learning, In The Hidden Cost of Reward, edited by M.R. Lepper and D. Greene, Hillsdale, New Jersey: Lawrence Erlbaum Associates, Inc., 1978.

Dufresne, R. J., Gerace, W. J., Leonard, W. J., Mestre, J. P., & Wenk, L., "Classtalk: A classroom communication system for active learning", *Journal of Computing in Higher Education,* 1996.

Hattie, J., Biggs, J., & Purdie, N., "Effects of learning skills interventions on student learning: A meta-analysis", *Review of Educational Research,* 1996.

3

Behaviouristic Learning Theories

Behaviourism is an approach to psychology based on the proposition that behaviour can be researched scientifically without recourse to inner mental states. It is a form of materialism, denying any independent significance for mind. Its significance for psychological treatment has been profound, making it one of the pillars of pharmacological therapy.

One of the assumptions of behaviourist thought is that free will is illusory, and that all behaviour is determined by the environment either through association or reinforcement.

There have been two major schools of thought and study within the Behaviourist orientation. The earlier "Classical Conditioning" school studied stimuli and responses to them. The later "Operant Conditioning" school noted that in addition to a stimulus spurring a response, it was also important to attend to the consequence that followed the response. The operant school, as with the earlier classical view focuses solely on observable actions displayed by individuals. Emotions and thoughts are not considered in the analysis of behaviour because they do not provide objective, observable data for evaluation.

3.1. Classical Conditioning

This earlier school of behaviourism studied the connection between a stimulus and the response it incites. Prominent researchers identified with this orientation noted that an event that formerly did not elicit a behaviour can be made to do so by pairing it with an unconditioned stimulus. This newly effective stimulusare said to be "conditioned".

Classical behaviourists also believed that the brain contains two systems, "excitation" and "inhibition". The excitation system increases neural activity in response to a stimulus or happening, and prompts a human or animal to display a certain behaviour. The inhibition system blocks other behaviours from being shown when that stimulus appears. For example, when the phone rings, the excitation system typically causes the response sequence of going to the phone, picking it up, and offering a greeting. The inhibition system prevents the display of other responses.

Individuals who display socially inappropriate behaviours were believed to be having problems discriminating between stimuli. Both of their systems become excited. For example, consider the case of a child who is physically abused by a male adult at home and cowers in fear at the approach of a male teacher who has not been abusive to the child. The child generalises instead of discriminates between the two stimuli. The inhibition system that should prevent the display of the fear response around non-abusive men instead becomes excited, allowing the "inappropriate" response to appear.

The different reactions to events that we witness in different people is believed to be due to the differing strengths of the two processes in each of us. Advertisers attempt to excite your inhibition system by causing a buying response to a stimuli that previously did not bring about such a response. Conversely, the process of "desensitisation", in which people attempt to overcome their phobias involves numbing an excited inhibition system. Clients are placed in non-threatening situations that progressively become more similar to the fear inducing situation. By handling low anxiety situations and discovering that there is no need for fear, the inhibition system is strengthened. Classical conditioning cannot explain all of human behaviour: some behaviours are developmental in nature, and higher level cognitive thought can often overrule the machine-like reflex responses that have been previously built. However, these early investigations helped to identify principles of human learning. The operant school of behaviourism would extend our understanding of behaviour.

3.1.1. Ivan Pavlov's Contributions

Ivan Pavlov was aware that food triggered salivation in his laboratory dogs. However, he noted that the dogs salivated before the standard feeding time. He was perplexed as to why dogs would salivate when there was no food present to be digested. He decided to investigate this "psychic secretion" phenomenon by manipulating circumstances. He "paired" the ringing of a bell with the presentation of the Unconditioned Stimulus (UCS). After about 10-20 pairings or "trials" the formerly neutral stimulus of the bell, activated salivation, even when no food was presented. The neutral stimulus became a Conditioned Stimulus (CS) that activated salivation.

Other research in Pavlov's laboratory made other principles of learning apparent. He noted that after several trials of ringing the bell with no presentation of the food, the CS no longer produced the Conditioned Response (CR). The salivation behaviour at the stimulus of the bell also extinguished if the time period between the bell and the presentation of the food was too great. The CS lost its ability to stimulate a response because it was no longer associated with the UCS.

3.1.2. John Watson's Contributions

John Watson is the acknowledged "father" of behaviourism. In 1913, his soon-to-be-famous article, "Psychology as the behaviourist views it" was published. This publication established the behaviourist school of behavioural investigation and intervention. Watson believed that psychologists should study actions, not feelings and thoughts. He desired a more objective science although he did believe in three innate emotions: fear, anger, and love. According to Watson, new responses shown by humans were either recently learned, simply old responses combined or sequenced to produce a new complex response, or the display of old responses to a new stimuli.

Watson's most famous research study involved "Albert", a young child of a laboratory worker. Albert was brought to the laboratory where he entertained himself by playing with the lab rats. During the experiment, Albert was presented with a rat that then brought about the play response. Then the investigator walked up behind Albert while he was enjoying his play with the rats, and stuck a metal bar with a hammer. This act created a loud sound that frightened Albert. After seven "pairings" of the original stimuli with the new stimuli, Albert showed a fear reaction at the presentation of the original stimuli. This fear response "generalised" to new stimuli: Albert also showed fear (CR) when things (CS) similar to the fuzzy lab rat were presented. This fear response extinguished after about a month of no loud sounds being made when lab rats were present. The lab rats were no longer associated with the frightening noise.

3.1.3. Edwin Guthrie's Contributions

Edwin Guthrie developed the principle of "all or none" learning. He believed that individuals forget or lose a previous response to a stimulus because a new behaviour is found to be more beneficial, and the inhibition system allows only one response to occur to a stimulus. He believed that disordered behaviour was due to responses competing to occur to a particular stimulus, thus causing stress and confusion.

Guthrie also described "one trial learning", pointing out that some new skills can be adopted after doing it only once. The benefits of the behaviour are quickly recognised, and the behaviour is shown again in the presence of the stimuli. Certainly, this type of learning does not apply to penmanship or video games in which multiple practice must be conducted to develop skill. However, if you step off of a curb and get hit by a bus, chances are that you'll learn to stop at the curb and look for vehicles next time. There is no need for repeated practice sessions.

3.1.4. Albert Bandura's Contributions

Albert Bandura pointed out that for some learning of new behaviours, not even one trial is needed. Sometimes people observe another engaging in an action they don't yet display, and then perform that behaviour well on the first attempt.

In a famous experiment, children watched an adult enter a preschool classroom, walk over to a table, pick up a hammer, and hit a large inflatable doll that had a weighted bottom. The adult then left and the child who had been watching was allowed into the room. Where did the child go? Directly to the doll to hit it with the hammer. A new behaviour was being displayed even though there had been no coaching or practice. Later studies found that the characteristics of the model had an effect on the chances of the behaviour being emulated. High status models and those who were reinforced for their behaviour were most likely to have their response modelled. Aggressive behaviour was more likely to be modelled than non-aggressive behaviour. Additionally, even if the behaviour was not initially demonstrated by the child in the presence of the stimulus, an offer of a reward would bring about that observed response.

3.2. OPERANT CONDITIONING

This later school of behaviourism emerged from the research of B.F. Skinner. This school of thought and practice focuses on the effect of environmental consequences. The term "operant" derives from Skinner's experiments in which rats and pigeons "operated" on the environment instead of being passive.

3.2.1. B.F. Skinner's Contributions

Skinner, the greatest behavioural psychologist of all time, is known as the "father" of operant conditioning. He rejected the idea of inner causes for behaviour, and placed emphasis on observable behaviour as opposed to the theorising, based on unverifiable evidence, often done by others. He discovered that whether a response to a stimulus continues to occur depends on the consequence that follows that behaviour. The promptness of administration of that consequence is also important. He also experimented with different "schedules of reinforcement", and devised a procedure known as "shaping".

3.2.2. Edward Thorndike's Contributions

Edward Thorndike is considered to be the originator of reinforcement theory and the "father" of educational psychology. He described several principles or laws regarding the effect of consequences upon behaviour. His "law of effect" stated that the strength of the connection between a stimuli and a response is an effect or result of the consequence that follows the behaviour. His "law of readiness" stated that an individual's physiology effects the influence of consequences. Individuals will be less affected by consequences when they are sleepy, inebriated, or otherwise pre-occupied by other things. The "law of exercise" stated that a connection between a stimulus and a response becomes stronger with practice.

3.2.3. Clark Hull's Contributions

Clark Hull devised perhaps the most complex, formal and systematic theory of behaviour ever presented. This formulation may have been the result of his background as a physicist and engineer. It is much too complicated to explain here, however, certain principles were identified. He noted that the strength of a stimulus is important in whether a response is displayed. For example, someone quickly whispering "boo" won't cause another person to flinch, but yelling it is more likely to do so.

The importance of the strength of the reinforcer on the display of the response was also described. For example, an adolescent who runs an errand for an adult and receives a penny in payment, may not agree to run another errand. However, payment of a dollar is more likely to result in a future errand running response to the request. Hull also described "secondary reinforcement" in which a previously neutral stimulus takes on reinforcing qualities. For example, giving a dollar to a six-month-old child is less likely to produce a reaction to a request than giving it to a six-year-old. An unknown actor's autograph may not bring any money until success makes that previously neutral stimuli become a desirable commodity.

3.2.4. Ivar Lovass's Contributions

Ivar Lovass is known as the "father" of applied behaviour analysis (ABA), the behaviourist procedures that involve the systematic environmental modifications used to understand and change the behaviours of humans. He worked with children with autism. These ABA procedures are the only ones proven to work with these impaired students. His programme of intensive one-to-one teaching with repeated trials was based on the work of Skinner and others.

3.3. Classical (Respondent) Conditioning

Classical conditioning was the first type of learning to be discovered and studied within the behaviourist tradition. The major theorist in the development of classical conditioning is Ivan Pavlov, a Russian scientist trained in biology and medicine. Pavlov was studying the digestive system of dogs and became intrigued with his observation that dogs deprived of food began to salivate when one of his assistants walked into the room. He began to investigate this phenomena and established the laws of classical conditioning. Skinner renamed this type of learning "respondent conditioning" since in this type of learning, one is responding to an environmental antecedent.

3.3.1. Major Concepts

Classical conditioning is Stimulus (S) elicits >Response (R) conditioning since the antecedent stimulus (singular) causes (elicits) the reflexive or involuntary response to occur. Classical conditioning starts with a reflex: an innate, involuntary behaviour elicited or caused by an antecedent environmental event. For example, if air is blown into your eye, you blink. You have no voluntary or conscious control over whether the blink occurs or not.

The specific model for classical conditioning is:

1. *Unconditioned Stimulus (US)* elicits > Unconditioned Response (UR): a stimulus will naturally (without learning) elicit or bring about a reflexive response.
2. *Neutral Stimulus (NS)* —> does not elicit the response of interest: this stimulus (sometimes called an orienting stimulus as it elicits an orienting response) is a neutral stimulus since it does not elicit the Unconditioned (or reflexive) Response.
3. The Neutral/Orientiing Stimulus (NS) is repeatedly paired with the Unconditioned/Natural Stimulus (US).
4. The NS is transformed into a Conditioned Stimulus (CS); that is, when the CS is presented by itself, it elicits or causes the CR (which is the same involuntary response as the UR; the name changes because it is elicited by a different stimulus. This is written CS elicits > CR.

In classical conditioning no new behaviours are learned. Instead, an association is developed between the NS and the US so that the animal / person responds to both events / stimuli (plural) in the same way; restated, after conditioning, both the US and the CS will elicit the same involuntary response.

The following is a restatement of these basic principles using figures of Pavlov's original experiments as an example.

3.3.1.1. Before conditioning

In order to have classical or respondent conditioning, there must exist a stimulus that will automatically or reflexively elicit a specific response. This stimulus is called the Unconditioned Stimulus or UCS because there is no learning involved in connecting the stimulus and response. There must also be a stimulus that will not elicit this specific response, but will elicit an orienting response. This stimulus is called a Neutral Stimulus or an Orienting Stimulus.

3.3.1.2. During conditioning

During conditioning, the neutral stimulus will first be presented, followed by the unconditioned stimulus. Over time, the learner will develop an association between these two stimuli.

3.3.1.3. After conditioning

After conditioning, the previously neutral or orienting stimulus will elicit the response previously only elicited by the unconditioned stimulus. The stimulus is now called a conditioned stimulus because it will now elicit a different response as a result of conditioning or learning. The response is now called a conditioned response because it is elicited by a stimulus as a result of learning. The two responses, unconditioned and conditioned, look the same, but they are elicited by different stimuli and are therefore given different labels.

In the area of classroom learning, classical conditioning primarily influences emotional behaviour. Things that make us happy, sad, angry, etc. become associated with neutral stimuli that gain our attention. For example, if a particular academic subject or remembering a particular teacher produces emotional feelings in you, those emotions are probably a result of classical conditioning.

3.4. Operant (Instrumental) Conditioning

The major theorists for the development of operant conditioning are Edward Thorndike, John Watson and B.F. Skinner. This approach to behaviourism played a major role in the development of the science of psychology, especially in the United States. They proposed that learning is the result of the application of consequences; that is, learners begin to connect certain responses with certain stimuli. This connection causes the probability of the response to change.

Thorndike labeled this type of learning instrumental. Using consequences, he taught kittens to manipulate a latch (e.g., an instrument). Skinner renamed instrumental as operant because it is more descriptive (i.e., in this learning, one is "operating" on, and is influenced by, the environment). Where classical conditioning illustrates S—>R learning, operant conditioning is often viewed as R—>S learning since it is the consequence that follows the response that influences whether the response is likely or unlikely to occur again. It is through operant conditioning that voluntary responses are learned.

The three-term model of operant conditioning (S—> R—>S) incorporates the concept that responses cannot occur without an environmental event preceding it. While the antecedent stimulus in operant conditioning does not elicit or cause the response, it can influence it. When the antecedent does influence the likelihood of a response occurring, it is technically called a discriminative stimulus.

It is the stimulus that follows a voluntary response that changes the probability of whether the response is likely or unlikely to occur again. There are two types of consequences: positive and negative. These can be added to or taken away from the environment in order to change the probability of a given response occurring again.

3.4.1. General Principles

There are four major techniques or methods used in operant conditioning. They result from combining the two major purposes of operant conditioning (increasing or decreasing the probability that a specific behaviour will occur in the future), the types of stimuli used (positive/pleasant or negative/aversive), and the action taken (adding or removing the stimulus).

3.4.1.1. Schedules of consequences

Stimuli are presented in the environment according to a schedule of which there are two basic categories: continuous and intermittent. Continuous reinforcement simply means that the behaviour is followed by a consequence each time it occurs. Intermittent schedules are based either on the passage of time or the number of correct responses emitted. The consequence can be delivered based on the same amount of passage of time or the same number of correct responses or it could be based on a slightly different amount of time or number of correct responses that vary around a particular number. This results in an four classes of intermittent schedules.

1. *Fixed interval* — the first correct response after a set amount of time has passed is reinforced. The time period required is always the same.

   Notice that in the context of positive reinforcement, this schedule produces a scalloping effect during learning. Also notice the number of behaviours observed in a 30-minute-time period.

2. *Variable interval*—the first correct response after a set amount of time has passed is reinforced. After the reinforcement, a new time period is set with the average equaling a specific number over a sum total of trials.

   Notice that this schedule reduces the scalloping effect and the number of behaviours observed in the 30-minute time period is slightly increased.

3. *Fixed ratio* — a reinforcer is given after a specified number of correct responses. This schedule is best for learning a new behaviour.

   Notice that behaviour is relatively stable between reinforcements, with a slight delay after a reinforcement is given. Also notice the number of behaviours observed during the 30-minute-time period is larger than that seen under either of the interval schedules.

4. *Variable ratio*—a reinforcer is given after a set number of correct responses. After reinforcement the number of correct responses necessary for reinforcement changes. This schedule is best for maintaining behaviour.

   Notice that the number of responses per time period increases as the schedule of reinforcement is changed from fixed interval to variable interval and from fixed ratio to variable ratio.

In summary, the schedules of consequences are often called schedules of reinforcements because there is only one schedule that is appropriate for administering response cost and punishment: continuous or fixed ratio of one. In fact, certainty of the application of a consequence is the most important aspect of using response cost and punishment. Learners must know, without a doubt, that an undesired or inappropriate target behaviour will be followed by removal of a positive/pleasant stimulus or the addition of a negative/aversive stimulus. Using an intermittent schedule when one is attempting to reduce a behaviour may actually lead to a strengthening of the behaviour, certainly an unwanted end result.

3.4.2. Premack Principle

The Premack Principle, often called "grandma's rule," states that a high frequency activity can be used to reinforce low frequency behaviour. Access to the preferred activity is contingent on completing the low-frequency behaviour. The high frequency behaviour to use as a reinforcer can be determined by:

1. asking students what they would like to do;
2. observing students during their free time; or
3. determing what might be expected behaviour for a particular age group.

3.4.3. Analysing Examples of Operant Conditioning

There are five basic processes in operant conditioning: positive and negative reinforcement strengthen behaviour; punishment, response cost, and extinction weaken behaviour.

1. *Postive reinforcement*— The term reinforcement always indicates a process that strengthens a behaviour; the word positive has two cues associated with it. First, a positive or pleasant stimulus is used in the process, and second, the reinforcer is added. In positive reinforcement, a positive reinforcer is added after a response and increases the frequency of the response.
2. *Negative reinforcement*— The term reinforcement always indicates a process that strengthens a behaviour; the word negative has two cues associated with it. First, a negative or aversive stimulus is used in the process, and second, the reinforcer is subtracted. In negative reinforcement, after the

response the negative reinforcer is removed which increases the frequency of the response.

3. *Response cost*— If positive reinforcement strengthens a response by adding a positive stimulus, then response cost has to weaken a behaviour by subtracting a positive stimulus. After the response the positive reinforcer is removed which weakens the frequency of the response.
4. *Punishment*— If negative reinforcement strengthens a behaviour by subtracting a negative stimulus, than punishment has to weaken a behaviour by adding a negative stimulus. After a response a negative or aversive stimulus is added which weakens the frequency of the response.
5. *Extinction*— No longer reinforcing a previously reinforced response results in the weakening of the frequency of the response.

Rules in analysing examples. The following questions can help in determining whether operant conditioning has occurred.

a) What behaviour in the example was increased or decreased?

b) Was the behaviour increased, or decreased.

c) What was the consequence / stimulus that followed the behaviour in the example?

d) Was the consequence / stimulus added or removed? If added the process was either positive reinforcement or punishment. If it was subtracted, the process was either negative reinforcement or response cost.

3.4.4. Applications of Operant Conditioning to Education

Our knowledge about operant conditioning has greatly influenced educational practices. Children at all ages exhibit behaviour. Teachers and parents are, by definition, behaviour modifiers if a child is behaviourally the same at the end of the academic year, you will not have done your job as a teacher; children are supposed to learn (i.e., produce relatively permanent change in behaviour or behaviour potential) as a result of the experiences they have in the school / classroom setting.

Behavioural studies in classroom settings have established principles that help teachers organise and arrange classroom experiences to facilitate both academic and social behaviour. Instruction itself has also been the focus of numerous studies, and has resulted in a variety of teaching models for educators at all levels. Programmed instruction is only one such model. Programmed instruction requires that learning be done in small steps, with the learner being an active participant (rather than passive), and that immediate corrective feedback is provided at each step.

3.5. Observational (Social) Learning

Observational or social learning is based primarily on the work of Albert Bandura. He and his colleagues were able to demonstrate through a variety of experiments that the application of consequences was not necessary for learning to take place. Rather learning could occur through the simple processes of observing someone else's activity.

Bandura formulated his findings in a four-step pattern which combines a cognitive view and an operant view of learning.

1. *Attention* — the individual notices something in the environment.
2. *Retention* — the individual remembers what was noticed.
3. *Reproduction* — the individual produces an action that is a copy of what was noticed.
4. *Motivation* — the environment delivers a consequence that changes the probability the behaviour will be emitted again (reinforcement and punishment)

Bandura's work draws from both behavioural and cognitive views of learning. He believes that mind, behaviour and the environment all play an important role in the learning process.

Three groups of children watched a film in which a child in a playroom behaved aggressively towards a "bobo doll." The film had three different endings. One group of children saw the child praised for his behaviour; a second group saw the child told to go sit down in a corner and was not allowed to play with the toys; a third group group saw a film with the child simply walking out of the room. Children were then allowed into the playroom and actions of aggression were noted.

Bandura and his colleagues also demonstrated that viewing aggression by cartoon characters produces more aggressive behaviour than viewing live or filmed aggressive behaviour by adults. Additionally, they demonstrated that having children view prosocial behaviour can reduce displays of aggressive behaviour.

References

Bates, John, and Theodore Wachs, eds., *Temperament: Individual Differences at the Interface of Biology and Behaviour,* Washington, DC: American Psychological Association, 1994.

Cohen, S. & Trostle, S.L., "Young children's preferences for school-related physical-environmental setting characteristics", *Environment and Behaviour,* 1990.

Dunn, R. Krimsky, J.S., Murray, J.B. & Quinn, P.J., "Light up their lives: A research on the effects of lighting on children's achievement and behaviour", *The Reading Teacher*, 1985.

Kuhn, D., *A developmental model of critical thinking*, Educational Researcher, 1999.

Vygotskii, L. S, *Educational psychology*, Trans. Robert Silverman. Boca Raton, FL: St. Lucie Press. 1997.

4

Cognitive Theories of Learning

Cognitivism is a theoretical approach in understanding the mind using quantitative, positivist and scientific methods, that describes mental functions as information processing models. It has two major components, one methodological, the other theoretical. Methodologically, cognitivism adopts a positivist approach and the belief that psychology can be fully explained by the use of experiment, measurement and the scientific method. This is also largely a reductionist goal, with the belief that individual components of mental function can be identified and meaningfully understood. The second is the belief that cognition consists of discrete, internal mental states whose manipulation can be described in terms of rules or algorithms.

Cognitivism became the dominant force in psychology in the late-20th century, replacing behaviourism as the most popular paradigm for understanding mental function. Cognitive psychology is not a wholesale refutation of behaviourism, but rather an expansion that accepts that mental states exist. This was due to the increasing criticism towards the end of the 1950s of behaviourist models. One of the most notable criticisms was Chomsky's argument that language could not be acquired purely through conditioning, and must be at least partly explained by the existence of internal mental states.

The main issues that interest cognitive psychologists are the inner mechanisms of human thought and the processes of knowing. Cognitive psychologists have attempted to throw light on the alleged mental structures that stand in a causal relationship to our physical actions.

Cognitivism has been criticised in a number of ways Phenomenologists and hermeneutic philosophers have criticised the positivist approach of cognitivism for reducing individual meaning to what they perceive as measurements stripped of all significance. They argue that by representing experiences and mental functions as measurements, cognitivism is ignoring the context and, therefore, the meaning of these measurements. They believe that it is this personal meaning of experience gained from the phenomenon as it is experienced by a person which is the fundamental aspect of our psychology that needs to be understood, therefore they argue that a context-free psychology is a contradiction in terms. They also argue in favour of holism: that positivist methods cannot be meaningfully used on something which is inherently irreducible to component parts. Humanistic psychology draws heavily on this philosophy, and practitioners have been among the most critical of cognitivism.

In the 1990s, various new theories emerged and challenged cognitivism and the idea that thought was best described as computation. Some of these new approaches, often influenced by phenomenological and post-modernist philosophy, include situated cognition, distributed cognition, dynamicism, embodied cognition. Some thinkers working in the field of artificial life have also produced non-cognitivist models of cognition.

4.1. Cognitive Learning

It is a common assumption that the effectiveness of a persuasive communication is, at least in part, a function of the extent to which its content is learned and retained by its audience. This assumed learning-persuasion relation is based on a reasonable analogy between the persuasive communication and an informational communication such as a classroom lecture. In the lecture, it is by defi-nition of the educational situation that retention of content is taken as a measure of effectiveness. In the persuasion situation, however, the essential criterion of effectiveness is acceptance of content. It remains an empirical question to determine whether acceptance of a persuasive communication is related to retention of its content.

The hypothesis that acceptance of a communication is, in some part, a function of learning or retention of its content has received explicit endorsement by a number of attitude researchers and theorists and has aroused no published opposition. Indeed, this cognitive learning model of persuasion is most reasonable. It is widely accepted that cognitions bearing on the object of an attitude form a major component of the structure of the attitude toward that object. Since the individual is not born with his cognitions, but acquires them, there seems to be no reasonable alternative to the assumption that cognitions bearing on attitude objects are learned. Further, the most obvious source of such cognitions is the wealth of persuasive messages to which one is exposed via the public communications media as well as through face-to-face communications.

In the light of the overpowering reasonableness of the persuasion-as-a-function-of-retention hypothesis, it is rather surprising how unsupporting the research evidence is. A few studies have directly examined the relation between the learning and attitudinal effects of persuasive communications. These studies have generally found that both communication retention and persuasion diminish with increasing time between communication and posttest, consistent with the hypothesis that retention is necessary for persuasion.

On the other hand, these same studies have found only weak and variable correlations between communication retention and persuasion among subjects tested at the same post test interval, suggesting that the relation between retention and persuasion is not a necessary one. There are separate memory systems for retention of a set of person-descriptive adjectives and of the person-impression derived from them; their results thus also suggest little or no necessary relation between a communication's retention and its effectiveness.

Additionally, in a number of studies scattered throughout the attitude literature, variables shown to affect opinion demonstrably — such as credibility, fear arousal, and organisation of arguments have not been found to have corresponding effects on retention of communicated arguments. Such negative findings on retention measures have typically been used to counter any possible interpretation for obtained attitude change differences in terms of unintentionally induced differences in attention to or retention of communication content. In sum, the research evidence must be interpreted as uncongenial to the hypothesis that persuasion is a function of retention of persuasive arguments. It must be concluded that either (a) learning of attitude-relevant cognitions is unrelated to attitude formation and change; or (b) persuasive communications can induce attitude change without necessarily providing the cognitive content on which the attitude is based. The first conclusion carries the implication that learned cognitions are not fundamental to the structure of attitudes. Rather than accept this conclusion, which runs counter to most conceptions of attitude, it seemed worth some effort to explore sources other than persuasive communications as possible origins of learned attitudinal cognitions.

4.2. Cognitive Responses to Persuasion

There is, of course, an important extracommunication source of cognitive content in the persuasion situation: the cognitive reactions of the communication recipient to incoming persuasive information. When a person receives a communication and is faced with the decision of accepting or rejecting the persuasion, he may be expected to attempt to relate the new information to his existing attitudes, knowledge, feelings, etc. In the course of doing this, he likely rehearses substantial cognitive content beyond that of the persuasive message itself. The present hypothesis is, then, that rehearsal and learning of cognitive responses to persuasion may provide a basis for explaining persisting effects of communications in terms of cognitive learning. The learning of cognitive response content may, indeed, be more fundamental to persuasion than is the learning of communication content.

Despite a number of speculations, there has been no direct experimental exploration of the role of cognitive responses in persuasion, and, in fact, there is not much research that is even relevant. The research on active participation in the communication process comes closest to being relevant. Elsewhere, isolated experiments have explored dependent variables approximating the present conception of cognitive responses to persuasion. Research in which cognitive responses to persuasion are employed as independent variables in experimental persuasion situations is particularly needed. Before proceeding to a consideration of evidence collected in the author's laboratory, it will be useful to state the present hypothesis with some precision.

It is proposed that the persuasion situation is usefully regarded as a complex stimulus that evokes in the recipient a complex cognitive response. The essential dimensions of the recipient's cognitive response are, at the least, (a) response content, i.e., degree of acceptance versus rejection of the position advocated in the communication, and (b) intensity, or vigour, of response. The latter dimension, as well as other possible dimensions of cognitive response, will not be considered further in this chapter. The essential components of the persuasion situation as a stimulus - that is, as determinant of the cognitive response content - are setting, source, and communication content. An additional major set of determinants of the cognitive response content is the set of characteristics brought by the recipient to the persuasion situation, including his existing repertory of attitude-relevant cognitions as well as personality traits and group memberships.

As in many other treatments of persuasion, the cognitive response analysis assumes that attitude change can be achieved by the modification, through learning, of the recipient's repertory of attitude-relevant cognitions. Such modification might include strengthening of existing cognitions as well as introduction of new ones. The present emphasis on the mediating role of the recipient's own cognitive responses to persuasion may be formulated as an assertion that cognitive modification of attitudes requires active rehearsal of attitude-relevant cognitions at a time when the attitude object or opinion issue is salient. Thus the effects of persuasive communications might range from persuasion—when the recipient rehearses content supporting the advocated position—to boomerang—when the recipient rehearses content opposing the advocated position.

As a consequence of the present emphasis on the recipient's rehearsal of his own responses to persuasion, it is assumed that learning of communication content does not play an essential role in mediating the effects of persuasive communications. The present formulation, therefore, is capable of maintaining an analysis of persuasion effects in terms of cognitive learning while being compatible with findings indicating no necessary relation between communication retention and persuasion.

It is possible to formulate the cognitive response analysis in terms of an analogy to the classical conditioning paradigm. In this analogy, the persuasion situation corresponds to the unconditioned stimulus in that it has a response evocation capacity; that is, it influences the content of the recipient's cognitive response. As an analog of the unconditioned response, the cognitive response becomes transferred to the attitude object, which is analogous to the conditioned stimulus of the classical paradigm. While this analogy may be decidedly useful, especially in relating the present analysis to other treatments that have invoked the classical conditioning model, it would be inappropriate currently to regard the model as more than a possibly suggestive analogy. A point of difficulty that would arise if the model is taken literally, for example, would concern the nature of the conditioned response in persuasion; it would be unnecessarily cumbersome, at this stage, to incorporate in the present analysis an analogy to the conditioning model's assumption that conditioned responses are either fractional components of unconditioned responses or preparatory adjustments to unconditioned stimuli.

4.2.1. Change and Content of Communication Content

Previous studies of the relationship between communication retention and opinion change have tested this relationship correlationally—subjects received a communication and were subsequently tested for both retention of content and acceptance of the viewpoint of the communication. A study was conducted in which communication retention was a manipulated independent variable, with opinion as the dependent variable. Such a design, it may be noted, is more appropriate to drawing a conclusion about the causal role of communication learning in attitude change than is a correlational design.

It must be said that learning of communication content is not a sufficient condition, and perhaps not even a necessary condition, for persuasion. The lack of opinion differences between conditions with decided retention differences in the present study suggests that such previously obtained across-cell correlations should not be interpreted in terms of a causal relation between communication retention and persuasion.

4.2.2. Acceptance and Recall of Improvised Arguments

If, as is presently supposed, attitudes change in the direction of cognitive content rehearsed during a persuasion situation, then procedures that manipulate the content of the recipient's cognitive responses should have persuasive effect. A traditional persuasion procedure that may be viewed as a manipulation of cognitive response content is the improvised role-playing procedure in which a subject is asked to deliver a persuasive message supporting a position initially unacceptable to him. The majority of research evidence indicates that role playing produces greater persuasion toward the unacceptable position than does passive receipt of a persuasive communication. Such results are quite compatible with the present point that a communication recipient's rehearsal of his own arguments may be more important in persuasion than is his rehearsal of arguments contained in a communication to which he is exposed. However, some commentators feel that the currently available evidence on role playing is equivocal. Because of this empirical uncertainty, the present research programme included an experiment intended to assess the effect of improvised role playing on both acceptance and retention of arguments.

In this experiment, each subject improvised five arguments in response to an assignment to advocate either specialised or general under-graduate education. Improvisation was obtained in response to five neutrally worded questions that could be answered with an argument supporting either viewpoint. Assignment to positions was random with approximately 90 subjects being assigned to each side. In addition to being exposed to their own improvised arguments supporting one side of the issue, subjects carefully read and studied-for about the same amount of time they had spent improvising-a set of arguments supporting the opposite side that was actually written by another subject in the study. Since each subject's improvisations served once as an improvised set of arguments and once as an externally originated set, this procedure served to equate quality of arguments for the two sets over the sample of subjects, although not necessarily for each subject. After a 20-minute irrelevant task, the subjects were tested for opinion on the general-specialised education issue and were then asked to recall as many arguments as they could of those to which they had been exposed-both their own and the ones that had been improvised by another subject.

4.3. Attitude-Relevant Cognitions

At present, knowledge concerning the determinants of learning of attitude-relevant cognitions is quite limited. Certainly, much is known theoretically about verbal learning, including learning of meaningful material. However, the particular variables involved in attitude-relevant learning—for example, covert rehearsal, preexisting attitudes, prior familiarity with information, and comprehension of persuasive messages—are not well understood in learning-theoretical terms. A number of presentations of a persuasive argument is about the only variable that is unequivocally established as a determinant of argument retention.

Until quite recently, another widely accepted principle of learning of persuasive arguments was that audiences would selectively attend to and remember information consonant with their pre-existing attitudes. Several studies had demonstrated effects of this nature. Recent attempts to replicate this phenomenon have met with absolutely no success, so that the phenomenon of selective learning of attitude-consonant information must currently be regarded as of dubious validity.

Other determinants of attitude-relevant learning that have been implicated by empirical research are information utility and novelty. Since utility and novelty are variables known to increase attention to persuasive information: it appears likely that their effects on learning of persuasive arguments may be mediated by these attentional effects rather than by any direct role in the learning process. The findings of the studies just mentioned, and of other relevant studies not cited here, do not require the supposition that any variable other than duration of exposure to persuasive information is a determinant of information learning. It seems likely also that comprehension of information is a determinant of retention; however, minimal evidence is available concerning this relationship. Additionally, conditions of practice, particularly distribution of practice over time, should be expected to affect learning of persuasive information in much the same manner that they affect learning of other verbal material; again, little pertinent evidence is available, although the literature concerned with primacy and recency effects in persuasion may be interpreted in terms of the conditions-of-practice variable.

The effects of rewards and punishments occurring in the persuasion situation are certainly relevant to theoretical interpretations of cognitive learning. However, although effects of rewards and punishments on attitude measures have frequently been demonstrated, the processes underlying such effects are poorly understood. Competing explanations in terms of classical conditioning, instrumental learning, dissonance reduction, and attention mechanisms, all can be justified by appeal to portions of the relevant literature.

The procedure of having subjects actively rehearse their own persuasive arguments was found to produce substantial enhancement of argument retention as well as noticeable self-persuasion. At the moment, it is unknown whether these effects were due to enhanced original attention to the improvised arguments or to other factors. None the less, the focus on learning of persuasive arguments actively rehearsed in a persuasion situation has provided the basis for presently reasserting the importance of cognitive learning in persua-sion. Thus, the study of determinants of persuasive-argument learning—a problem area in which, to summarise the present brief literature review, current ignorance is considerable—can be justified not only as an interesting exercise in learning theory, but in terms of its practical value in interpreting the basis for effective and durable persuasion.

4.4. Cognitive Theory of Multimedia Learning

Research on educational technologies—ranging from motion pictures to computer-based tutoring systems—documents a disapointing history in which strong claims for a new technology are followed by large-scale implementations which eventually fail. For example, in 1922, the famous inventor Thomas Edison proclaimed that "the motion picture is destined to revolutionise our educational system and that in a few years it will supplant...the use of textbooks." Yet, in reviewing the role of motion pictures in schools over the decades since Edison's grand predictions, most teachers used films infrequently in classrooms. Similarly, 50 years later in the 1970s, the game-like computer-assisted instruction (CAI) programs that were tauted as the wave of the future in education eventually proved to be no more effective than teacher based modes of instruction.

Today, similarly strong claims are being made for the potential of multimedia learning environments. How can we avoid a trail of broken promises concerning the educational benefits of new educational technologies such as multimedia learning evironments? A reasonable solution is to use instructional technology in ways that are grounded in research-based theory. Effective use of a new instructional technology must be guided by a research-based theory of how students learn. Fortunately, advances in cognitive psychology provide the starting point for such theories. One of the most important avenues of cognitive psychology is to understand how technology—such as multimedia—can be used to foster student learning. As an example, a research-based review of five principles of multimedia design are dealt with here. The theory draws on dual coding theory, working memory, cognitive load theory, generative theory, and SOI model of meaningful learning. According to the theory, the learner possesses a visual information processing system and a verbal information processing, such that auditory narration goes into the verbal system whereas animation goes into the visual system.

In multimedia learning the learner engages in three important cognitive processes. The first cognitive progress, selecting, is applied to incoming verbal information to yield a text base and is applied to incoming visual information to yield an image base. The second cognitive process, organising, is applied to the word base to create a verbally-based model of the to-beexplained system and is applied to the image base to create a visually-based model of the tobe-explained system. Finally, the third process, integrating, occurs when the learner builds connections between corresponding events in the verbally-based model and the visually-based model. The model has generated a series of experiments yielding five major principles of how to use multimedia to help students understand a scientific explanation. Each principle of multimedia design is subject to further research.

Multiple Representation Principle: The first principle is simply that it is better to present an explanation using two modes of representation rather than one. For example, students who listened to a narration explaining how a bicycle tyre pump works while also viewing a corresponding animation generated twice as many useful solutions to subsequent problem solving transfer questions than did students who listened to the same narration without viewing any animation. Similarly, students who read a text containing captioned illustrations placed near the corresponding words generated about 65 percent more useful solutions on a subsequent problem-solving transfer test than did students who simply read the text. We call this result a multimedia effect.

The multimedia effect is consistent with a cognitive theory of multimedia learning because students given multimedia explanations are able to build two different mental representations—a verbal model and a visual model—and build connections between them.

Contiguity principle: (When giving a multimedia explanation, present corresponding words and pictures contiguously rather than separately.) The second principle is that students better understand an explanation when corresponding words and pictures are presented at the same time than when they are separated in time.

For example, students who listened to a narration explaining how a bicycle tyre pump works while also viewing a corresponding animation generated 50 percent more useful solutions to subsequent problem-solving transfer questions than did students who viewed the animation before or after listening to the narration. Similarly, students who read a text explaining how tyre pumps work that included captioned illustrations placed near the text generated about 75 percent more useful solutions on problem-solving transfer questions than did students who read the same text and illustrations presented on separate pages.

We call this result a contiguity effect, and similar patterns have been noted by other researchers. This result is consistent with the cognitive theory of multimedia learning because corresponding words and pictures must be in working memory at the same time in order to facilitate the construction of referential links between them.

Split-attention principle: (When giving a multimedia explanation, present words as auditory narration rather than as visual on-screen text.) The third principle is that words should be presented auditorily rather than visually. For example, students who viewed an animation depicting the formation of lightning while also listening to a corresponding narration generated approximately 50 percent more useful solutions on a subsequent problem-solving transfer test than did students who viewed the same animation with corresponding on-screen text consisting of the same words as the narration. This is called a split attention effect. This result is consistent with the cognitive theory of multimedia learning because the on-screen text and animation can overload the visual information processing system whereas narration is processed in the verbal information processing system and animation is processed in the visual information processing system.

Individual differences principle: (The foregoing principles are more important for lowknowledge than high-knowledge learners, and for high-spatial rather than low-spatial learners.) The fourth principle is that multimedia effects, contiguity effects, and split-attention effects depend on individual differences in the learner. For example, students who lack prior knowledge tended to show stronger multimedia effects and contiguity effects than students who possessed high levels of prior knowledge. According to a cognitive theory of multimedia learning, students with high prior knowledge may be able to generate their own mental images while listening to an animation or reading a verbal text so having a contiguous visual presentation is not needed. Additionally, students who scored high on tests of spatial ability showed greater multimedia effects than did students who scored low on spatial ability. According to a cognitive theory of multimedia learning, students with high spatial ability are able to hold the visual image in visual working memory and thus are more likely to benefit from contiguous presentation of words and pictures.

Coherence principle: (When giving a multimedia explanation, use few rather than many extraneous words and pictures.) The fifth principle is that students learn better from a coherent summary which highlights the relevant words and pictures than from a longer version of the summary. For example, students who read a passage explaining the steps in how lightning forms along with corresponding illustrations generated 50 percent more useful solutions on a subsequent problem-solving transfer test than did students who read the same information with additional details inserted in the materials. Sweller and his colleagues refer to this as the redundancy effect and they have found a similar pattern of results. This result is consistent with a cognitive theory of multimedia learning, in which a shorter presentation primes the learner to select relevant information and organise it productively.

By beginning with a theory of how learners process multimedia information, we have been able to conduct focused research that yields some preliminary principles of multimedia design. Although all of the principles are subject to further testing, this work demonstrates how it is possible to take a learner-centred approach to instructional technology. This work can be considered a success to the extent that this line of research contributes to the implementation of successful multimedia instruction.

4.5. Theory of Cognitive Development

The Theory of Cognitive Development, one of the most historically influential theories was developed by Jean Piaget, a Swiss psychologist. His theory provided many central concepts in the field of developmental psychology and concerned the growth of intelligence, which for Piaget, meant the ability to more accurately represent the world and perform logical operations on representations of concepts grounded in the world.

The theory concerns the emergence and acquisition of schemata—schemes of how one perceives the world—in "developmental stages", times when children are acquiring new ways of mentally representing information. The theory is considered "constructivist", meaning that, unlike nativist theories (which describe cognitive development as the unfolding of innate knowledge and abilities) or empiricist theories (which describe cognitive development as the gradual acquisition of knowledge through experience), it asserts that we construct our cognitive abilities through self-motivated action in the world. For his development of the theory, Piaget was awarded the Erasmus Prize. Piaget divided schemes that children use to understand the world through four main periods, roughly correlated with and becoming increasingly sophisticated with age:

- Sensorimotor period (years 0–2)
- Preoperational period (years 2–7)
- Concrete operational period (years 7–11)
- Formal operational period (years 11–adulthood)

4.5.1. Sensorimotor Period

According to Piaget, this child is in the *sensorimotor period* and primarily explores the world with senses rather than through mental operations.

Infants are born with a set of congenital reflexes, according to Piaget, in addition to a drive to explore their world. Their initial schemas are formed through differentiation of the congenital reflexes

The *sensorimotor period* is the first of the four periods. According to Piaget, this stage marks the development of essential spatial abilities and understanding of the world in six sub-stages:

The first sub-stage, known as *the reflex schema* stage, occurs from birth to six weeks and is associated primarily with the development of reflexes.

The second sub-stage, *primary circular reaction phase*, occurs from six weeks to four months and is associated primarily with the development of habits.

The third sub-stage, the *secondary circular reactions phase*, occurs from four to nine months and is associated primarily with the development of coordination between vision and prehension.

The fourth sub-stage, called *the co-ordination of secondary circular reactions stage*, which occurs from nine to twelve months, is when Piaget (1954) thought that object permanence developed.

The fifth sub-stage, *the tertiary circular reactions phase*, occurs from twelve to eighteen months and is associated primarily with the discovery of new means to meet goals.

The sixth sub-stage, considered "beginnings of symbolic representation", is associated primarily with the beginnings of insight, or true creativity.

4.5.2. Preoperational Stage

The Preoperational stage is the second of four stages of cognitive development. By observing sequences of play, Piaget was able to demonstrate that towards the end of the second year a qualitatively new kind of psychological functioning occurs.

(Pre)Operatory Thought in Piagetian theory is any procedure for mentally acting on objects. The hallmark of the preoperational stage is sparse and logically inadequate mental operations. During this stage the child learns to use and to represent objects by images and words, in other words they learn to use symbolic thinking. Thinking is still egocentric: The child has difficulty taking the viewpoint of others.

The child can classify objects by a single feature: e.g. groups together all the red blocks regardless of shape or all the square blocks regardless of color. According to Piaget, the Pre-Operational stage of development follows the Sensorimotor stage and occurs between 2–7 years of age. In this stage, children develop their language skills. They begin representing things with words and images. However, they still use intuitive rather than logical reasoning. At the beginning of this stage, they tend to be egocentric, that is, they are not aware that other people do not think, know and perceive the same as them. Children have highly imaginative minds at this time and actually assign emotions to inanimate objects. The theory of mind is also critical to this stage.

The Preoperational Stage can be further broken down into the Preconceptual Stage and the Intuitive Stage

The Preconceptual stage (2-4 years) is marked by egocentric thinking and animistic thought. A child who displays animistic thought tends to assign living attributes to inanimate objects, for example that a glass would feel pain if it were broken.

The Intuitive(4-7 years) stage is when children start employing mental activities to solve problems and obtain goals but they are unaware of how they came to their conclusions. For example a child is shown 7 dogs and 3 cats and asked if there are more dogs than cats. The child would respond positively. However when asked if there are more dogs than animals the child would once again respond positively. Such fundamental errors in logic show the transition between intuitiveness in solving problems and true logical reasoning acquired in later years.

4.5.3. Concrete Operational Stage

The Concrete operational stage is the third of four stages of cognitive development in Piaget's theory. This stage, which follows the Preoperational stage, occurs between the ages of 7 and 12 years and is characterized by the appropriate use of logic. Important processes during this stage are:

Seriation—the ability to sort objects in an order according to size, shape, or any other characteristic. For example, if given different-shaded objects they may make a color gradient.

Classification—the ability to name and identify sets of objects according to appearance, size or other characteristic, including the idea that one set of objects can include another. A child is no longer subject to the illogical limitations of animism (the belief that all objects are alive and therefore have feelings).

Decentering—where the child takes into account multiple aspects of a problem to solve it. For example, the child will no longer perceive an exceptionally wide but short cup to contain less than a normally-wide, taller cup.

Reversibility—where the child understands that numbers or objects can be changed, then returned to their original state. For this reason, a child will be able to rapidly determine that if 4+4 equals 8, 8-4 will equal 4, the original quantity.

Conservation—understanding that quantity, length or number of items is unrelated to the arrangement or appearance of the object or items. For instance, when a child is presented with two equally-sized, full cups they will be able to discern that if water is transferred to a pitcher it will conserve the quantity and be equal to the other filled cup.

Elimination of Egocentrism—the ability to view things from another's perspective (even if they think incorrectly). For instance, show a child a comic in which Jane puts a doll under a box, leaves the room, and then Melissa moves the doll to a drawer, and Jane comes back. A child in the concrete operations stage will say that Jane will still think it's under the box even though the child knows it is in the drawer.

4.5.4. Formal Operational Stage

The formal operational period is the fourth and final of the periods of cognitive development in Piaget's theory. This stage, which follows the Concrete Operational stage, commences at around 11 years of age (puberty) and continues into adulthood. It is characterized by acquisition of the ability to think abstractly, reason logically and draw conclusions from the information available. During this stage the young adult is able to understand such things as love, "shades of gray", logical proofs, and values.

Lucidly, biological factors may be traced to this stage as it occurs during puberty (the time at which another period of neural pruning occurs), marking the entry to adulthood in Physiology, cognition, moral judgement (Kohlberg), Psychosexual development (Freud), and psychosocial development (Erikson). Some two thirds of people do not develop this form of reasoning fully enough that it becomes their normal mode for cognition, and so they remain, even as adults, concrete operational thinkers.

These four stages have been found to have the following characteristics:

— Although the timing may vary, the sequence of the stages does not.

— Universal (not culturally specific)

— *Generalizable*: the representational and logical operations available to the child should extend to all kinds of concepts and content knowledge

— Stages are logically organized wholes

— Hierarchical nature of stage sequences (each successive stage incorporates elements of previous stages, but is more differentiated and integrated)

— Stages represent qualitative differences in modes of thinking, not merely quantitative differences

Piagetians accounts of development have been challenged on several grounds. First, as Piaget himself noted, development does not always progress in the smooth manner his theory seems to predict. 'Decalage', or unpredicted gaps in the developmental progression, suggest that the stage model is at best a useful approximation. More broadly, Piaget's theory is 'domain general', predicting that cognitive maturation occurs concurrently across different domains of knowledge (such as mathematics, logic, understanding of physics, of language, etc).

However, more recent cognitive developmentalists have been much influenced by trends in cognitive science away from domain generality and towards domain specificity or modularity of mind, under which different cognitive faculties may be largely independent of one another and thus develop according to quite different timetables. In this vein, many current cognitive developmentalists argue that rather than being domain general learners, children come equipped with domain specific theories, sometimes referred to as 'core knowledge', which allows them to break into learning within that domain. For example, even young infants appear to understand some basic principles of physics (e.g. that one object cannot pass through another) and human intention (e.g. that a hand repeatedly reaching for an object has that object, not just a particular path of motion, as its goal). These basic assumptions may be the building block out of which more elaborate knowledge is constructed.

References

Ausubel, D. P., "A cognitive structure view of word and concept meaning", In R. C. Anderson & D. P. Ausubel (Eds.), *Readings in the psychology of cognition,* New York: Holt, Rinehart and Winston, Inc., 1965.

Cameron, J., Pierce, W. D., Banko, K. M., & Gear, A., "Achievement-based rewards and intrinsic motivation: A test of cognitive mediators", *Journal of Educational Psychology,* 2005.

Geary, D. C., "Evolution and cognitive development", In R. Burgess & K. MacDonald (Eds.), *Evolutionary perspectives on human development* (pp. 99-133). Thousand Oaks, CA: Sage Publications, 2004.

Neisser, U., *Cognitive psychology*, New York: Appleton-Century Crofts, 1967.

Wertsch, J.V. (ed), *Culture, communication and cognition*, Cambridge: Cambridge University Press, 1985.

5

Intelligence

Intelligence is an umbrella term used to describe a property of the mind that encompasses many related abilities, such as the capacities to reason, to plan, to solve problems, to think abstractly, to comprehend ideas, to use language, and to learn. There are several ways to define intelligence. In some cases, intelligence may include traits such as creativity, personality, character, knowledge, or wisdom. However, most psychologists prefer not to include these traits in the definition of intelligence.

Theories of intelligence can be divided into those based on a unilinear construct of general intelligence and those based on multiple intelligences. Francis Galton, influenced by his cousin Charles Darwin, was the first to advance a theory of general intelligence. For Galton, intelligence was a real faculty with a biological basis that could be studied by measuring reaction times to certain cognitive tasks. Galton's research on measuring the head size of British scientists and ordinary citizens led to the conclusion that head size had no relationship with the person's intelligence.

Alfred Binet and the French school of intelligence believed that intelligence was an average of numerous dissimilar abilities, rather than a unitary entity with specific identifiable properties. The Stanford-Binet intelligence test has been used by both theorists of general intelligence and multiple intelligence.

Our hominid and human ancestors evolved large and complex brains exhibiting an ever-increasing intelligence through a long and mostly unknown evolutionary process. This process was either driven by the direct adaptive benefits of intelligence, or alternatively, driven by its indirect benefits within the context of sexual selection as a reliable signal of genetic resistance against pathogens.

5.1. Theories of Intelligence

The most widely accepted theory of intelligence is based on psychometrics testing or intelligence quotient (IQ) tests. However, dissatisfaction with traditional IQ tests has led to the development of a number of alternative theories, all of which suggest that intelligence is the result of a number of independent abilities that uniquely contribute to human performance.

5.1.1. Psychometric Approach

Despite the variety of concepts of intelligence, the approach to understanding intelligence with the most supporters and published research over the longest period of time is based on psychometrics testing. Such intelligence quotient (IQ) tests include the Stanford-Binet, Raven's Progressive Matrices, the Wechsler Adult Intelligence Scale and the Kaufman Assessment Battery for Children.

All forms of IQ tests correlate highly with one another. The traditional view is that these tests measure *g*, or "general intelligence factor". However, this is by no means universally accepted. One common view is that these abilities are hierarchically arranged with g at the vertex. *g* itself is sometimes considered to be a two part construct, *gF* and *gC*, which stand for fluid and crystallised intelligence.

Intelligence, as measured by IQ and other aptitude tests, is widely used in educational, business, and military settings due to its efficacy in predicting behaviour. *g* is highly correlated with many important social outcomes— individuals with low IQs are more likely to be divorced, have a child out of marriage, be incarcerated, and need long term welfare support, while individuals with high IQs are associated with more years of education, higher status jobs and higher income. Intelligence is significantly correlated with successful training and performance outcomes, and *g* is the single best predictor of successful job performance.

Critics of the psychometric approach point out that people in the general population have a somewhat different and broader conception of intelligence than what is measured in IQ tests. In turn, they argue that the psychometric approach measures only a part of what is commonly understood as intelligence. Furthermore, sceptics argue that even though tests of mental abilities are correlated, people still have unique strengths and weaknesses in specific areas. Consequently they argue that psychometric theorists over-emphasize.

Researchers in the field of human intelligence have encountered a considerable amount of public concern and criticism - much more than scientists in other areas normally receive. A number of critics have challenged the relevance of psychometric intelligence in the context of everyday life. There have also been controversies over genetic factors in intelligence, particularly questions regarding the relationship between race and intelligence and sex and intelligence. Another controversy in the field is how to interpret the increases in test scores that have occurred over time, the so-called Flynn effect.

5.1.2. Triarchic Theory of Intelligence

The triarchic theory of intelligence proposes three fundamental aspects of intelligence—analytic, creative, and practical—of which only the first is measured to any significant extent by mainstream tests. There is a need for a balance between analytic intelligence, on the one hand, and creative and especially practical intelligence on the other.

5.1.3. Emotional Intelligence

The concept of emotional intelligence is at least as "important" as more traditional sorts of intelligence. These theories grew from observations of human development and of brain injury victims who demonstrate an acute loss of a particular cognitive function—e.g. the ability to think numerically, or the ability to understand written language—without showing any loss in other cognitive areas.

5.1.4. Empirical Evidence

IQ proponents have pointed out that IQ's predictive validity has been repeatedly demonstrated, for example in predicting important non-academic outcomes such as job performance, whereas the various multiple intelligence theories have little or no such support. Meanwhile, the relevance and even the existence of multiple intelligences have not been borne out when actually tested. A set of ability tests that do not correlate together would support the claim that multiple intelligences are independent of each other.

5.2. Factors Affecting Intelligence

Intelligence is an ill-defined, difficult to quantify concept. Accordingly, the IQ tests used to measure intelligence provide only approximations of the posited 'real' intelligence. In addition, a number of theoretically unrelated properties are known to correlate with IQ such as race, gender and height but since correlation does not imply causation the true relationship between these factors is uncertain. Factors affecting IQ may be divided into biological and environmental.

5.2.1. Biological

Evidence suggests that genetic variation has a significant impact on IQ, accounting for threefourths in adults. Despite the high heritability of IQ, few genes have been found to have a substantial effect on IQ, suggesting that IQ is the product of interaction between multiple genes.

Other biological factors correlating with IQ include ratio of brain weight to body weight and the volume and location of gray matter tissue in the brain.

Because intelligence appears to be at least partly dependent on brain structure and the genes shaping brain development, it has been proposed that genetic engineering could be used to enhance the intelligence of animals, a process sometimes called biological uplift in science fiction. Experiments on mice have demonstrated superior ability in learning and memory in various behavioural tasks.

5.2.2. Environmental

Evidence suggests that family environmental factors may have an effect upon childhood IQ, accounting for up to a quarter of the variance. On the other hand, by late adolescence this correlation disappears, such that adoptive siblings are no more similar in IQ than strangers. Moreover, adoption studies indicate that, by adulthood, adoptive siblings are no more similar in IQ than strangers, while twins and full siblings show an IQ correlation.

Consequently, in the context of the nature versus nurture debate, the "nature" component appears to be much more important than the "nurture" component in explaining IQ variance in the general population. There are indications that, in middle age, intelligence is influenced by lifestyle choices. Cultural factors also play a role in intelligence.

5.2.3. Ethical Issues

Since intelligence is susceptible to modification through the manipulation of environment, the ability to influence intelligence raises ethical issues. Transhumanist theorists study the possibilities and consequences of developing and using techniques to enhance human abilities and aptitudes, and ameliorate what it regards as undesirable and unnecessary aspects of the human condition; eugenics is a social philosophy which advocates the improvement of human hereditary traits through various forms of intervention. The perception of eugenics has varied throughout history, from a social responsibility required of society, to an immoral, racist stance.

Neuroethics considers the ethical, legal and social implications of neuroscience, and deals with issues such as difference between treating a human neurological disease and enhancing the human brain, and how wealth impacts access to neurotechnology. Neuroethical issues interact with the ethics of human genetic engineering.

5.3. Fluid Intelligence

Fluid intelligence is tied to biology. It is defined as our "on-the-spot reasoning ability, a skill not basically dependant on our experience." This type of intelligence is active when the central nervous system (CNS) is at its physiological peak.

Fluid intelligence is measured by the performance subtasks on the Wechsler Adult Intelligence Scale (WAIS).

Fluid intelligence is important to psychologists as it relates to the study of aging. There is ongoing intense debate among psychologists as to whether or not intelligence declines with aging. Fluid intelligence reaches a peak in early adulthood and then regularly declines. This is because of the physiological changes that accompany aging. The development of CNS structures is exceeded by the rate of CNS breakdown.

5.4. Crystallised Intelligence

Crystallised intelligence can be defined as "the extent to which a person has absorbed the content of culture." It is the store of knowledge or information that a given society has accumulated over time.

Crystallised intelligence is measured by most of the verbal subtests of the Wechsler Adult Intelligence Scale (WAIS).

Crystallised intelligence is important to psychologists as it relates to the study of aging. There is ongoing intense debate among psychologists as to whether or not intelligence declines with aging. As one claims, because crystallised intelligence is based on learning and experience, it remains relatively stable over time. It may even increase as the rate at which we acquire or learn new information in the course of living balances out or exceeds the rate at which we forget. On the other side of the debate, another claims crystallised intelligence in fact declines with age. Why? Because, at a certain time of life the cumulative effect of losses - of job, of health, of relationships - cause disengagement from the culture, and so forgetting finally exceeds the rate at which knowledge is acquired.

5.4.1. Brain Development in Children and Adults

One of the beliefs in our culture is that the brain and its intellectual capacity is developed in early childhood and this has important implications for cognitive development over the lifespan.

It is widely believed that if children's early childhood development is not properly stimulated, then there is likely to be underdevelopment of the brain and that can lead to lower intellectual ability, poor school learning and to a life characterised by social problems such as unemployment, criminal activity, teenage pregnancy and welfare. It will be difficult if not impossible to overcome the disadvantages of deficiencies in early childhood stimulation later in adulthood. And so, some might argue, "Why should we invest in adult literacy education? Let's put our money into early childhood programs. An ounce of prevention is worth a pound of cure!"

But now trends in both brain science and cognitive science have converged to bring about revisions to these ideas from the conventional wisdom. James S. McDonnell Foundation in St. Louis has written articles to explain the findings of brain science and their relevance, or lack thereof, for early childhood and in-school education. Following is a brief summary from the 1998 article of what Bruer regards as major misconceptions that educators have of brain science.

1) Enriched early childhood environments causes synapses to multiply rapidly.
2) More synapses mean more brainpower.
3) The plateau period of high synaptic density and high brain metabolism is the optimal period for learning.

Is it possible to measure the intelligence of young infants in a similar way? Conventional tests of "infant intelligence" do not predict later test scores very well, but certain experimental measures of infant attention and memory that were originally developed for other purposes have turned out to be more successful. In the most common procedure, a particular visual pattern is shown to a baby over and over again. The experimenter records how long the infant subject looks at the pattern on each trial; these looks get shorter and shorter as the baby becomes "habituated" to it. The time required to reach a certain level of habituation, or the extent to which the baby now "prefers" a new pattern, are regarded as measures of some aspect of his or her information-processing capability.

These habituation-based measures, obtained from babies at ages ranging from three months to a year, are significantly correlated with the intelligence test scores of the same children when they get to be two or four or six years old. A few studies have found such correlations even at ages eight or 11. A recent meta analysis, based on 31 different samples, estimates the average magnitude of the correlations at about r=.36. It is possible that these habituation scores do indeed reflect real cognitive differences, perhaps in 'speed of information proçessing". It is also possible, however, that—to a presently unknown extent—they reflect early differences in temperament or inhibition.

It is important to understand what remains stable and what changes in the development of intelligence. A child whose IQ score remains the same from age 6 to age 18 does not exhibit the same performance throughout that period. On the contrary, steady gains in general knowledge vocabulary, reasoning ability, etc. will be apparent. What does not change is his or her score in comparison to that of other individuals of the same age. A six-year old with an IQ of 100 is at the mean of six-year-olds; an 11-year-old with that score is at the mean of 18-year-olds.

Factors and g. The patterns of intercorrelation among tests are complex. Some pairs of tests are much more closely related than others, but all such correlations are typically positive and form what is called a "positive manifold." In any such manifold, some portion of the variance of scores on each test can be mathematically attributed to a "general factor" or *g*. Given this analysis, the overall pattern of correlations can be roughly described as produced by individual differences in *g* plus differences in the specific abilities sampled by particular tests. In addition, however, there are usually patterns of intercorrelation among groups of tests. These commonalities.

While some psychologists today still regard g as the most fundamental measure of intelligence, others prefer to emphasize the distinctive profile of strengths and weaknesses present in each person's performance. A recently published review identifies over 70 different abilities that can be distinguished by currently available tests. One way to represent this structure is in terms of a hierarchical arrangement with a general intelligence factor at the apex and various more specialised abilities arrayed below it.

Different specialised abilities might also be correlated for other reasons, such as the effects of education. Thus while the *g*-based factor hierarchy is the most widely accepted current view of the structure of abilities, some theorists regard it as misleading. Moreover, a wide range of human abilities, including many that seem to have intellectual components, are outside the domain of standard psychometric tests.

5.4.2. Tests as Predictors

5.4.2.1. School performance

Intelligence tests were originally devised by Alfred Binet to measure children's ability to succeed in school. They do in fact predict school performance fairly well: the correlation between IQ scores and grades is about .50. They also predict scores on school achievement tests, designed to measure knowledge of the curriculum. Note, however, that correlations of this magnitude account for only about 25 percent of the overall variance. Successful school learning depends on many personal characteristics other than intelligence, such as persistence, interest in school, and willingness to study. The encouragement for academic achievement that is received from peers, family and teachers may also be important, together with more general cultural factors.

The relationship between test scores and school performance seems to be ubiquitous. Wherever it has been studied, children with high scores on tests of intelligence tend to learn more of what is taught in school than their lower-scoring peers. There may be styles of teaching and methods of instruction that will decrease or increase this correlation, but none that consistently eliminates it has yet been found.

What children learn in school depends not only on their individual abilities but also on teaching practices and on what is actually taught. Recent comparisons among pupils attending school in different countries have made this especially obvious. Children in Japan and China, for example, know a great deal more math than American children even though their intelligence test scores are quite similar. This difference may result from many factors, including cultural attitudes toward schooling as well as the sheer amount of time devoted to the study of mathematics and how that study is organised.

5.4.2.2. Years of education

Some children stay in school longer than others; many go on to college and perhaps beyond. Two variables that can be measured as early as elementary school correlate with the total amount of education individuals will obtain: test scores and social class background. Correlations between IQ scores and total years of education are about .55, implying that differences in psychometric intelligence account for about 30 percent of the outcome variance. The correlations of years of education with social class background are also positive, but somewhat lower.

There are a number of reasons why children with higher test scores tend to get more education. They are likely to get good grades, and to be encouraged by teachers and counselors; often they are placed in "college preparatory" classes, where they make friends who may also encourage them. In general, they are likely to find the process of education rewarding in a way that many low-scoring children do not. These influences are not omnipotent: some high scoring children do drop out of school. Many personal and social characteristics other than psychometric intelligence determine academic success and interest, and social privilege may also play a role. Nevertheless, test scores are the best single predictor of an individual's years of education.

In contemporary American society, the amount of schooling that adults complete is also somewhat predictive of their social status. Occupations considered high in prestige usually require at least a college degree-16 or more years of education-as a condition of entry. It is partly because intelligence test scores predict years of education so well that they also predict occupational status, and even income to a smaller extent. Moreover, many occupations can only be entered through professional schools which base their admissions at least partly on test scores: the MCAT, the GMAT, the LSAT, etc. Individual scores on admission-related tests such as these are certainly correlated with scores on tests of intelligence.

5.4.2.3. Social status and income

How well do IQ scores predict such outcome measures as the social status or income of adults? This question is complex, in part because another variable also predicts such outcomes: namely, the socio economic status (SES) of one's parents. Unsurprisingly, children of privileged families are more likely to attain high social status than those whose parents are poor and less educated. These two predictors are by no means independent of one another; the correlation between them is around .33.

One way to look at these relationships is to begin with SES. Measures of parental SES predict about one-third of the variance in young adults' social status and about one-fifth of the variance in their income. About half of this predictive effectiveness depends on the fact that the SES of parents also predicts children's intelligence test scores, which have their own predictive value for social outcomes; the other half comes about in other ways.

We can also begin with IQ scores, which by themselves account for about one-fourth of the social status variance and one-sixth of the income variance. Statistical controls for parental SES eliminate only about a quarter of this predictive power. One way to conceptualise this effect is by comparing the occupational status of adult brothers who grew up in the same family and hence have the same parental SES. In such cases, the brother with the higher adolescent IQ score is likely to have the higher adult social status and income. This effect, in turn, is substantially mediated by education: the brother with the higher test scores is likely to get more schooling, and hence to be better credentialled as he enters the workplace.

Do these data imply that psychometric intelligence is a major determinant of social status or income? That depends on what one means by major. In fact, individuals who have the same test scores may differ widely in occupational status and even more widely in income. Consider for a moment the distribution of occupational status scores for all individuals in a population, and then consider the conditional distribution of such scores for just those individuals who test at some given IQ. The standard deviation of the latter distribution may still be quite large; in some cases it amounts to about 88 percent of the standard deviation for the entire population. Viewed from this perspective, psychometric intelligence appears as only one of a great many factors that influence social outcomes.

5.4.2.4. Job performance

Scores on intelligence tests predict various measures of job performance: supervisor ratings, work samples, etc. Such correlations, which typically lie between r=.30 and r=.50, are partly restricted by the limited reliability of those measures themselves. They become higher when ris statistically corrected for this unreliability: in one survey of relevant studies, the mean of the corrected correlations was .54. This implies that, across a wide range of occupations, intelligence test performance accounts for some 29 percent of the variance in job performance.

Although these correlations can sometimes be modified by changing methods of training or aspects of the job itself, intelligence test scores are at least weakly related to job performance in most settings. Sometimes IQ scores are described as the 'best available predictor" of that performance. It is worth noting, however, that such tests predict considerably less than half the variance of job-related measures. Other individual characteristics such as interpersonal skills, aspects of personality, etc., are probably of equal or greater importance, but at this point we do not have equally reliable instruments to measure them.

5.4.2.5. Social outcomes

Psychometric intelligence is negatively correlated with certain socially undesirable outcomes. For example, children with high test scores are less likely than lower-scoring children to engage in juvenile crime. The correlations for most "negative outcome" variables are typically smaller than .20, which means that test scores are associated with less than 4% of their total variance. It is important to realise that the causal links between psychometric ability and social outcomes may be indirect. Children who are unsuccessful in-and hence alienated from-school may be more likely to engage in delinquent behaviours for that very reason, compared to other children who enjoy school and are doing well.

In summary, intelligence test scores predict a wide range of social outcomes with varying degrees of success. Correlations are highest for school achievement, where they account for about a quarter of the variance. They are somewhat lower for job performance, and very low for negatively valued outcomes such as criminality.

5.4.3. Test Scores and Measures of Processing Speed

Many recent studies show that the speeds with which people perform very simple perceptual and cognitive tasks are correlated with psychometric intelligence. In general, people with higher intelligence test scores apprehend, scan, retrieve, and respond to stimuli more quickly than those who score lower.

5.4.3.1. Cognitive correlates

The modern study of these relations began in the 1970s, as part of the general growth of interest in chronometric measures of cognition. Many of the new cognitive paradigms required subjects to make same/

different judgments or other types of speeded responses to visual displays. Although those paradigms had not been devised with individual differences in mind, they could be interpreted as providing measures of the speed of certain information processes. Those speeds turned out to correlate with psychometrically-measured verbal ability. In some problem solving tasks, it was possible to analyse the subjects' overall response times into theoretically motivated 'cognitive components'; component times could then be correlated with test scores in their own right.

Although the size of these correlations was modest, they did increase as the basic tasks were made more complex by requiring increased memory or attentional capacity. For instance, the correlation between paired associate learning and intelligence increased as the pairs were presented at faster rates.

5.4.3.2. Choice reaction time

In another popular cognitive paradigm, the subject simply moves his or her finger from a 'home" button to one of eight others arranged in a semicircle around it; these are marked by small lights that indicate which one is the target on a given trial. Various aspects of the choice reaction times obtained in this paradigm are correlated with scores on intelligence tests, sometimes with values of r as high as .30 or -.40 (r is negative because higher test scores go with shorter times). Nevertheless it has proved difficult to make theoretical sense of the overall pattern of correlations, and the results obtained in this paradigm are still hard to interpret. A later modification, seems to be more promising.

5.4.3.3. Inspection time

A more recently developed measure of processing speed, which seems relatively independent of response factors, is the method of "inspection time" (IT). In the standard version of this paradigm, two vertical lines are shown very briefly on each trial, followed by a pattern mask; the subject must judge which line was shorter. For a given subject, IT is defined as the minimum exposure duration for which the lines must be displayed if he or she is to meet a pre established criterion of accuracy, e.g., nine correct trials out of ten.

Inspection times defined in this way are consistently correlated with measures of psychometric intelligence. A recent meta-analysis reported an overall correlation of -.30 between IQ scores and IT; this rose to -.55 when corrected for measurement error and attenuation. More recent findings confirm this general result. IT usually correlates best with performance subtests of intelligence; its correlation with verbal intelligence is usually weaker and sometimes zero.

One apparent advantage of IT over other chronometric methods is that the task itself seems particularly simple. At first glance, it is hard to imagine that any differences in response strategies or stimulus familiarity could affect the outcome. Nevertheless, it seems that they do. Some subjects use apparent-movement cues in the basic IT task while others do not; only in the latter group is IT correlated with intelligence test scores. Moreover, standard IT paradigms require an essentially spatial judgment; it is not surprising, then, that they correlate with intelligence tests which emphasize spatial ability. It is clear that the apparently simple IT task actually involves complex modes of information processing that are as yet poorly understood.

5.4.3.4. Neurological measures

Recent research has begun to explore what seem to be still more direct measures of neural processing. Visual evoked potential (VEP) techniques have been used to assess nerve conduction velocity (NCV). To estimate this velocity, each subject's head length is divided by the mean latency of an early component (N70 or P100) in his or her VEP pattern. In a study with 147 college-student subjects, this measure correlated r =.26 with scores on an unspeeded test of intelligence. Some researchers have also reported correlations between VEP parameters and intelligence test scores. Interestingly, however, the same "conduction velocities" were not correlated with the same subjects' choice reaction times. Other researchers have also reported correlations between VEP parameters and intelligence test scores.

5.4.3.5. Problems of interpretation

Some researchers believe that psychometric intelligence, especially g, depends directly on the 'neural efficiency" of the brain. They regard the observed correlations between test scores and measures of processing speed as evidence for their view. If choice reaction times, inspection times, and VEP latencies actually reflect the speed of basic neural processes, such correlations are only to be expected. In fact, however, the observed patterns of correlation are rarely as simple as this hypothesis would predict.

Moreover, it is quite possible that high- and low-IQ individuals differ in other ways that affect speeded performance. Those variables include motivation, response criteria, perceptual strategies, attentional strategies, and in some cases differential familiarity with the material itself. Finally, we do not know the direction of causation that underlies many of these correlations. Do high levels of neural efficiency" promote the development of intelligence, or do more intelligent people just find faster ways to carry out perceptual tasks? Or both? These questions are still open.

5.5. Genes and Intelligence

The focus here is on the relative contributions of genes and environments to individual differences in particular traits. To avoid misunderstanding, it must be emphasized from the outset that gene action always involves an environment-at least a biochemical environment, and often an ecological one. Thus all genetic effects on the development of observable traits are potentially modifiable by environmental input, though the practicability of making such modifications may be another matter. Conversely, all environmental effects on trait development involve the genes or structures to which the genes have contributed. Thus there is always a genetic aspect to the effects of the environment.

5.5.1. Sources of Individual Differences

Individuals differ from one another on a wide variety of traits: familiar examples include height. intelligence, and aspects of personality. Those differences are often of considerable social importance. Many interesting questions can be asked about their nature and origins. One such question is the extent to which they reflect differences among the genes of the individuals involved, as distinguished from differences among the environments to which those individuals have been exposed. The issue here is not whether genes and environments are both essential for the development of a given trait, and it is not about the genes or environment of any particular person. We are concerned only with the observed variation of the trait across individuals in a given population. A figure called the "heritability" (h^2) of the trait represents the proportion of that variation that is associated with genetic differences among the individuals. The remaining variation ($1-h^2$] is associated with environmental differences and with errors of measurement.

Sometimes special interest attaches to those aspects of environments that family members have in common. The part of the variation that derives from this source, called "shared" variation or c^2, can also be estimated. Still more refined estimates can be made: c^2 is sometimes subdivided into several kinds of shared variation; h^2 is sometimes subdivided into so-called "additive" and "non-additive" portions /the part that is transmissible from parent to child vs. the part expressed anew in each generation by a unique patterning of genes. Variation associated with correlations and statistical interactions between genes and environments may also be identifiable. In theory, any of the above estimates may vary with the age of the individuals involved.

A high heritability does not mean that the environment has no impact on the development of a trait, or that learning is not involved. Vocabulary size, for example, is very substantially heritable although every word in an individual's vocabulary is learned. In a society in which plenty of words are available in everyone's environment, especially for individuals who are motivated to seek them out, the number of words that individuals actually learn depends to a considerable extent on their genetic predispositions.

Behaviour geneticists have often emphasized the fact that individuals can be active in creating or selecting their own environments. Some describe this process as active or reactive genotype-environment correlation. Others suggest that these forms of gene-environment relationship are typical of the way that genes are normally expressed, and simply include them as part of the genetic effect. This is a matter of terminological preference, not a dispute about facts.

5.5.2. Estimates of Individual Differences

Estimates of the magnitudes of these sources of individual differences are made by exploiting natural and social 'experiments" that combine genotypes and environments in informative ways. Monozygotic (MZ) and dyzygotic (DZ) twins, for example, can be regarded as experiments of nature. MZ twins are paired individuals of the same age growing up in the same family who have all their genes in common; DZ twins are otherwise similar pairs who have only half their genes in common.

Adoptions, in contrast, are experiments of society. They allow one to compare genetically unrelated persons who are growing up in the same family as well as genetically related persons who are growing up in different families. They can also provide information about genotype-environment correlations: in ordinary families genes and environments are correlated because the same parents provide both, whereas in adoptive families one set of parents provides the genes and another the environment.

An experiment involving both nature and society is the study of monozygotic twins who have been reared apart. Relationships in the families of monozygotic twins also offer unique possibilities for analysis. Because these comparisons are subject to different sources of potential error, the results of studies involving several kinds of kinship are often analysed together to arrive at robust overall conclusions.

5.5.2.1. Parameter Estimates

Across the ordinary range of environments in modern Western societies, a sizable part of the variation in intelligence test scores is associated with genetic differences among individuals. Quantitative estimates vary from one study to another, because many are based on small or selective samples. If one simply combines all available correlations in a single analysis, the heritability (h^2) works out to about .50 and the between-family variance (c^2) to about .25. These overall figures are misleading, however, because most of the relevant studies have been done with children. We now know that the heritability of IQ changes with age: h^2 goes up and c^2 goes down from infancy to adulthood. In childhood h^2 and C^2 for IQ are of the order of .45 and .35;

by late adolescence h2 is around .75 and c^2 is quite low. Substantial environmental variance remains, but it primarily reflects within-family rather than between-family differences.

These particular estimates derive from samples in which the lowest socioeconomic levels were under represented, so the range of between family differences was smaller than in the population as a whole. This means that we should be cautious in generalising the findings for between-family effects across the entire social spectrum. The samples were also mostly white, but available data suggest that twin and sibling correlations in African-American and similarly selected White samples are more often comparable than not.

Why should individual differences in intelligence reflect genetic differences more strongly in adults than they do in children's One possibility is that as individuals grow older their transactions with their environments are increasingly influenced by the characteristics that they bring to those environments themselves, decreasingly by the conditions imposed by family life and social origins. Older persons are in a better position to select their own effective environments, a form of genotype-environment correlation. In any case the popular view that genetic influences on the development of a trait are essentially frozen at conception while the effects of the early environment cumulate inexorably is quite misleading, at least for the trait of psychometric intelligence.

5.5.2.2. Implications

Estimates of h^2 and c^2 for IQ are descriptive statistics for the populations studied. They are outcome measures, summarizing the results of a great many diverse, intricate, individually variable events and processes, but they can nevertheless be quite useful. They can tell us how much of the variation in a given trait the genes and family environments explain, and changes in them place some constraints on theories of how this occurs. On the other hand they have little to say about specific mechanisms, i.e., about how genetic and environmental differences get translated into individual physiological and psychological differences. Many psychologists and neuroscientists are actively studying such processes; data on heritabilities may give them ideas about what to look for and where or when to look for it.

A common error is to assume that because something is heritable it is necessarily unchangeable This is wrong. Heritability does not imply immutability. As previously noted, heritable traits can depend on learning, and they may be subject to other environmental effects as well. The value of h^2 can change if the distribution of environments in the population is substantially altered. On the other hand, there can be effective environmental changes that do not change heritability at all.

If the environment relevant to a given trait improves in a way that affects all members of the population equally, the mean value of the trait will rise without any change in its heritability. This has evidently happened for height: the heritability of stature is high, but average heights continue to increase.

In theory, different subgroups of a population might have different distributions of environments or genes and hence different values of h^2. This seems not to be the case for high and low IQ levels, for which adult heritabilities appear to be much the same. It is also possible that an impoverished or suppressive environment could fail to support the development of a trait, and hence restrict individual variation. This could affect estimates of h^2, c^2, Or both, depending on the details of the process. Again, an environmental factor that affected every member of a subgroup equally might alter the group's mean without affecting heritabilities at all.

Where the heritability of IQ is concerned, it has sometimes seemed as if the findings based on differences between group means were in contradiction with those based on correlations. For example, children adopted in infancy into advantaged families tend to have higher IQs in childhood than would have been expected if they had been reared by their birth mothers; this is a mean difference implicating the environment. Yet at the same time their individual resemblance to their birth mothers persists, and this correlation is most plausibly interpreted in genetic terms. There is no real contradiction: the two findings simply call attention to different aspects of the same phenomenon. A sensible account must include both aspects: there is only a single developmental process, and it occurs in individuals. By looking at means or correlations one learns somewhat different but compatible things about the genetic and environmental contributions to that process.

As far as behaviour genetic methods are concerned, there is nothing unique about psychometric intelligence relative to other traits or abilities. Any reliably measured trait can be analysed by these methods, and many traits including personality and attitudes have been. The methods are neutral with regard to genetic and environmental sources of variance: if individual differences on a trait are entirely due to environmental factors, the analysis will reveal this.

These methods have shown that genes contribute substantially to individual differences in intelligence test performance, and that their role seems to increase from infancy to adulthood. They have also shown that variations in the unique environments of individuals are important, and that between-family variation contributes significantly to observed differences in IQ scores in childhood although this effect diminishes later on. All these conclusions are wholly consistent with the notion that both genes and environment, in complex interplay, are essential to the development of intellectual competence.

5.6. Environmental Effects on Intelligence

The ‘environment" includes a wide range of influences on intelligence. Some of those variables affect whole populations, while others contribute to individual differences within a given group. Some of them are social, some are biological; at this point some are still mysterious. It may also happen that the proper interpretation of an environmental variable requires the simultaneous consideration of genetic effects. Nevertheless, a good deal of solid information is available.

5.6.1. Social Variables

It is obvious that the cultural environment—how people live, what they value, what they do—has a significant effect on the intellectual skills developed by individuals. Rice farmers in Liberia are good at estimating quantities of rice; children in Botswana, accustomed to storytelling, have excellent memories for stories. Both these groups were far ahead of American controls on the tasks in question. On the other hand Americans and other Westernised groups typically outperform members of traditional societies on psychometric tests, even those designed to be "culture-fair."

Cultures typically differ from one another in so many ways that particular differences can rarely be ascribed to single causes. Even comparisons between subpopulations are often difficult to interpret. If we find that groups living in different environments differ in their test scores, it is easy to suppose that the environmental difference causes the IQ difference. But there is also an opposite direction of causation: individuals may come to be in one environment or another because of differences in their own abilities, including the abilities measured by intelligence tests. Sons whose IQ scores are above those of their fathers also tend to achieve a higher social class status; conversely, those with scores below their fathers' tend to achieve lower status.

5.6.1.1. Occupation

Intelligence test scores predict occupational level, not only because some occupations require more intelligence than others but also because admission to many professions depends on test scores in the first place. There can also be an effect in the opposite direction, i.e. workplaces may affect the intelligence of those who work in them. More "intellectual flexibility" in the individuals who hold them. Although the issue of direction of effects complicates the interpretation of this theory, this remains a plausible suggestion.

5.6.1.2. Schooling

Attendance at school is both a dependent and an independent variable in relation to intelligence. On the one hand, children with higher test scores are less likely to drop out, more likely to be promoted from grade to grade and then to attend college. Thus the number of years of education that adults complete is roughly predictable from their childhood scores on intelligence tests. On the other hand schooling itself changes mental abilities, including those abilities measured on psychometric tests. This is obvious for tests like the SAT that are explicitly designed to assess school learning, but it is almost equally true of intelligence tests themselves.

The evidence for the effect of schooling on intelligence test scores takes many forms. When children of nearly the same age go through school a year apart, those who have been in school longer have higher mean scores. Children who attend school intermittently score below those who go regularly, and test performance tends to drop over the summer vacation.

Schools affect intelligence in several ways, most obviously by transmitting information. The answers to questions like "Who wrote Hamlet?" and "What is the boiling point of water?" are typically learned in school, where some pupils learn them more easily and thoroughly than others. Perhaps at least as important are certain general skills and attitudes: systematic problem-solving, abstract thinking, categorisation, sustained attention to material of little intrinsic interest, repeated manipulation of basic symbols and operations. There is no doubt that schools promote and permit the development of significant intellectual skills, which develop to different extents in different children. It is because tests of intelligence draw on many of those same skills that they predict school achievement as well as they do.

To achieve these results, the school experience must meet at least some minimum standard of quality. In very poor schools, children may learn so little that they fall farther behind the national IQ norms for every year of attendance. When this happens, older siblings have systematically lower scores than their younger counterparts.

5.6.1.3. Interventions

Intelligence test scores reflect a child's standing relative to others in his or her age cohort. Very poor or interrupted schooling can lower that standing substantially; are there also ways to raise it? In fact many interventions have been shown to raise test scores and mental ability 'in the short run", but long-run gains have proved more elusive. One noteworthy example of success was the Venezuelan Intelligence Project, in which hundreds of seventh-grade children from underprivileged backgrounds in that country were exposed to an extensive, theoretically based curriculum focused on thinking skills. The intervention produced substantial gains on a wide range of tests, but there has been no follow-up.

Children who participate in "Head Start" and similar programs are exposed to various school-related materials and experiences for one or two years. Their test scores often go up during the course of the programme, but these gains fade with time. By the end of elementary school, there are usually no significant I9 or achievement-test differences between children who have been in such programmes and controls who have not. There may, however, be other differences. Follow-up studies suggest that children who participated in such programs as preschoolers are less likely to be assigned to special education, less likely to be held back in grade, and more likely to finish high school than matched controls.

More extensive interventions might be expected to produce larger and more lasting effects, but few such programmes have been evaluated systematically.

5.6.1.4. Family Environment

No one doubts that normal child development requires a certain minimum level of responsible care. Severely deprived, neglectful, or abusive environments must have negative effects on a great many aspects of development, including intellectual aspects. Beyond that minimum, however, the role of family experience is now in serious dispute. Psychometric intelligence is a case in point. Do differences between children's family environments produce differences in their intelligence test performance? The problem here is to disentangle causation from correlation. There is no doubt that such variables as resources of the home and parents' use of language are correlated with children's IQ scores, but such correlations may be mediated by genetic as well as environmental factors.

Behaviour geneticists frame such issues in quantitative terms. Environmental factors certainly contribute to the overall variance of psychometric intelligence. But how much of that variance results from differences between families, as contrasted with the varying experiences of different children in the same family? Between-family differences create what is called "shared variance" or c^2. Recent twin and adoption studies suggest that while the value of c^2 is substantial in early childhood, it becomes quite small by late adolescence.

These findings suggest that differences in the life styles of families whatever their importance may be for many aspects of children's lives make little long-term difference for the skills measured by intelligence tests. We should note, however, that low-income and non-white families are poorly represented in existing adoption studies as well as in most twin samples. Thus it is not yet clear whether these surprisingly small values of c^2 apply to the population as a whole. It remains possible that, across the full range of income and ethnicity, between-family differences have more lasting consequences for psychometric intelligence.

5.6.2. Biological Variables

Every individual has a biological as well as a social environment, one that begins in the womb and extends throughout life. Many aspects of that environment can affect intellectual development. We now know that a number of biological factors, including malnutrition, exposure to toxic substances, and various prenatal and perinatal stressors, result in lowered psychometric intelligence under at least some conditions.

5.6.2.1. Nutrition

There has been only one major study of the effects of prenatal malnutrition on long-term intellectual development. The test scores of Dutch 19-year-old males were analysed in relation to a wartime famine that had occurred in the winter of 1944-45, just before their birth. In this very large sample, exposure to the famine had no effect on adult intelligence. Note, however, that the famine itself lasted only a few months; the subjects were exposed to it prenatally but not after birth.

In contrast, prolonged malnutrition during childhood does have long-term intellectual effects. These have not been easy to establish, in part because many other unfavorable socioeconomic conditions are often associated with chronic malnutrition. In one intervention study, however, pre-schoolers in two Guatemalan villages were given ad lib access to a protein dietary supplement for several years. A decade later, many of these children scored significantly higher on school related achievement tests than comparable controls. It is worth noting that the effects of poor nutrition on intelligence may well be indirect. Malnourished children are typically less responsive to adults, less motivated to learn, and less active in exploration than their more adequately nourished counterparts.

Although the degree of malnutrition prevalent in these villages rarely occurs in the United States, there may still be nutritional influences on intelligence. In studies of so-called "micro-nutrients," experimental groups of children have been given vitamin/mineral supplements while controls got placebos. in many of these studies, the experimental children showed test-score gains that significantly exceeded the controls.

In a somewhat different design, pregnant women who were thought to be at risk for delivering low birth-weight babies dietary supplements of liquid protein were given. At one year of age, the babies born to these mothers showed faster habituation to visual patterns than did control infants. Although these results are encouraging, there has been no long-term follow-up of such gains.

5.6.2.2. Lead

Certain toxins have well established negative effects on intelligence. Exposure to lead is one such factor. In one long-term study, the blood lead levels of children growing up near a lead smelting plant were substantially and negatively correlated with intelligence test scores throughout childhood. No "threshold dose" for the effect of lead appears in such studies.

5.6.2.3. Alcohol

Extensive prenatal exposure to alcohol can give rise to fetal alcohol syndrome, which includes mental retardation as well as a range of physical symptoms. Smaller "doses" of prenatal alcohol may have negative effects on intelligence even when the full syndrome does not appear. Mothers who reported consuming more than 1.5 oz, of alcohol daily during pregnancy had children who scored some five points below controls at age four. Prenatal exposure to aspirin and antibiotics had similar negative effects in this study.

5.6.3. Perinatal Factors

Complications at delivery and other negative perinatal factors may have serious consequences for development. Nevertheless, because they occur only rarely, they contribute relatively little to the population variance of intelligence. Down's syndrome, a chromosomal abnormality that produces serious mental retardation, is also rare enough to have little impact on the overall distribution of test scores.

The correlation between birth weight and later intelligence deserves particular discussion. In some cases low birth weight simply reflects premature delivery; in others, the infant's size is below normal for its gestational age. Both factors apparently contribute to the tendency of low-birth-weight infants to have lower test scores in later childhood. These correlations are small, ranging from .05 to .13 in different groups. The effects of low birth weight are substantial only when it is very low indeed. Premature babies born at these very low birth weights are behind controls on most developmental measures; they often have severe or permanent intellectual deficits.

5.6.4. Continuously Rising Test Scores

Perhaps the most striking of all environmental effects is the steady worldwide rise in intelligence test performance. Although many psychometricians had noted these gains, it was James Flynn who first described them systematically. His analysis shows that performance has been going up ever since testing began. The "Flynn Effect" is now very well documented, not only in the United States but in many other technologically advanced countries. The average gain is about three IQ points per decade; more than a full standard deviation since, say, 1940.

Although it is simplest to describe the gains as increases in population IQ, this is not exactly what happens. Most intelligence tests are "re-standardised" from time to time, in part to keep up with these very gains. As part of this process the mean score of the new standardisation sample is typically set to 100 again, so the increase more or less disappears from view. In this context, the Flynn effect means that if twenty years have passed since the last time the test was standardised, people who now score 100 on the new version would probably average about 106 on the old one.

The sheer extent of these increases is remarkable, and the rate of gain may even be increasing. The scores of nineteen-year-olds in the Netherlands, for example, went up more than 8 points-over half a standard deviation-between 1972 and 1982. What's more, the largest gains appear on the types of tests that were specifically designed to be free of cultural influence. One of these is Raven's Progressive Matrices, an untimed non-verbal test that many psychometricians regard as a good measure of g.

These steady gains in intelligence test performance have not always been accompanied by corresponding gains in school achievement. Indeed, the relation between intelligence and achievement test scores can be complex. This is especially true for the Scholastic Aptitude Test (SAT), in part because the ability range of the students who take the SAT has broadened over time. That change explains some portion, but not all, of the prolonged decline in SAT scores that took place from the mid nineteen-sixties to the early eighties, even as IQ scores were continuing to rise.

Meanwhile, however, other more representative measures show that school achievement levels have held steady or in some cases actually increased.

The consistent IQ gains documented by Flynn seem much too large to result from simple increases in test sophistication. Their cause is presently unknown, but three interpretations deserve our consideration. Perhaps the most plausible of these is based on the striking cultural differences between successive generations. Daily life and occupational experience both seem more "complex" today than in the time of our parents and grandparents. The population is increasingly urbanised; television exposes us to more information and more perspectives on more topics than ever before; children stay in school longer; almost everyone seems to be encountering new forms of experience. These changes in the complexity of life may have produced corresponding changes in complexity of mind, and hence in certain psychometric abilities.

A different hypothesis attributes the gains to modern improvements in nutrition. Large nutritionally-based increases in height have occurred during the same period as the IQ gains; perhaps there have been increases in brain size as well. As we have seen, however, the effects of nutrition on intelligence are themselves not firmly established.

The third interpretation addresses the very definition of intelligence. Real intelligence, whatever it may be, cannot have increased as much as these data would suggest. Consider, for example, the number of individuals who have IQ scores of 140 or more. In 1952 only 0.38 pewrcent of Dutch test takers had IQs over 140; in 1982, scored by the same norms, 9.12 percent exceeded this figure! Judging by these criteria, the Netherlands should now be experiencing "...a cultural renaissance too great to be overlooked". So too should France, Norway, the United States, and many other countries. Because James Flynn finds this conclusion implausibie or absurd, he argues that what has risen cannot be intelligence itself but only a minor sort of "abstract problem solving ability." The issue remains unresolved.

5.5.5. Individual Life Experiences

Although the environmental variables that produce large differences in intelligence are not yet well understood, genetic studies assure us that they exist. With a heritability well below 1.00, IQ must be subject to substantial environmental influences. Moreover, available heritability estimates apply only within the range of environments that are well-represented in the present population. We already know that some relatively rare conditions, like those reviewed earlier, have large negative effects on intelligence. Whether there are conditions that have large positive effects is not known.

There is both a biological and a social environment. For any given child, the social factors include not only an overall cultural/social/school setting and a particular family but also a unique "micro-environment" of experiences that are shared with no one else. The adoption studies show that family variables, such as differences in parenting style, in the resources of the home, etc., have smaller long-term effects than we once supposed. At least among people who share a given SES level and a given culture, it seems to be unique individual experience that makes the largest environmental contribution to adult IQ differences.

References

Binet A; Simon T *The development of intelligence in children*. Baltimore: Williams & Wilkins (original); Kessinger Publishing. 2007.

Wake, Warren K.; Gardner, Howard; Kornhaber, Mindy L. *Intelligence: Multiple perspectives*. Fort Worth, TX: Harcourt Brace College Publishers. 1996

Blakeslee, Sandra; Hawkins, Jeff. *On intelligence*. New York: Times Books. 2004.

Terman, L. *The measurement of intelligence*. Boston: Houghton Mifflin. 1916.

6

Student Motivation

Motivation is typically defined as the forces that account for the arousal, selection, direction, and continuation of behaviour. Nevertheless, many teachers have at least two major misconceptions about motivation that prevent them from using this concept with maximum effectiveness. One misconception is that some students are unmotivated. Strictly speaking, that is not an accurate statement. As long as a student chooses goals and expends a certain amount of effort to achieve them, he is, by definition, motivated. What teachers really mean is that students are not motivated to behave in the way teachers would like them to behave.

The second misconception is that one person can directly motivate another. This view is inaccurate because motivation comes from within a person. What you can do, with the help of the various motivation theories discussed in this chapter, is create the circumstances that influence students to do what you want them to do.

Many factors determine whether the students in your classes will be motivated or not motivated to learn. You should not be surprised to discover that no single theoretical interpretation of motivation explains all aspects of student interest or lack of it. Different theoretical interpretations do, however, shed light on why some students in a given learning situation are more likely to want to learn than others. Furthermore, each theoretical interpretation can serve as the basis for the development of techniques for motivating students in the classroom.

Sometimes it is useful to think of motivation not as something "inside" a student driving the student's behaviour, but as equivalent to the student's outward behaviours. In its most thorough-going form, behaviourism focuses almost completely on what can be directly seen or heard about a person's behaviour, and has relatively few comments about what may lie behind the behaviour. When it comes to motivation, this perspective means minimising or even ignoring the distinction between the inner drive or energy of students, and the outward behaviours that express the drive or energy. The two are considered the same, or nearly so.

Equating the inner and the outward might seem to violate common sense. How can a student do something without some sort of feeling or thought to make the action happen? This very question has led to alternative models of motivation that are based on cognitive rather than behaviourist theories of learning.

Sometimes the circumstances of teaching limit teachers' opportunities to distinguish between inner motivation and outward behaviour. Certainly teachers see plenty of student behaviours-signs of motivation of some sort. But the multiple demands of teaching can limit the time needed to determine what the behaviours mean. If a student asks a lot of questions during discussions, for example, is he or she is curious about the material itself, or just wanting to look intelligent in front of classmates and the teacher? In a class with many students and a busy agenda, there may not be a lot of time for a teacher to decide between these possibilities. In other cases, the problem may not be limited time as much as communication difficulties with a student.

Consider a student who is still learning English, or who belongs to a cultural community that uses patterns of conversation that are unfamiliar to the teacher, or who has a disability that limits the student's general language skill. In these cases discerning the student's inner motivations may take more time and effort. It is important to invest the extra time and effort for such students, but while a teacher is doing so, it is also important for her to guide and influence the students' behaviour in constructive directions. That is where behaviourist approaches to motivation can help.

6.1. Operant Conditioning as a Way of Motivating

The most common version of the behavioural perspective on motivation is the theory of operant conditioning associated with B. F. Skinner. The description in that chapter focused on behavioural learning, but the same operant model can be transformed into an account of motivation. In the operant model, you may recall, a behaviour being learned increases in frequency or likelihood because performing it makes a reinforcement available.

To understand this model in terms of motivation, think of the likelihood of response as the motivation and the reinforcement as the motivator. Imagine, for example, that a student learns by operant conditioning to answer questions during class discussions: each time the student answers a question, the teacher praises this behaviour. In addition to thinking of this situation as behavioural learning, however, you can also think of it in terms of motivation: the likelihood of the student answering questions is increasing because of the teacher's praise.

Many concepts from operant conditioning, in fact, can be understood in motivational terms. The decrease in performance frequency can be thought of as a loss of motivation, and removal of the reinforcement can be thought of as removal of the motivator.

6.2. Behavioural Perspectives on Motivation

As we mentioned, behaviourist perspectives about motivation do reflect a classroom reality: that teachers sometimes lack time and therefore must focus simply on students' appropriate outward behaviour. But there are none the less cautions about adopting this view. An obvious one is the ambiguity of students' specific behaviours; what looks like a sign of one motive to the teacher may in fact be a sign of some other motive to the student. If a student looks at the teacher intently while she is speaking, does it mean the student is motivated to learn, or only that the student is daydreaming? If a student invariably looks away while the teacher is speaking, does it mean that the student is disrespectful of the teacher, or that student comes from a family or cultural group where avoiding eye contact actually shows more respect for a speaker than direct eye contact?

Another concern about behaviourist perspectives, including operant conditioning, is that it leads teachers to ignore students' choices and preferences, and to "play God" by making choices on their behalf. According to this criticism, the distinction between "inner" motives and expressions of motives in outward behaviour does not disappear just because a teacher chooses to treat a motive and the behavioural expression of a motive as equivalent. Students usually do know what they want or desire, and their wants or desires may not always correspond to what a teacher chooses to reinforce or ignore. Approaches that are exclusively behavioural, it is argued, are not sensitive enough to students' intrinsic, self-sustaining motivations.

There is truth to this allegation if a teacher actually does rely on rewarding behaviours that she alone has chosen, or even if she persists in reinforcing behaviours that students already find motivating without external reinforcement. In those cases reinforcements can backfire: instead of serving as an incentive to desired behaviour, reinforcement can become a reminder of the teacher's power and of students' lack of control over their own actions.

A classic research study of intrinsic motivation illustrated the problem nicely. In the study, researchers rewarded university students for two activities—solving puzzles and writing newspaper headlines—that they already found interesting. Some of the students, however, were paid to do these activities, whereas others were not. Under these conditions, the students who were paid were less likely to engage in the activities following the experiment than were the students who were not paid, even though both groups had been equally interested in the activities to begin with. The extrinsic reward of payment, it seemed, interfered with the intrinsic reward of working the puzzles.

Later studies confirmed this effect in numerous situations, though they have also found certain conditions where extrinsic rewards do not reduce intrinsic rewards. Extrinsic rewards are not as harmful, for example, if a person is paid "by the hour" rather than piecemeal. They also are less harmful if the task itself is relatively well-defined and high-quality performance is expected at all times. So there are still times and ways when externally determined reinforcements are useful and effective. In general, however, extrinsic rewards do seem to undermine intrinsic motivation often enough that they need to be used selectively and thoughtfully. As it happens, help with being selective and thoughtful can be found in the other, more cognitively oriented theories of motivation. These use the goals, interests, and beliefs of students as ways of explaining differences in students' motives and in how the motives affect engagement with school. We turn to these cognitively oriented theories next, beginning with those focused on students' goals.

6.3. Motives

One way motives vary is by the kind of goals that students set for themselves, and by how the goals support students' academic achievement.

In addition to holding different kinds of goals-with consequent differences in academic motivation-students show obvious differences in level of interest in the topics and tasks of the classroom.

Attributions are perceptions about the causes of success and failure. Suppose that you get a low mark on a test and are wondering what caused the low mark.

In addition to being influenced by their goals, interests, and attributions, students' motives are affected by specific beliefs about the student's personal capacities. In self-efficacy theory the beliefs become a primary, explicit explanation for motivation.

Motivation is affected by several factors, including reinforcement for behaviour, but especially also students' goals, interests, and sense of self-efficacy and self-determination. The factors combine to create two general sources of motivation: students' expectation of success and the value that students place on a goal. Viewing motivation in this way is often called the expectancy-value model.

6.4. Importance of Motivation

Most motivation theorists assume that motivation is involved in the performance of all learned responses; that is, a learned behaviour will not occur unless it is energised. The major question among psychologists, in general, is whether motivation is a primary or secondary influence on behaviour. That is, are changes in behaviour better explained by principles of environmental/ecological influences, perception, memory, cognitive development, emotion, explanatory style, or personality or are concepts unique to motivation more pertinent.

For example, we know that people respond to increasingly complex or novel events in the environment up to a point and then responses decrease. This inverted-U-shaped curve of behaviour is well-known and widely acknowledged.

6.5. Relationship of Motivation and Emotion

Emotion is different from motivation in that there is not necessarily a goal orientation affiliated with it. Emotions occur as a result of an interaction between perception of environmental stimuli, neural/hormonal responses to these perceptions, and subjective cognitive labeling of these feelings. Evidence suggests there is a small core of core emotions that are uniquely associated with a specific facial expression. This implies that there are a small number of unique biological responses that are genetically hard-wired to specific facial expressions.

A further implication is that the process works in reverse: if you want to change your feelings, you can do so by changing your facial expression. That is, if you are motivated to change how you feel and your feeling is associated with a specific facial expression, you can change that feeling by purposively changing your facial expression. Since most of us would rather feel happy than otherwise, the most appropriate facial expression would be a smile.

In general, explanations regarding the source(s) of motivation can be categorised as either extrinsic (outside the person) or intrinsic. Intrinsic sources and corresponding theories can be further subcategorised as either body/physical, mind/mental or transpersonal/spiritual.

In current literature, needs are now viewed as dispositions toward action. Action or overt behaviour may be initiated by either positive or negative incentives or a combination of both. The following chart provides a brief overview of the different sources of motivation that have been studied. While initiation of action can be traced to each of these domains, it appears likely that initiation of behaviour may be more related to emotions and/or the affective area while persistence may be more related to conation or goal-orientation.

6.5.1. Sources of Motivational Needs

6.5.1.1. Behavioural/external

a) elicited by stimulus associated/connected to innately connected stimulus
b) obtain desired, pleasant consequences (rewards) or escape/avoid undesired, unpleasant consequences

6.5.1.2. Social

a) imitate positive models
b) be a part of a group or a valued member

6.5.1.3. Biological

a) increase/decrease stimulation (arousal)
b) activate senses (taste, touch, smell, etc.
c) decrease hunger, thirst, discomfort, etc.
d) maintain homeostasis, balance

6.5.1.4. Cognitive

a) maintain attention to something interesting or threatening
b) develop meaning or understanding
c) increase/decrease cognitive disequilibrium; uncertainty
d) solve a problem or make a decision
e) figure something out
f) eliminate threat or risk

6.5.1.5. Affective

a) increase/decrease affective dissonance
b) increase feeling good

c) decrease feeling bad
d) increase security of or decrease threats to self-esteem
e) maintain levels of optimism and enthusiasm

6.5.1.6. Conative

a) meet individually developed/selected goal
b) obtain personal dream
c) develop or maintain self-efficacy
d) take control of one's life
e) eliminate threats to meeting goal, obtaining dream
f) reduce others' control of one's life

6.5.1.7. Spiritual

a) understand purpose of one's life
b) connect self to ultimate unknowns

6.6. Theories of Motivation

Many of the theories of motivation address issues introduced previously in these materials. The following provides a brief overview to any terms or concepts that have not been previously discussed.

6.6.1. Behavioural

Each of the major theoretical approaches in behavioural learning theory posits a primary factor in motivation. Classical conditioning states that biological responses to associated stimuli energise and direct behaviour. Operant learning states the primary factor is consequences: the application of reinforcers provides incentives to increase behaviour; the application of punishers provides disincentives that result in a decrease in behaviour.

6.6.2. Cognitive

There are several motivational theories that trace their roots to the information processing approach to learning. These approaches focus on the categories and labels people use help to identify thoughts, emotions, dispositions, and behaviours.

The first is cognitive dissonance theory which is in some respects similar to disequilibrium in Piaget's theory of cognitive development. The implication is that if we can create the appropriate amount of disequilibrium, this will in turn lead to the individual changing his or her behaviour which in turn will lead to a change in thought patterns which in turn leads to more change in behaviour.

A second cognitive approach is attribution theory. This theory proposes that every individual tries to explain success or failure of self and others by offering certain "attributions." These attributions are either internal or external and are either under control or not under control.

In a teaching/learning environment, it is important to assist the learner to develop a self-attribution explanation of effort. If the person has an attribution of ability as soon as the individual experiences some difficulties in the learning process, he or she will decrease appropriate learning behaviour. If the person has an external attribution, then nothing the person can do will help that individual in a learning situation. In this case, there is nothing to be done by the individual when learning problems occur.

A third cognitive approach is expectancy theory which proposes the following equation:

Motivation = Perceived Probability of Success (Expectancy)

Connection of Success and Reward (Instrumentality)

Value of Obtaining Goal (Valance, Value)

Since this formula states that the three factors of Expectancy, Instrumentality, and Valance or Value are to be multiplied by each other, a low value in one will result in a low value of motivation. Therefore, all three must be present in order for motivation to occur. That is, if an individual doesn't believe he or she can be successful at a task OR the individual does not see a connection between his or her activity and success OR the individual does not value the results of success, then the probability is lowered that the individual will engage in the required learning activity. From the perspective of this theory, all three variables must be high in order for motivation and the resulting behaviour to be high.

6.7. Psychoanalytic Theories

The psychoanalytic theories of motivation propose a variety of fundamental influences. Freud suggested that all action or behaviour is a result of internal, biological instincts that are classified into two categories: life and death.

6.7.1. Humanistic Theories

One of the most influential writers in the area of motivation is Abraham Maslow.

Abraham Maslow attempted to synthesize a large body of research related to human motivation. Prior to Maslow, researchers generally focused separately on such factors as biology, achievement, or power to explain what energises, directs, and sustains human behaviour. Maslow posited a hierarchy of human needs based on two groupings: deficiency needs and growth needs. Within the deficiency needs, each lower need must be met before moving to the next higher level. Once each of these needs has been satisfied, if at some future time a deficiency is detected, the individual will act to remove the deficiency. The first four levels are:

1) *Physiological*: hunger, thirst, bodily comforts, etc.;
2) *Safety/security*: out of danger;
3) *Belongingness and Love*: affiliate with others, be accepted; and
4) *Esteem*: to achieve, be competent, gain approval and recognition.

According to Maslow, an individual is ready to act upon the growth needs if and only if the deficiency needs are met. Maslow's initial conceptualisation included only one growth need—self-actualisation. Self-actualised people are characterised by: (1) being problem-focused; (2) incorporating an ongoing freshness of appreciation of life; (3) a concern about personal growth; and (4) the ability to have peak experiences. Maslow later differentiated the growth need of self-actualisation, specifically naming two lower-level growth needs prior to general level of self-actualisation and one beyond that level. They are:

5) *Cognitive:* to know, to understand, and explore;
6) *Aesthetic:* symmetry, order, and beauty;
7) *Self-actualisation:* to find self-fulfilment and realise one's potential; and
8) *Self-transcendence:* to connect to something beyond the ego or to help others find self-fulfilment and realise their potential.

Maslow's basic position is that as one becomes more self-actualised and self-transcendent, one becomes more wise and automatically knows what to do in a wide variety of situations.

Maslow's hierarchy can be used to describe the kinds of information that individual's seek at different levels. For example, individuals at the lowest level seek coping information in order to meet their basic needs. Information that is not directly connected to helping a person meet his or her needs in a very short time span is simply left unattended. Individuals at the safety level need helping information. They seek to be assisted in seeing how they can be safe and secure.

Enlightening information is sought by individuals seeking to meet their belongingness needs. Quite often this can be found in books or other materials on relationship development. Empowering information is sought by people at the esteem level. They are looking for information on how their ego can be developed. Finally, people in the growth levels of cogntive, aesthetic, and self-actualisation seek edifying information.

Maslow recognised that not all personalities followed his proposed hierarchy. While a variety of personality dimensions might be considered as related to motivational needs, one of the most often cited is that of introversion and extroversion. Reorganising Maslow's hierarchy and considering the introversion/extraversion dimension of personality results in three levels, each with an introverted and extroverted component. This organisation suggests there may be two aspects of each level that differentiate how people relate to each set of needs. Different personalities might relate more to one dimension than the other. For example, an introvert at the level of Other/Relatedness might be more concerned with his or her own perceptions of being included in a group, whereas an extrovert at that same level would pay more attention to how others value that membership.

At this point there is little agreement about the identification of basic human needs and how they are ordered.

Notice that bonding and relatedness are a component of every theory. However, there do not seem to be any others that are mentioned by all theorists. This lack of accord may be a result of different philosophies of researchers rather than differences among human beings. A person's explanatory or attributional style will modify the list of basic needs. Therefore, it seems appropriate to ask people what they want and how their needs could be met rather than relying on an unsupported theory.

Maslow's work lead to additional attempts to develop a grand theory of motivation, a theory that would put all of the factors influencing motivation into one model. An example proposes five factors as the sources of motivation: (1) Instrumental Motivation, (2) Intrinsic Process Motivation, (3) Goal Internalisation, (4) Internal Self Concept-based Motivation, (5) External Self Concept-based Motivation. Individuals are influenced by all five factors, though in varying degrees that can change in specific situations.

Factors one and five are both externally-oriented. The main difference is that individuals who are instrumentally motivated are influenced more by immediate actions in the environment whereas individuals who are self-concept motivated are influenced more by their constructions of external demands and ideals.

Factors two, three, and four are more internally-oriented. In the case of intrinsic process, the specific task is interesting and provides immediate internal reinforcement. The individual with a goal-internalisation orientation is more task-oriented whereas the person with an internal self-concept orientation is more influenced by individual constructions of the ideal self.

6.7.2. Social Learning

Social learning theory suggests that modeling and vicarious learning are important motivators of behaviour.

6.7.3. Social Cognition

Social cognition theory proposes reciprocal determination as a primary factor in both learning and motivation. In this view, the environment, an individual's behaviour, and the individual's characteristics both influence and are influenced by each other two components. Bandura highlights self-efficacy and self-regulation the establishment of goals, the development of a plan to attain those goals, the commitment to implement that plan, the actual implementation of the plan, and subsequent actions of reflection and modification or redirection.

6.8. Achievement of Motivation

One classification of motivation differentiates among achievement, power, and social factors. In the area of achievement motivation, the work on goal-theory has differentiated three separate types of goals: mastery goals which focus on gaining competence or mastering a new set of knowledge or skills; performance goals which focus on achieving normative-based standards, doing better than others, or doing well without a lot of effort; and social goals which focus on relationships among people. In the context of school learning, which involves operating in a relatively structured environment, students with mastery goals outperform students with either performance or social goals. However, in life success, it seems critical that individuals have all three types of goals in order to be very successful.

One aspect of this theory is that individuals are motivated to either avoid failure or achieve success. In the former situation, the individual is more likely to select easy or difficult tasks, thereby either achieving success or having a good excuse for why failure occurred. In the latter situation, the individual is more likely to select moderately difficult tasks which will provide an interesting challenge, but still keep the high expectations for success.

6.8.1. Impacting Motivation in the Classroom

There are a variety of reasons why individuals may be lacking in motivation and provides a list of specific behaviours associated with high academic achievement. This is an excellent checklist to help students develop the conative component of their lives. In addition, as stated previously in these materials, teacher efficacy is a powerful input variable related to student achievement. There are a variety of specific actions that teachers can take to increase motivation on classroom tasks. In general, these fall into the two categories discussed above: intrinsic motivation and extrinsic motivation.

6.8.1.1. Intrinsic

a) Explain or show why learning a particular content or skill is important.

b) Create and/or maintain curiosity.

c) Provide a variety of activities and sensory stimulations.

d) Provide games and simulations.

e) Set goals for learning.

f) Relate learning to student needs.

g) Help student develop plan of action.

6.8.1.2. Extrinsic

a) Provide clear expectations.

b) Give corrective feedback.

c) Provide valuable rewards.

d) Make rewards available.

As a general rule, teachers need to use as much of the intrinsic suggestions as possible while recognising that not all students will be appropriately motivated by them. The extrinsic suggestions will work, but it must be remembered that they do so only as long as the student is under the control of the teacher. When outside of that control, unless the desired goals and behaviours have been internalised, the learner will cease the desired behaviour and operate according to his or her internal standards or to other external factors.

6.8.2. Operant Conditioning and Social Learning Theory

After demonstrating that organisms tend to repeat actions that are reinforced and that behaviour can be shaped by reinforcement, Skinner developed the technique of programmed instruction to make it possible for students to be reinforced for every correct response. According to him, supplying the correct answer—and being informed by the programme that it is the correct answer—motivates the student to go on to the next frame; and as the student works through the programme, the desired terminal behaviour is progressively shaped.

Following Skinner's lead, many behavioural learning theorists devised techniques of behaviour modification on the assumption that students are motivated to complete a task by being promised a reward of some kind. Many times the reward takes the form of praise or a grade. Sometimes it is a token that can be traded in for some desired object; and at other times the reward may be the privilege of engaging in a self-selected activity.

Operant conditioning interpretations of learning may help reveal why some students react favourably to particular subjects and dislike others. For instance, some students may enter a required math class with a feeling of delight, while others may feel that they have been sentenced to prison. Skinner suggests that such differences can be traced to past experiences. He would argue that the student who loves math has been shaped to respond that way by a series of positive experiences with maths. The maths hater, in contrast, may have suffered a series of negative experiences.

The Power of Persuasive Models Social learning theorists, such as Albert Bandura, call attention to the importance of observation, imitation, and vicarious reinforcement. A student who identifies with and admires a teacher of a particular subject may work hard partly to please the admired individual and partly to try becoming like that individual. A student who observes an older brother or sister reaping benefits from earning high grades may strive to do the same with the expectation of experiencing the same or similar benefits. A student who notices that a classmate receives praise from the teacher after acting in a certain way may decide to imitate such behaviour to win similar rewards.

6.9. Cognitive Views of Motivation

Cognitive views stress that human behaviour is influenced by the way people think about themselves and their environment. The direction that behaviour takes can be explained by four influences: the inherent need to construct an organised and logically consistent knowledge base, one's expectations for successfully completing a task, the factors that one believes account for success and failure, and one's beliefs about the nature of cognitive ability.

6.9.1. Impact of Cognitive Development

This view is based on Jean Piaget's principles of equilibration, assimilation, accommodation, and schema formation. Piaget proposes that children possess an inherent desire to maintain a sense of organisation and balance in their conception of the world. A sense of equilibration may be experienced if a child assimilates a new experience by relating it to an existing scheme, or the child may accommodate by modifying an existing scheme if the new experience is too different.

In addition, individuals will repeatedly use new schemes because of an inherent desire to master their environment. This explains why young children can, with no loss of enthusiasm, sing the same song, tell the same story, and play the same game over and over and why they repeatedly open and shut doors to rooms and cupboards with no seeming purpose. It also explains why older children take great delight in collecting and organising almost everything they can get their hands on and why adolescents who have begun to attain formal operational thinking will argue incessantly about all the unfairness in the world and how it can be eliminated.

6.9.2. Need for Achievement

Have you ever decided to take on a moderately difficult task and then found that you had somewhat conflicting feelings about it? On the one hand, you felt eager to start the course, confident that you would be pleased with your performance. But on the other hand, you also felt a bit of anxiety because of the small possibility of failure. Now try to imagine the opposite situation. In reaction to a suggestion to take a course outside your major, you flatly refuse because the probability of failure seems great, while the probability of success seems quite small.

Individuals with a high need for achievement have a stronger expectation of success than they do a fear of failure for most tasks and therefore anticipate a feeling of pride in accomplishment. When given a choice, high-need achievers seek out moderately challenging tasks because they offer an optimal balance between challenge and expected success. By contrast, individuals with a low need for achievement avoid such tasks because their fear of failure greatly outweighs their expectation of success, and they therefore anticipate feelings of shame. When faced with a choice, they typically opt either for relatively easy tasks because the probability of success is high or rather difficult tasks because there is no shame in failing to achieve a lofty goal.

For people to succeed at life in general, they must first experience success in one important aspect of their lives. For most children, that one important part should be school. But the traditional approach to evaluating learning, which emphasizes comparative grading, allows only a minority of students to achieve A's and B's and feel successful. The self-worth of the remaining students suffers, which depresses their motivation to achieve on subsequent classroom tasks.

6.9.3. Maslow's Theory of Growth Motivation

Maslow describes 17 propositions, that he believes would have to be incorporated into any sound theory of growth motivation to meet them. Referring to need gratification as the most important single principle underlying all development, he adds that "the single, holistic principle that binds together the multiplicity of human motives is the tendency for a new and higher need to emerge as the lower need fulfills itself by being sufficiently gratified". He elaborates on this basic principle by proposing a five-level hierarchy of needs. Physiological needs are at the bottom of the hierarchy, followed in ascending order by safety, belongingness and love, esteem, and self-actualisation needs. This order reflects differences in the relative strength of each need. The lower a need is in the hierarchy, the greater is its strength because when a lower-level need is activated, people will stop trying to satisfy a higher-level need and focus on satisfying the currently active lower-level need.

The first four needs are often referred to as deficiency needs because they motivate people to act only when they are unmet to some degree. Self-actualisation, by contrast, is often called a growth need because people constantly strive to satisfy it. Basically, self-actualisation refers to the need for self-fulfilment — the need to develop all of one's potential talents and capabilities. For example, an individual who felt she had the capability to write novels, teach, practise medicine, and raise children would not feel self-actualised until all of these goals had been accomplished to some minimal degree. Because it is at the top of the hierarchy and addresses the potential of the whole person, self-actualisation is discussed more frequently than the other needs.

In addition to the five basic needs that compose the hierarchy, Maslow describes cognitive needs and aesthetic needs. While not part of the basic hierarchy, these two classes of needs play a critical role in the satisfaction of basic needs. Maslow maintains that such conditions as the freedom to investigate and learn, fairness, honesty, and orderliness in interpersonal relationships are critical because their absence makes satisfaction of the five basic needs impossible.

6.10. Impact of Cooperative Learning on Motivation

Classroom tasks can be structured so that students are forced to compete with one another, work individually, or cooperate with one another to obtain the rewards that teachers make available for successfully completing these tasks.

Traditionally, competitive arrangements have been assumed to be superior to the other two in increasing motivation and learning. But reviews of the research literature found cooperative arrangements to be far superior in producing these benefits.

6.10.1. Types of Classroom Reward Structures

Competitive goal structures are typically norm referenced. This traditional practice of grading on the curve predetermines the percentage of A, B, C, D, and F grades regardless of the actual distribution of test scores. Because only a small percentage of students in any group can achieve the highest rewards and because this accomplishment must come at some other students' expense, competitive goal structures are characterised by negative interdependence. Students try to outdo one another, view classmates' failures as an advantage, and come to believe that the winners deserve their rewards because they are inherently better.

Some researchers have argued that competitive reward structures lead students to focus on ability as the primary basis for motivation. This orientation is reflected in the question, "Am I smart enough to accomplish this task?" When ability is the basis for motivation, competing successfully in the classroom may be seen as relevant to self-esteem, difficult to accomplish, and uncertain. These perceptions may cause some students to avoid challenging subjects or tasks, to give up in the face of difficulty, to reward themselves only if they win a competition, and to believe that their own successes are due to ability, whereas the successes of others are due to luck.

Individualistic goal structures are characterised by students working alone and earning rewards solely on the quality of their own efforts. The success or failure of other students is irrelevant. All that matters is whether the student meets the standards for a particular task. Thirty students working by themselves at computer terminals are functioning in an individual reward structure. Individual structures lead students to focus on task effort as the primary basis for motivation. Whether a student perceives a task as difficult depends on how successful she has been with that type of task in the past.

Cooperative goal structures are characterised by students working together to accomplish shared goals. What is beneficial for the other students in the group is beneficial for the individual and vice versa. Because students in cooperative groups can obtain a desired reward only if the other students in the group also obtain the same reward, cooperative goal structures are characterised by positive interdependence. Also, all groups may receive the same rewards, provided they meet the teacher's criteria for mastery. For example, a teacher might present a lesson on map reading, then give each group its own map and a question-answering exercise. Students then work with each other to ensure that all know how to interpret maps. Each student then takes a quiz on map reading. All teams whose average quiz scores meet a preset standard receive special recognition.

Cooperative structures lead students to focus on effort and cooperation as the primary basis of motivation. This orientation is reflected in the statement "We can do this if we try hard and work together." In a cooperative atmosphere, students are motivated out of a sense of obligation: one ought to try, contribute, and help satisfy group norms.

6.10.1.1. Motivating Students to Learn

1. Use behavioural techniques to help students exert themselves and work toward remote goals.
2. Make sure that students know what they are to do, how to proceed, and how to determine when they have achieved goals.
3. Do everything possible to satisfy deficiency needs: physiological, safety, belongingness and esteem.
   a) Accommodate the instructional programme to the physiological needs of your students.
   b) Make your room physically and psychologically safe.
   c) Show your students that you take an interest in them and that they belong in your classroom.
   d) Arrange learning experiences so that all students can gain at least a degree of esteem.
4. Enhance the attractions and minimise the dangers of growth choices.
5. Direct learning experiences toward feelings of success in an effort to encourage an orientation toward achievement, a positive self-concept, and a strong sense of self-efficacy.
6. Try to encourage the development of need achievement, self-confidence, and self-direction in students who need these qualities.
7. Try to make learning interesting by emphasizing activity, investigation, adventure, social interaction and usefulness.

References

Ames, Carole A., "Motivation: What Teachers Need to Know", Teachers College Record 91, 3, Spring 1990.

Brophy, Jere, "On Motivating Students", *Occasional Paper* No. 101, East Lansing, Michigan: Institute for Research on Teaching, Michigan State University, October 1986.

Maehr, Martin L., and Carol Midgley, "Enhancing Student Motivation: A Schoolwide Approach", *Educational Psychologist*, 1991.

Weiner, B., "Interpersonal and intrapersonal theories of motivation from an attributional perspective", *Educational Psychology Review,* 2000.

7

Managing Student Diversity

All of us, including the students, have preferred ways of learning. Teachers often call these differences learning styles, though this term may imply more consistency across situations than is really the case. One student may like to make diagrams to help remember a reading assignment, whereas another student may prefer to write a sketchy outline instead. Yet in many cases the students could in principle reverse the strategies and still learn the material: if coaxed (or perhaps required), the diagram-maker could takes notes for a change and the note-taker could draw diagrams. Both might still learn using the alternate style, even if neither felt as comfortable as with the strategies they prefer.

This reality suggests that a balanced, middle-of-the-road approach may be a teacher's best response to students' learning styles. Or to put it another way: it is good to support students' preferred learning strategies where possible and appropriate, but neither necessary nor desirable to do so all of the time. Most of all, it is neither necessary nor possible to classify or label students according to seemingly fixed learning styles and then allow them to learn only according to those styles. A student may prefer to hear new material rather than see it; he may prefer for you to explain something orally, for example, rather than to see it demonstrated in a video. But he may nonetheless tolerate or sometimes even prefer to see it demonstrated. In the long run, in fact, he may learn it best by encountering the material in both ways, regardless of his habitual preferences.

That said, there is evidence that individuals, including students, do differ in how they habitually think. These differences are more specific than learning styles or preferences, and psychologists sometimes call them cognitive styles, meaning typical ways of perceiving and remembering information, and typical ways of solving problems and making decisions. In a style of thinking called field dependence, for example, individuals perceive patterns as a whole rather than focus on the parts of the pattern separately. In a complementary tendency, called field independence, individuals are more inclined to analyze overall patterns into their parts. Cognitive research from the 1940s to the present has found field dependence/independence differences to be somewhat stable for any given person across situations, though not completely so. Someone who is field dependent (perceives globally or "wholistically") in one situation, that is, tends to a modest extent to perceive things globally or wholistically in other situations. Field dependence and independence can be important understanding students because the styles affect students' behaviours and preferences in school and classrooms. Field dependent persons tend to work better in groups, it seems, and to prefer "open-ended" fields of study like literature and history. Field independent persons, on the other hand, tend to work better alone and to prefer highly analytic studies like math and science. The differences are only a tendency, however, and there are a lot of students who contradict the trends. As with the broader notion of learning styles, the cognitive styles of field dependence and independence are useful for tailoring instruction to particular students, but their guidance is only approximate. They neither can nor should be used to "lock" students to particular modes of learning or to replace students' own expressed preferences and choices about curriculum.

Another cognitive style is impulsivity as compared to reflectivity. As the names imply, an impulsive cognitive style is one in which a person reacts quickly, but as a result makes comparatively more errors. A reflective style is the opposite: the person reacts more slowly and therefore makes fewer errors. As you might expect, the reflective style would seem better suited to many academic demands of school. Research has found that this is indeed the case for academic skills that clearly benefit from reflection, such as mathematical problem solving or certain reading tasks. Some classroom or school-related skills, however, may actually develop better if a student is relatively impulsive. Being a good partner in a cooperative learning group, for example, may depend partly on responding spontaneously (i.e. just a bit "impulsively") to others' suggestions; and being an effective member of an athletic team may depend on not taking time to reflect carefully on every move that you or your team mates make.

There are two major ways to use knowledge of students' cognitive styles. The first and the more obvious is to build on students' existing style strengths and preferences. A student who is field independent and reflective, for example, can be encouraged to explore tasks and activities that are relatively analytic and that require relatively independent work. One who is field dependent and impulsive, on the other hand, can be encouraged and supported to try tasks and activities that are more social or spontaneous. But a second, less obvious way to use knowledge of cognitive styles is to encourage more balance in cognitive styles for students who need it. A student who lacks field independence, for example, my need explicit help in organizing and analyzing key academic tasks (like organizing a lab report in a science class). One who is already highly reflective may need encouragement to try ideas spontaneously, as in a creative writing lesson.

7.1. Multiple Intelligences

For nearly a century, educators and psychologists have debated the nature of intelligence, and more specifically whether intelligence is just one broad ability or can take more than one form. Many classical definitions of the concept have tended to define intelligence as a single broad ability that allows a person to solve or complete many sorts of tasks, or at least many academic tasks like reading, knowledge of vocabulary, and the solving of logical problems. There is research evidence of such a global ability, and the idea of general intelligence often fits with society's everyday beliefs about intelligence. Partly for these reasons, an entire mini-industry has grown up around publishing tests of intelligence, academic ability, and academic achievement.

But there are also problems with defining intelligence as one general ability. One way of summing up the problems is to say that conceiving of intelligence as something general tends to put it beyond teachers' influence. When viewed as a single, all-purpose ability, students either have a lot of intelligence or they do not, and strengthening their intelligence becomes a major challenge, or perhaps even an impossible one. This conclusion is troubling to some educators, especially in recent years as testing school achievement has become more common and as students have become more diverse.

But alternate views of intelligence also exist that portray intelligence as having multiple forms, whether the forms are subparts of a single broader ability or are multiple "intelligences" in their own right. For various reasons such this perspective has gained in popularity among teachers in recent years, probably because it reflects many teachers' beliefs that students cannot simply be rated along a single scale of ability, but are fundamentally diverse .

One of the most prominent of these models is Howard Gardner's theory of multiple intelligences. Gardner proposes that there are eight different forms of intelligence, each of which functions independently of the others. Each person has a mix of all eight abilities—more of one but less of another—that helps to constitute that person's individual cognitive profile. Since most tasks—including most tasks in classrooms— require several forms of intelligence and can be completed in more than one way, it is possible for people with various profiles of talents to succeed on a task equally well. In writing an essay, for example, a student with high interpersonal intelligence but rather average verbal intelligence might use his or her interpersonal strength to get a lot of help and advice from classmates and the teacher. A student with the opposite profile might work well alone, but without the benefit of help from others. Both students might end up with essays that are good, but good for different reasons.

As evidence for the possibility of multiple intelligences, Gardner cites descriptions of individuals with exceptional talent in one form of intelligence (for example, in playing the piano) but who are neither above nor below average in other areas. He also cites descriptions of individuals with brain damage, some of whom lose one particular form of intelligence (like the ability to talk) but retain other forms. In the opinion of many psychologists, however, the evidence for multiple intelligences is not strong enough to give up the "classical" view of general intelligence. Part of the problem is that the evidence for multiple intelligences relies primarily on anecdotes—examples or descriptions of particular individuals who illustrate the model—rather than on more widespread information or data.

Nonetheless, whatever the status of the research evidence, the model itself can be useful as a way for teachers to think about their work. Multiple intelligences suggest the importance of diversifying instruction in order to honor and to respond to diversity in students'. talents and abilities. Viewed like this, whether Gardner's classification scheme is actually accurate is probably less important than the fact there is (or may be) more than one way to be "smart." In the end, as with cognitive and learning styles, it may not be important to label students' talents or intellectual strengths. It may be more important simply to provide important learning and knowledge in several modes or styles ways that draw on more than one possible form of intelligence or skill. A good example of this principle is your own development in learning to teach. It is well and good to read books about teaching , but it is even better to read books and talk with classmates and educators about teaching and get actual experience in classrooms. The combination both invites and requires a wide range of your talents and usually proves more effective than any single type of activity, whatever your profile of cognitive styles or intellectual abilities happens to be.

7.2. Gender differences

Gender roles are the patterns of behaviours, attitudes, and expectations associated with a particular sex—with being either male or female. For clarity, psychologists sometimes distinguish gender differences, which are related to social roles, from sex differences, which are related only to physiology and anatomy. Using this terminology, gender matters more than sex when teaching. Although there are many exceptions, boys and girls do differ on average in ways that parallel conventional gender stereotypes and that affect how the sexes behave at school and in class. The differences have to do with physical behaviours, styles of social interaction, academic motivations, behaviours, and choices. They have a variety of sources—primarily parents, peers, and the media. Teachers are certainly not the primary cause of gender role differences, but sometimes teachers influence them by their responses to and choices made on behalf of students.

7.2.1. Physical Differences in Gender Roles

Physically, boys tend to be more active than girls, and by the same token more restless if they have to sit for long periods. They are also more prone than girls to rely on physical aggression if they are frustrated. Both tendencies are inconsistent with the usual demands of classroom life, of course, and make it a little more likely that school will be a difficult experience for boys, even for boys who never actually get in trouble for being restless or aggressive.

During the first two or three years of elementary school, gross motor skills develop at almost the same average rate for boys and girls. As a group, both sexes can run, jump, throw a ball, and the like with about equal ease, though there are of course wide significant differences among individuals of both sexes. Toward the end of elementary school, however, boys pull ahead of girls at these skills even though neither sex has begun yet to experience puberty. The most likely reason is that boys participate more actively in formal and informal sports because of expectations and support from parents, peers, and society. Puberty eventually adds to this advantage by making boys taller and stronger than girls, on average, and therefore more suited at least for sports that rely on height and strength.

In thinking about these differences, keep in mind that they refer to average trends and that there are numerous individual exceptions. Every teacher knows of individual boys who are not athletic, for example, or of particular girls who are especially restless in class. The individual differences mean, among other things, that it is hard to justify providing different levels of support or resources to boys than to girls for sports, athletics, or physical education. The differences also suggest, though, that individual students who contradict gender stereotypes about physical abilities may benefit from emotional support or affirmation from teachers, simply because they may be less likely than usual to get such affirmation from elsewhere.

7.2.2. Social Differences in Gender Roles

When relaxing socially, boys more often gravitate to large groups. Whether on the playground, in a school hallway, or on the street, boys' social groups tend literally to fill up a lot of space, and often include significant amounts of roughhousing as well as organized and "semi-organized" competitive games or sports. Girls, for their part, are more likely to seek and maintain one or two close friends and to share more intimate information and feelings with these individuals. To the extent that these gender differences occur, they can make girls less visible or noticeable than boys, at least in leisure play situations where children or youth choose their companions freely. As with physical differences, however, keep in mind that differences in social interactions do not occur uniformly for all boys and girls. There are boys with close friends, contradicting the general trend, and girls who play primarily in large groups.

Differences in social interaction styles happen in the classroom as well. Boys, on average, are more likely to speak up during a class discussion—sometimes even if not called on, or even if they do not know as much about the topic as others in the class. When working on a project in a small co-ed group, furthermore they have a tendency to ignore girls' comments and contributions to the group. In this respect co-ed student groups parallel interaction patterns in many parts of society, where men also have a tendency to ignore women's comments and contributions.

7.2.3. Academic and Cognitive Differences in the Genders

On average, girls are more motivated than boys to perform well in school, at least during elementary school. By the time girls reach high school, however, some may try to down play their own academic ability in order make themselves more likeable by both sexes. Even if this occurs, though, it does not affect their grades: from kindergarten through twelfth grade, girls earn slightly higher average grades than boys. This fact does not lead to similar achievement, however, because as youngsters move into high school, they tend to choose courses or subjects conventionally associated with their gender—math and science for boys, in particular, and literature and the arts for girls. By the end of high school, this difference in course selection makes a measurable difference in boys' and girls' academic performance in these subjects.

But again, consider my caution about stereotyping: there are individuals of both sexes whose behaviours and choices run counter to the group trends. Differences within each gender group generally are far larger than any differences between the groups. A good example is the "difference" in cognitive ability of boys and girls. Many studies have found none at all. A few others have found small differences, with boys slightly better at math and girls slightly better at reading and literature. Still other studies have found the differences not only to be small, but to be getting smaller in recent years than compared to earlier studies. Collectively the findings about cognitive abilities are virtually "non-findings," and it is worth asking why gender differences have therefore been studied and discussed so much for so many years.

7.2.4. How Teachers Influence Gender Roles

Teachers often intend to interact with both sexes equally, and frequently succeed at doing so. Research has found, though, that they do sometimes respond to boys and girls differently, perhaps without realizing it. Three kinds of differences have been noticed. One is the overall amount of attention paid to each sex; the second is the visibility or "publicity" of conversations; and the third is the type of behaviour that prompts teachers to support or criticize students.

7.2.5. Attention Paid

In general teachers interact with boys more often than with girls by a margin of 10 to 30 percent, depending on the grade level of the students and the personality of the teacher. One possible reason for the difference is related to the greater assertiveness of boys that I already noted; if boys are speaking up more frequently in discussions or at other times, then a teacher may be "forced" to pay more attention to them. Another possibility is that some teachers may feel that boys are especially prone to getting into mischief, so they may interact with them more frequently to keep them focused on the task at hand. Still another possibility is that boys, compared to girls, may interact in a wider variety of styles and situations, so there may simply be richer opportunities to interact with them. This last possibility is partially supported by another gender difference in classroom interaction, the amount of public versus private talk.

7.2.6. Public Talk versus Private Talk

Teachers have a tendency to talk to boys from a greater physical distance than when they talk to girls. The difference may be both a cause and an effect of general gender expectations expressive nurturing is expected more often of girls and women, and a businesslike task orientation is expected more often of boys and men, particularly in mixed-sex groups. Whatever the reason, the effect is to give interactions with boys more "publicity." When two people converse with each other from across the classroom, many others can overhear them; when they are at each other's elbows, though, few others can overhear.

7.2.7. Distributing Praise and Criticism

In spite of most teachers' desire to be fair to all students, it turns out that they sometimes distribute praise and criticism differently to boys and girls.The tendency is to praise boys more than girls for displaying knowledge correctly, but to criticize girls more than boys for displaying knowledge incorrectly. Another way of stating this difference is by what teachers tend to overlook: with boys, they tend to overlook wrong answers, but with girls, they tend to overlook right answers. The result (which is probably unintended) is a tendency to make boys' knowledge seem more important and boys themselves more competent. A second result is the other side of this coin: a tendency to make girls' knowledge less visible and girls themselves less competent.

Gender differences also occur in the realm of classroom behaviour. Teachers tend to praise girls for "good" behaviour, regardless of its relevance to content or to the lesson at hand, and tend to criticize boys for "bad" or inappropriate behaviour. This difference can also be stated in terms of what teachers overlook: with girls, they tend to overlook behaviour that is not appropriate, but with boys they tend to overlook behaviour that is appropriate. The net result in this case is to make girls' seem more good than they may really be, and also to make their "goodness" seem more important than their academic competence. By the same token, the teacher's patterns of response imply that boys are more "bad" than they may really be.

At first glance, the gender differences in interaction can seem discouraging and critical of teachers because they imply that teachers as a group are biased about gender. But this conclusion is too simplistic for a couple of reasons. One is that like all differences between groups, interaction patterns are trends, and as such they hide a lot of variation within them. The other is that the trends suggest what often tends in fact to happen, not what can in fact happen if a teacher consciously sets about to avoid interaction patterns like the ones I have described. Fortunately for us all, teaching does not need to be unthinking; we have choices that we can make, even during a busy class!

7.3. Differences in Cultural Expectations

A culture is the system of attitudes, beliefs, and behaviours that constitute the distinctive way of life of a people. Although sometimes the term is also used to refer specifically to the artistic, intellectual and other "high-brow" aspects of life, I use it here more broadly to refer to everything that characterizes a way of life—baseball games as well as symphony concerts, and McDonald's as well as expensive restaurants. In this broad sense culture is nearly synonymous with ethnicity, which refers to the common language, history, and future experienced by a group within society. Culture has elements that are obvious, like unique holidays or customs, but also features that are subtle or easy for outsiders to overlook, like beliefs about the nature of intelligence or about the proper way to tell a story. When a classroom draws students from many cultures or ethnic groups, therefore, the students bring to it considerable diversity. Teachers need to understand that diversity—understand how students' habitual attitudes, beliefs, and behaviours differ from each other, and especially how they differ from the teacher's.

But this kind of understanding can get complicated. To organize the topic, therefore, I will discuss among aspects of cultural diversity according to how directly that relate to language differences compared to differences in other social and psychological features of culture. The distinction is convenient, but it is also a bit arbitrary because, as you will see, the features of a culture overlap and influence each other.

7.3.1. Bilingualism: Language Differences in the Classroom

Although monolingual speakers often do not realize it, the majority of children around the world are bilingual, meaning that they understand and use two languages. Even in the United States, which is a relatively monolingual society, more than 47 million people speak a language other than English at home, and about 10 million of these people were children or youth in public schools. The large majority of bilingual students (75%) are Hispanic, but the rest represent more than a hundred different language groups from around the world. In larger communities throughout the United States, it is therefore common for a single classroom to contain students from several language backgrounds at once.

In classrooms as in other social settings, bilingualism exists in different forms and degrees. At one extreme are students who speak both English and another language fluently; at the other extreme are those who speak only limited versions of both languages. In between are students who speak their home (or heritage) language much better than English, as well as others who have partially lost their heritage language in the process of learning English. Commonly, too, a student may speak a language satisfactorily, but be challenged by reading or writing it—though even this pattern has individual exceptions. Whatever the case, each bilingual student poses unique challenges to teachers.

7.3.2. Balanced or Fluent Bilingualism

The student who speaks both languages fluently has a definite cognitive advantage. As you might suspect and as research has confirmed, a fully fluent bilingual student is in a better position than usual to express concepts or ideas in more than one way, and to be aware of doing so.

7.3.3.Unbalanced Bilingualism

Unfortunately, the bilingualism of many students is "unbalanced" in the sense that they are either still learning English, or else they have lost some earlier ability to use their original, heritage language—or occasionally a bit of both. The first sort of student—sometimes called an English language learner (ELL) or limited English learner (LEL)—have received the greatest attention and concern from educators, since English is the dominant language of instruction and skill with it obviously helps prepare a student for life in American society. ELL students essentially present teachers with this dilemma: how to respect the original language and culture of the student while also helping the student to join more fully in the mainstream—i.e. English-speaking—

culture? Programs to address this question have ranged from total immersion in English from a young age (the "sink or swim" approach) to phasing in English over a period of several years (sometimes called an additive approach to bilingual education). In general, evaluations of bilingual programs have favored the more additive approaches. Both languages are developed and supported, and students ideally become able to use either language permanently, though often for different situations or purposes. A student may end up using English in the classroom or at work, for example, but continue using Spanish at home or with friends, even though he or she is perfectly capable of speaking English with them.

7.3.4. Language Loss

What about the other kind of imbalance, in which a student is acquiring English but losing ability with the student's home or heritage language? This sort of bilingualism is quite common in the United States and other nations with immigrant populations. Imagine this situation. First-generation immigrants arrive, and they soon learn just enough English to manage their work and daily needs, but continue using their original language at home with family and friends from their former country. Their children, however, experience strong expectations and pressure to learn and use English, and this circumstance dilutes the children's experience with the heritage language. By the time the children become adults, they are likely to speak and write English better than their heritage language, and may even be unable or unwilling to use the heritage language with their own children (the grandchildren of the original immigrants).

This situation might not at first seem like a problem for which we, as teachers, need to take responsibility, since the children immigrants, as students, are acquiring the dominant language of instruction. In fact, however, things are not that simple. Research finds that language loss limits students' ability to learn English as well or as quickly as they otherwise can do. Having a large vocabulary in a first language, for example, has been shown to save time in learning vocabulary in a second language. But students can only realize the savings if their first language is preserved. Preserving the first language is also important if a student has impaired skill in all languages and therefore needs intervention or help from a speech-language specialist. Research has found, in such cases, that the specialist can be more effective if the specialist speaks and uses the first language as well as English. More generally, though also more indirectly, minimizing language loss helps all bilingual students' education because preservation tends to enrich students' and parents' ability to communicate with each other. With two languages to work with, parents can stay "in the loop" better about their children's educations and support the teacher's work—for example, by assisting more effectively with homework.

Note that in the early years of schooling, language loss can be minimized to some extent by the additive or parallel track bilingual programs that I mentioned above. For a few years, though not forever, young students are encouraged to use both of their languages. In high school, in addition, some conventional foreign language classes—notably in Spanish—can be adjusted to include and support students who are already native speakers of the language alongside students who are learning it for the first time). But for heritage languages not normally offered as "foreign" languages in school, of course, this approach will not work. Such languages are especially at risk for being lost.

7.3.5. Cultural Differences in Language Use

Cultures and ethnic groups differ not only in languages, but also in how languages are used. Since some of the patterns differ from those typical of modern classrooms, they can create misunderstandings between teachers and students. Consider these examples:

In some cultures, it is considered *polite or even intelligent not to speak* unless you have something truly important to say. "Chitchat," or talk that simply affirms a personal tie between people, is considered immature or intrusive. In a classroom, this habit can make it easier for a child to learn not to interrupt others, but it can also make the child seem unfriendly.

Eye contact varies by culture. In many African American and Latin American communities, it is considered appropriate and respectful for a child not to look directly at an adult who is speaking to them. In classrooms, however, teachers often expect a lot of eye contact (as in "I want all eyes on me!") and may be tempted to construe lack of eye contact as a sign of indifference or disrespect.

Social distance varies by culture. In some cultures, it is common to stand relatively close when having a conversation; in others, it is more customary to stand relatively far apart. Problems may happen a teacher and a student prefer different social distances. A student who expects a closer distance than does the teacher may seem overly familiar or intrusive, whereas one who expects a longer distance may seem overly formal or hesitant.

Wait time varies by culture. Wait time is the gap between the end of one person's comment or question and the next person's reply or answer. In some cultures wait time is relatively long—as long as three or four seconds. In others it is a "negative" gap, meaning that it is acceptable, even expected, for a person to interrupt before the end of the previous comment. In classrooms the wait time is customarily about one second; after that, the teacher is likely to move on to another question or to another student. A student who habitually expects a wait time long than one second may seem hesitant, and not be given many chances to speak. A student who expects a "negative" wait time, on the other hand, may seem overeager or even rude.

7.3.6. Cultural Differences in Attitudes and Beliefs

In addition to differences in language and in practices related to language, cultural groups differ in a variety of other attitudes and beliefs. Complete descriptions of the details of the differences have filled entire books of encyclopedias. For teachers, however, the most important ones center on beliefs about identity, or the sense of self or of "who you are." A number of other cultural beliefs and practices can be understood as resulting from how members of a culture think about personal identity.

In white, middle-class American culture, the self is usually thought of as unique and independent—a unitary, living source of decisions, choices, and actions that stands (or should eventually stand) by itself. This view of the self is well entrenched in schools, as for example when students are expected to take responsibility for their own successes or failures and when they are tested and evaluated individually rather than as a group or team. As teachers, furthermore, most of us subscribe to the idea that ali students are unique, even if we cannot implement this idea fully in teaching because of the constraints of large classes. Whatever the circumstances, teachers tend to believe in an independent self.

To a greater or lesser extent, however, the majority of non-white cultures and ethnic groups believe in something closer to an interdependent self, or a belief that it is your relationships and responsibilities, and not uniqueness and autonomy, that defines a person. In these cultures, the most worthy person is not the one is unusual or who stands out in a crowd. Such a person might actually be regarded as lonely or isolated. The worthy person is instead the one who gets along well with family and friends, and who meets obligations to them reliably and skillfully. At some level, of course, we all value interpersonal skill and to this extent think of ourselves as interdependent. The difference between individual and interdependent self is one of emphasis, with many non-white cultures emphasizing interdependence significantly more than white middle-class society in general and more than schools in particular.

There can be consequences of the difference in how the students respond to school. Here are some of the possibilities — though keep in mind that there are also differences among students as individuals, whatever their cultural background. I am talking about tendencies, not straightforward predictions.

Preference for activities that are cooperative rather than competitive: Many activities in school are competitive, even when teachers try to de-emphasize the competition. Once past the first year or two of school, students often become attentive to who receives the highest marks on an assignment, for example, or who is the best athlete at various sports or whose contributions to class discussion the most verbal recognition from the teacher. Suppose, in addition, that a teacher deliberately organizes important activities or assignments competitively (as in "Let's see who finishes the math sheet first"). Classroom life can then become explicitly competitive, and the competitive atmosphere can interfere with cultivating supportive relationships among students or between students and the teacher. For students who give priority to these relationships, competition can seem confusing at best and threatening at worst. What sort of sharing or help with answers, the student may ask, is truly legitimate? If the teacher answers this question more narrowly than does the student, then what the student views as cooperative sharing may be seen by the teacher as laziness, "freeloading", or even cheating.

Avoidance of standing out publicly: Even when we, as teachers, avoid obvious forms of competition, we may still interact frequently with students one at a time while allowing or inviting many others to observe the conversation. An especially common pattern for such conversations is sometimes called the IRE cycle, an abbreviation for the teacher initiating, a student responding, and the teacher then evaluating the response. What is sometimes taken for granted is how often IRE cycles are witnessed publicly, and how much the publicity can be stressful or embarrassing for students who do not value standing out in a group but who do value belonging to the group. The embarrassment can be especially acute if they feel unsure about whether they have correct knowledge or skill to display. To keep such students from "clamming up" completely, therefore, teachers should consider limiting IRE cycles to times when they are truly productive. IRE conversations may often work best when talking with a student privately, or when confirming knowledge that the student is likely to be able to display competently already, or when "choral" speaking (responding together in unison) is appropriate.

Interpersonal time versus clock time: In order to function all schools rely on fairly precise units of time as measured on clocks. Teachers typically allot a fixed number of minutes to one lesson or class, another fixed number of minutes for the next, another for recess or lunch time, and so on. In more ways than one, therefore, being on time becomes especially valued in schools, as it is in many parts of society. Punctuality is not always conducive, however, to strong personal relationships, which develop best when individuals do not end joint activities unilaterally or arbitrarily, but allow activities to "finish themselves," so to speak—to finish naturally. If personal relationships are a broad, important priority for a student, therefore, it may take effort and practice by the student to learn the extent to which schools and teachers expect punctuality. Punctuality includes the obvious, like showing up for school when school is actually scheduled to begin. But it also includes subtleties, like starting and finishing tasks when the teacher tells students to do so, or answering a question promptly at the time it is asked rather than sometime later when discussion has already moved on.

7.4. Accommodating Diversity in Practice

Briefly, then, here is what this chapter said: Students differ in a multitude of ways, both individually and as groups. Individually, for example, students have *preferred learning styles* as well as preferred *cognitive or thinking styles*. They also have unique *cognitive profiles,* intelligence or competence that affect how and what they learn most successfully.

In addition to individual diversity, students tend to differ according to *behaviours associated with gender*, although there are many individual exceptions. *Motor abilities* as well as *motivation* and experience with athletics gradually differentiate boys and girls, especially when they reach high school and begin high school. *Socially,* boys tend to adopt relationships that are more active and wide-ranging than do girls. *Academically,* girls tend to be a bit more motivated and to receive slightly higher marks in school. *Teachers sometimes contribute to gender role differences*—perhaps without intending—by paying attention to boys more frequently and more publicly in class, and by distributing praise and criticism in ways differentiated by sex.

Students also differ according to *cultures, language, and ethnic groups* of their families. Many students are *bilingual,* with educational consequences that depend on their fluency in each of their two languages. If they have more difficulty with English, then programs that add their first language together with English have proved to be helpful. If they have more difficulty with their first language, they are risk for language loss, and the consequences are also negative even if more hidden from teachers' views.

In addition to language differences as such, students differ according to *how they use language*—in taking turns at speaking, in eye contact, social distance, wait time, and the use of questions. Some of these differences stem from cultural differences about self-identity, with non-Anglo culturally sometimes (but not always) supporting a more interdependent view of the self than Anglo culture or the schools. Differences in attitudes and in use of language have several consequences for teachers. In particular—where appropriate—they should consider using cooperative activities, avoid highlighting individuals' accomplishments or failures, and be patient about students' learning to be punctual. Hopefully, therefore, we have persuaded you—if you ever really needed persuading—that students are indeed diverse. The question that follows from this point is *what to do* about the diversity. We partially answered that question by making a number of teaching-related suggestions throughout this chapter. But there is obviously more to be said about accommodating diversity—about actually working with students' differences and making them a resource rather than a burden or challenge. In the rest of this book therefore we offer more suggestions, not only about knowing how different one student can be from another, but also about diversifying teaching to acknowledge this fact. Differences among students are inevitably a challenge during all phases of teaching, from planning instruction, to implementing lessons and activities, to assessing students' learning after lessons or activities are all finished.

7.5. Curricular Congruence

To successfully reach out to a diversity of learners requires substantial support. Although budget-minded critics will argue that such support is costly, they need to be reminded that an investment in prevention today will eliminate or lessen the expense of remediation tomorrow. Not surprisingly, educators who receive substantial help are more effective when carrying out worthwhile innovations that increase all students' potential for success. This notion of support is vitally important because students' "at-riskness" will not disappear and because the government and educational community continue to believe in the efficacy of raising academic standards.

At-risk learners benefit from instructional activities that are carefully planned and mutually supported by classroom teachers and learning centre staff. Unfortunately, many schools provide separate instruction in both settings. For example, in the English classroom, students may explore the theme of good and evil by reading and discussing William Golding's *Lord of the Flies*, whereas in the learning centre, at-risk students may complete workbook exercises and other fragmented activities unrelated to the instructional theme. Clearly, at-risk learners are more likely to be successful when classroom and learning centre teachers provide them with congruent goals, resources, strategies, and skills.

A model that can be adapted to both push-in and pull-out efforts represents an ambitious approach, but it can be a major source of support for at-risk learners. Specifically, these learners receive language arts instruction seven periods a week. Twice a week, the majority of students experience a double period of instruction, while the at-risk learners are enriched with activities that support the language arts program. If *Lord of the Flies* is being highlighted, the classroom teacher might immerse students in interactive activities concerning important themes, concepts, and vocabulary of the novel. Meanwhile, the learning centre teacher might engage individuals in a similar instructional focus, while providing support through a prereading plan, structured overview, semantic mapping, or semantic feature analysis.

An important part of this classroom/learning center connection is cooperative planning time that is built into the teaching assignments of the English staff. These professionals are scheduled weekly for 20-minute periods of teaching and for one period of mutual planning with the learning centre staff. During the planning session, the key players discuss their community of learners and organise congruent activities that support effective learning.

Creating a closer link between the classroom and the learning centre makes sense. This approach increases transfer of learning and simultaneously lessens the incidence of fragmented, reductionistic teaching. Thus, at-risk learners have more opportunities to engage in cohesive instruction directly related to their learning strengths and needs. Although curricular congruence is not a cure-all, it is a serious source of support for helping at-risk learners to be successful and independent.

7.6. Special Education Teacher As Team Teacher

Similar to the intent of curricular congruence is the changing role of the special education teacher serving as a team teacher. This inclusionary perspective helps learners with mild, moderate, and severe disabilities to be successful in the heterogeneous classroom and, thus, to be genuine members of the learning community. In a chapter of Villa and Thousand's "Creating an Inclusive School", middle grades science teacher Nancy Keller and special educator Lia Cravedi-Cheng describe their bonding as team teachers, which led to the social and academic growth of themselves and their students. Initially, the key players decided to meet at least one period each week for mutual planning. During this time, they focused on building a trusting relationship as they defined and redefined professional roles, discussed content to be covered, planned related instructional activities, and assessed student outcomes. These and other planning agendas set the stage for continued growth with a variety of joint responsibilities.

While reflecting on their professional growth, Keller and Cravedi-Cheng realised that successful inclusion occurs when both teachers and students receive support. Planning cooperatively, developing goals, maintaining personal accountability helped the teachers to merge their talents, to reaffirm their commitment to all students, and to reach their audience academically and socially. As was expected, both special needs students and their nondisabled peers became contributing members of the learning community.

Cheryl Jorgensen describes an interdisciplinary programme at Souhegan High School in New Hampshire. The learning environment for grades 9 and 10 involves two teams for each grade level, with approximately 85 students in each team. Social studies, science, English, and special education teachers share daily blocks of time morning and afternoon, and these professionals may organise instruction in a variety of ways to accommodate students' learning needs. An important part of these efforts is collaborative planning time for content area teachers and special educators. Interestingly, special needs students at Souhegan High do not usually require instructional modifications in their heterogeneously grouped classes; however, when support is needed for nurturing full participation, it may be provided by peers, adults, adapted resources, or assistive technology. Individuals also benefit from modified expectations—for example, a physically disabled learner may have his or her lines in a play tape-recorded by a classmate.

7.7. Volunteers and Paraprofessionals

Another source of help for students and teachers in a heterogeneous learning environment is an "extra set of hands." Specifically, these individuals may nurture learning by functioning as effective role models, reading to students, listening to them read, listening to their retellings after silent reading, asking challenging questions concerning their reading, coaching their efforts, sharing and monitoring reading and writing, developing instructional materials, administering interest and attitude inventories, organising a classroom newspaper, assisting with bulletin boards and classroom displays that encourage reading and writing, and serving as a resource during field trips.

Volunteers and aides can make valuable contributions to the classroom context, and their support is vitally needed to accommodate the diversity of learning needs which has increased markedly in recent years. Well-constructed questionnaires surveying parents and potential volunteers can provide useful information that can lead to a functional plan of action for eliciting, managing, and developing effective volunteers and aides.

7.8. Instructional Resources

Students' journey toward success also involves natural immersion in authentic resources. All learners, including those at risk of failing, benefit from literacy-rich classrooms cluttered with paperbacks, anthologies, fiction and non fiction works, dramas and comedies, poetry, illustrated books, "how-to" manuals, bibliotherapeutic stories, talking books, large-print books, dictionaries, magazines, newspapers, and pamphlets. Students are more apt to respond positively to these materials when they are permitted to choose from a wide variety of options, when they observe teachers respecting their choices, and when they are encouraged to read at their own comfortable pace in the classroom.

Being sensitive to students' interests and strengths will also help them to meet content area expectations, especially if teaching and learning are organised around important themes and concepts. For example, if the instructional unit concerns the Civil War, and individual may demonstrate his or her preferred learning style by reading illustrated materials and by creating a flow chart showing important battles. Others may respond to thematic and conceptual aspects of the study unit in ways that represent their unique styles, as the teacher guides them to focus on instructional outcomes that fulfil curricular expectations. These flexible considerations not only provide immediate learning benefits, but also promote a lifelong love of learning.

Not surprisingly, this flexibility also applies to technological resources, which play a major role in helping students to be successful. Disabled learners, in particular, may benefit from adaptive hardware, such as seating devices, switches, electronic communication aids, and computers that scan printed materials and read the text aloud.

Although appropriate instructional resources can facilitate learning in heterogeneous classrooms, a problematic economy has caused school administrators to allocate budgets for the basic curricula. Administrators need to work with parents and the community to provide a wide variety of resources to support students and teachers. This effort increases the chances that special needs students and their nondisabled classmates will respond positively to literacy learning and will use it throughout their lives.

What may be considered to be typical undergraduate behaviour in the United States does not apply to all students. As in all cultures, individual styles exist. It is important to remember that student academic performance can increase when methods of instruction match the learning styles and cognitive styles of individual students.

7.8.1. Varying Instructions

One of the most effective ways to deal with student diversity within group instruction is to vary teaching methods. Instruction can be varied within one class session and from session to session.

Some students learn easily via auditory methods and others via visual or kinesthetic means. A teacher who is aware of these different modes of learning can help students learn more efficiently and effectively. For example, the teacher can give an explanation, show slides depicting the subject or draw a diagram of what was explained, and then have students use the information by asking them to solve a problem, give an example of how to apply the concepts explained, summarise the explanation, or physically manipulate equipment.

Another way to vary instruction is to vary the use of inductive and deductive teaching methods. In the deductive approach, students are given information and then asked to perform a task or answer questions based on the information given. In the inductive approach, students are asked to perform a task before they are given information about the task. Explanations can be given after students either discover how to do the task or discover that they are unable to perform the task. For some students, explanations are more meaningful once they have had some experience in working with or thinking about a particular idea or concept.

7.8.2. Student Participation

Student diversity can also be addressed by increasing the degree of student participation. Students are more attentive when they are asked to actively participate in the class. Students can be asked to participate in a discussion by responding to structured and focused discussion questions with the teacher as leader and facilitator.

Instructional variety and student participation can also be increased by asking students to respond to questions within particular theoretical frameworks, ideologies, or their own personal experiences. Further variety can be introduced by asking students to debate an issue, roleplay situations, or engage in group activities.

Involving students directly with the material to be learned not only varies instruction but can also enhance learning and retention of information. Some students need a great deal of personal involvement with course material in order to learn and understand it well.

7.8.3. Individual Needs

Teaching to student diversity also requires taking individual student needs into account, identifying the various levels of student understanding and providing encouragement to students.

Although it is important for the teacher to endeavour to meet the diverse needs of students, some students will need more help than can reasonably be given during class and office hours. Most colleges and universities have student services such as academic and study skill centres or a tutorial office that these students can be referred to. In referring the student, it is helpful to inform him or her of the specific skills that need improvement.

7.9. Diversity and Learning Styles

It is also important for teachers to be aware of diverse student learning styles: Learning styles refer to how students learn and study. Two extreme types of learning styles that have been called the "deep" or global approach and the "surface" or atomistic approach have been identified. The global approach is a holistic style of learning in which the student integrates the main points of the lesson into a structural whole. On the opposite end of the continuum is the atomistic approach in which students concentrate on parts of the lesson, often without interrelating or integrating the information. Although both styles are important in learning, the predominant use of one style over another can be detrimental to the learning process.

In terms of study habits, students who tend to use the global approach spend a longer time studying, find the material more interesting, and feel that studying is gratifying students who use the atomistic approach spend a great deal of time on rote memorisation of facts and may find studying tedious and unrewarding.

Successful learning depends on the student's ability to combine the best of both learning styles. The global approach learner must learn to pay attention to details and the atomistic approach learner needs to view the details in relation to the larger picture.

Students tend to have a preference for one learning style over another. However, the method of teaching, the type of testing and the nature of the subject matter can influence student choice of learning style. For instance, in large survey courses, it is easy for students to be overwhelmed by the amount of factual information and turn to a more atomistic approach. Consequently, they may focus on the details of the course and lose sight of the overall implications of the conceptual and theoretical course material. When this happens, students need to be directed toward developing a deeper approach to studying the subject matter. On the other hand, students predominantly using a global approach may need to be reminded that a certain amount of factual and detailed information is needed to support conceptual and theoretical assertions.

7.9.1. Learning Styles Chart

There appears to be a relationship between student learning styles and the subjects they choose to study in college. Atomistic learners tend to be attracted to departments in which knowledge is hierarchically structured and related to accepted paradigms. Students who favor the global approach are most often found in departments in which knowledge is more subject to personal interpretation.

Teachers can help students to become more aware of their own characteristic learning styles as well as show them how they might most effectively capitalise on their intellectual strengths. For example, he might help students to recognise their ability to memorise facts, and then help them to explore how they might make use of these facts in explaining an overall concept. The goal is to encourage the students to try to go beyond the limitations of one particular style.

Through an awareness of learning styles, a teacher can effectively balance instruction to include both learning approaches. Probably the most effective technique a teacher can use is to vary teaching strategies to include examples and discussions that utilise both the atomistic approach and the global approach. In this way students can be encouraged to practice both styles and learn to use the best of each when most appropriate.

The teacher's teaching methods and the course testing procedures tend to encourage and expect certain learning; therefore, students should be informed of these expectations so that they can direct their learning process according to the most appropriate style. The teacher can help students choose the expected learning style by clearly explaining testing formats, grading procedures and course content requirements.

Knowledge of these different approaches may also help the teacher to explain puzzling student behaviour. For example, when students ask extensive questions about the exam it might be easy to assume that these students don't want to study or are not interested in learning, and therefore want to be given answers. However, in light of the research on learning styles, students may just be trying to find out what is expected of them so they can concentrate their efforts on the appropriate learning style necessary for success in each particular course and on each type of exam.

7.9.2. Diversity, Learning Style and Culture

Educators do not believe that all learners are the same. Yet visits to schools throughout the world might convince us otherwise. Too often, educators continue to treat all learners alike while paying lip service to the principle of diversity.

Teachers know that students learn in different ways; the experience in the classroom confirms this every day. In addition, well-accepted theories and extensive research illustrate and document learning differences. Most educators can talk about learning differences, whether by the name of learning styles, cognitive styles, psychological type, or multiple intelligences. Learners bring their own individual approach, talents and interests to the learning situation.

We also know that an individual learner's culture, family background, and socioeconomic level affect his or her learning. The context in which someone grows and develops has an important impact on learning.

These beliefs, principles and theories have an important impact on the opportunities for success for every student in our schools.

7.9.3. Diversity, Uniformity and School Practices

Despite acknowledgment of important differences among learners, uniformity continues to dominate school practices. Most schools still function as if all students were the same. Students use the same textbooks and the same materials for learning. They work at the same pace on the same quantity of material. They study the same content and work through the same curriculum on the same schedule. Teachers talk with whole groups of students, delivering the same information at the same time to everyone. And, of course, schools use the same tests for all to measure the success of the learning.

Is this kind of sameness always wrong? Surely, given the task of educating large numbers of people, efficiency justifies some consistency and uniformity in the process. Even more valid is the argument for general standards and equality across schools, districts, and states. This is a realistic perspective, but to better match beliefs about diversity with practice, we must address the imbalance between uniformity and diversity.

At present, schools are heavily biased toward uniformity over diversity. An appropriate balance must be determined thoughtfully with attention to beliefs, theories, and research rather than efficiency.

In one sense, the current imbalance is easily understood. Sameness is always easier to accommodate than difference, and education practices often have been developed to consciously promote the same education for all students. We have few teaching models that appropriately accommodate both consistent educational values and human diversity.

A clarification is needed here. Attention to diversity does not mean "anything goes." Honouring diversity does not imply a lack of clear beliefs and strong values. There are indeed some absolutes in education. Every learner benefits from an outstanding teacher and an engaging learning experience. Every student and teacher deserves to be treated with respect. Every student should have an opportunity to reach his or her individual potential. Every student should master specific basic skills. The challenge is to identify what should be the same in schools and what should be different. We need appropriate uniform standards but not standardisation.

7.10. Attending to Diversity

The need to address the balance between uniformity and diversity is urgent because the current imbalance is consistently damaging to many learners and teachers.

The emphasis on uniformity is a serious disadvantage for students whose culture has taught them behaviours and beliefs that are different from the norms of the majority culture most often emphasized in schools. Students whose families value collaboration are told to be independent. Students whose culture values spontaneity are told to exercise self- control. Students who are rewarded in their families for being social are told to work quietly and alone.

A limited acknowledgment of individual learning differences also encourages a continual search for the one "best" way for students to learn, teachers to teach, and the curriculum to be studied. There is ample proof over the years—in reading, mathematics, writing, and foreign language instruction, for example, that it is futile to search for the single best way to achieve a broad educational outcome, in large part because learners do not fit a single mold.

Students who do not learn through whatever the current "best approach" happens to be are too often labeled "disabled" because their way of learning does not respond to that particular method. To further complicate the situation, the method becomes the identified deficit and the target for remediation. For example, in reading, remediation in phonics, which is a strategy, often becomes the target for learning. In a typical situation, a young learner who initially was not successful learning to read with a phonic approach receives additional instruction in phonics. The overarching goal, in this case the ability to read, is lost as the instruction emphasizes the specific practice of the deficit technique. Remediating a deficit technique rather than teaching the desired skill through the student's strength is the norm in too many schools.

The same pattern is evident in behavioural areas where, for example, an active, hands- on learner who does not have the opportunity to use that approach in a positive way in the classroom is described as lacking self-control and labeled disruptive or hyperactive. It disturbs many educators to see the tremendous increase in the number of students medicated for attention deficit disorder (ADD) and attention deficit hyperactivity disorder (ADHD) without an examination of their learning styles.

The traits that are associated with ADD- hyperactivity, distractibility, and impulsiveness- can result from a number of causes. For example, a child may be hyperactive or inattentive because of being bored with a lesson, anxious about a bully, upset about a divorce, allergic to milk, temperamental by nature, or a hundred other things. Research suggests, though, that once adults have labelled and medicated the child—and the medication works—these more complex questions are all too often forgotten. By rushing to drugs and labels, we may be leaving more difficult problems to fester under the surface.

Teachers, too, suffer from the imbalance between uniformity and diversity, especially when they are evaluated with uniform processes. Numerous educators, have written eloquently about the value of diversity of teaching styles. We do not have evidence of one best way to teach, just as we don't know of one best way to learn.

An emphasis on uniformity creates competition rather than collaboration among teachers. While identification of specific teaching skills can be uniform, diversity of teaching styles can and should be a school's strength. For example, all teachers can be held accountable for thoughtful planning, but that planning could be linear and sequential for one teacher and holistic and conceptual for another. The plan books of these teachers would look very different, and they should be evaluated differently, too.

Distinct approaches to teaching methods, content instruction, curriculum organisation, and special education programming come and go over the years. It is unrealistic to expect that a particular approach will be successful for all learners. This expectation only leads to disappointment and another swing of the education pendulum. Instead of an either-or mentality, many experienced teachers know that using the best of a variety of approaches benefits many learners. Instructional tools must be carefully and intentionally adapted to accommodate individual learners. Only in this way will all students have an opportunity for success.

7.10.1. Defining Learning Style

To understand people's behaviours, we need to look at the roots of their actions. One way to do this is to consider several basic ways in which we all interact with a situation, a person, information, or ideas. First we take in the occurrence; then we think about it; react to it; and ultimately act upon it. These basic functions imply four categories of style differences.

1) *Style is concerned with cognition:* People perceive and gain knowledge differently.
2) *Style is concerned with conceptualisation:* People form ideas and think differently.
3) *Style is concerned with affect:* People's emotional responses and values differ.
4) *Style is concerned with behaviour:* People act differently.

These categories help organise the diverse aspects of style, but they are not meant to be rigid. The complexity and subtlety of human behaviour makes any organisation of individual differences accurate in one instance but arbitrary in the next. To understand styles and their implications for education, it is best to view these categories in conjunction with all the characteristics that are integrated in the total personality of each human being.

7.10.2. Cognition

Perception, the initial stage of cognition, involves receiving, obtaining, taking possession of, and discerning information, ideas, and concepts. Some of us best perceive what is real; others clearly see possibilities with their imaginations. Some people see parts of a whole, separating ideas from their context, while others see the whole, not unlike the difference between seeing the forest or the trees.

These perceptual differences affect what and how something is received. A gifted artist can describe the gestalt of a painting, but some viewers will be struck by, and confined to, a single image in the work. The artist can plead, cajole, and discuss the entire painting in detail, but to little avail if the viewer's perception governs a certain view.

Consider how it would be if you hiked through the woods with a friend who suddenly became fascinated with a mushroom. At first, you might not even see the mushroom; your friend must point it out. Then, even when you physically see it, it doesn't mean the same thing to the two of you. You never eat mushrooms, and besides, you're on the hike mainly to enjoy your friend's company. But your friend is an accomplished gourmet chef who is looking to a new challenge: learning to cook with wild mushrooms he himself gathers. He'll soon be taking a class to learn to distinguish between edible and poisonous varieties. Your perceptions about the mushroom, obviously, are different.

Two people listening to the same music respond differently to the nuances of the sound, reflecting the depth of their musical experiences and their personal perceptions. Perhaps one is tuned to certain subtleties, while the other listens more generally. Two people sitting next to each other at a movie will recall different things when they discuss the film later. Students in a class often hear the teacher's directions in very different ways.

Gaining knowledge is another part of cognition. People get information in different ways. Some people use abstract sources, reading about things and listening to others' descriptions. Others need concrete experiences. The concrete person often will depend directly on the senses for information: "I see it; now I know what it is." The abstract person is more receptive to secondhand sources of knowledge. Some people have to touch something or see it operate before they accept it as real, while others can imagine a vivid reality without needing to experience it. There are also sensory specialists, those people who rely on one sense more than another to gather information. Again, these different ways of getting information and gaining knowledge reflect distinct personal styles.

7.10.3. Conceptualisation

People also exhibit differences in what they do with the knowledge they gain: how they process information and how they think. Some people are always looking for connections and ways to tie things together. Others are more divergent: One thought, idea, or fact triggers a multitude of new directions. Some people order ideas, information, and experiences in a linear, sequential way, while others organise their thoughts in clusters and random patterns. Some people think aloud; they verbalise ideas as a way of understanding them. Others concentrate on understanding concepts and experiences privately in their own minds. Some people think quickly, spontaneously and impulsively; others are deliberate and reflective.

We see these and other examples every day. You may have had the experience of asking someone, "Whatever made you say that?" Then you realise the person was thinking about something in a very different way than you were. The important point is that these differences form patterns for each person and affect their total behaviour.

7.10.4. Affect

Differences in motivation, judgments, values, and emotional responses also characterise individual style. Some people are motivated internally; others seek external rewards. Some people actively seek to please others: children to please their parents and teachers, adults to please bosses and spouses. Some people simply are not attuned to others' expectations, and still others will rebel against any such demands. Some people make decisions logically, rationally, objectively, and coolly. Others decide things subjectively, focusing on their own and others' perceptions and emotions. Some people seek frequent feedback on their ideas and work; some are crushed by slight criticism. Others welcome analytical comments, and still others would never ask an outsider for a critique.

For some people, the medium is the message; others focus directly on the content. Some people are emotionally involved in everything they do, and others are neutral. The emotional learner prefers a classroom with a high emotional energy while another learner works best in a low-key environment. These affective differences are also stylistic and interrelated with the conceptual and cognitive characteristics discussed above.

The discussion of differences in affective style does not contradict basic humanistic beliefs in education. Everyone does best in a supportive atmosphere free from excessive criticism. But an awareness of stylistic differences can help administrators and teachers recognise that every person does not seek the same affective response and understand the kinds of support students, parents, and coworkers want.

7.10.5. Behaviour

Cognitive, conceptual, and affective patterns are the roots of behaviour, and pervasive and consistent stylistic characteristics will be reflected in a person's actions. The reflective thinker, for example, can be expected to act in a reflective way in a variety of situations from decision making to relating to people. Some people scan a situation to get the overall gist before tackling a problem; others focus on, a certain part of the problem immediately and start with it. Some people approach a task randomly; others are very systematic. Some people need explicit structure; others prefer and perform best in a more open-ended situation. Some people prefer to work alone, and others like groups. Many people prefer working in certain kinds of physical environments.

In education, we recognise a variety of differences in how people learn and how these basic styles affect the individual learner's behaviour. Reflective students are slow to respond to questions and need to think through a response carefully. Impulsive learners respond quickly and blurt out their thoughts. The step-by-step person learns best when each stage is clear and the transitions are spelled out. Another kind of learner makes intuitive leaps. After several weeks of struggling with division of fractions, this student may suddenly announce, "I've got it!" This same intuitive learner also will be impatient with sounding out parts of a word and doing phonetic worksheets when she has already grasped the essence of a story.

In sum, people differ in the ways they perceive, think, feel, and behave. Researchers have identified many specific examples of these differences, as summarised in the chart which follows. Equally important, the personal and professional experiences of educators provide constant evidence that style differences exist and that they affect many aspects of learning and teaching each day.

To provide an equal opportunity for all students to be successful in school, educators must first develop a deep understanding of individual differences in learning. The research and theories on culture and learning style adequately document learning differences among individuals.

While these theories are familiar to many educators, and generally accepted, their application is relatively shallow. For example, many teachers know that it is important to provide a "visual" learner with visual information. But if the visual is words on an overhead projector mimicking the words spoken orally, this is a superficial accommodation of the learner's style. Far more significant would be an image, symbol, or visual representation of the information so that the visual learner could learn through his or her strengths.

Many teachers know that the active, kinesthetic learner needs hands-on experiences. A deeper understanding of these learners tells us that the experiences should come early in the process while the initial understanding of the concepts and skills are being developed, not just during practice time. Yet many times these learners are asked to "understand" first, then "do" later.

The kinesthetic learner needs to manipulate the science equipment to understand the concepts, and she will learn abstract math concepts while doing the measurement project or even after it's completed. The kinesthetic learners' impatience to get started sometimes causes teachers to demand that they explain what they will do before they start. This is difficult for these students, since the doing leads to the understanding and the explaining.

Learning styles research and resources are rich with examples to help develop appropriate activities for different learners. But if the activities are not guided by a consistent and deep understanding of the significance of learning differences, the activities will be a cursory attempt to implement these concepts. Learning styles labels are simply a tool; the diverse behaviours we see in the classroom are reflections of much deeper cognitive processes.

Not all learners who share a certain label are alike. A "visual" learner who is also "concrete sequential" seeks visual order and would benefit from a linear diagram of material. A "visual" learner who is also "abstract random" responds to design and would be drawn to a mind-map format for organising information. A careful study of the major concepts of learning styles is necessary for the practical application of these theories in schools.

7.10.6. Culture and Learner Diversity

We know that culture and learning are connected in important ways. Early life experiences and the values of a person's culture affect both the expectations and the processes of learning. If this relationship is true, could we then assume that students who share cultural characteristics have common ways of learning? Does culture create a way of learning, and how would we know this? Do African American students have similar ways of learning? Do girls learn differently than boys? These questions are both important and controversial. They are important because we need all the information we can get to help every learner succeed in school, and because a deep understanding of the learning process should provide a framework for curriculum and instructional decisions. They also are important questions because success for the diverse student populations in schools calls for continual re-examination of educators' assumptions, expectations, and biases.

Such questions are controversial because information about a group of people often leads to naive inferences about individual members of that group. Additionally, in the search for explanations of the continued achievement difference between students of color and mainstream white students, there is an understandable sensitivity about causes and effects. It is all too easy to confuse descriptions of differences with explanations for deficits. The questions also are controversial because they force us to confront philosophical issues in the uniformity versus diversity debate.

A deep understanding of both culture and learning style differences is important for all educators, though the subject must be addressed carefully. The relationship of the values of the culture in which a child is currently living, or from which a child has roots, and the learning expectations and experiences in the classroom is directly related to the child's school success academically, socially, and emotionally.

7.10.7. Nature vs. Nurture Issue

If a classroom teacher is to facilitate successful learning opportunities for all learners, he or she must "know" the learner. This includes knowing about innate personality and also learned cultural values that affect behaviour. The learner, of any age, is a product of nature and nurture. We each are born with predisposition for learning in certain ways. We also are products of external influences, especially within our immediate family, extended community, and culture.

Researchers confirm that learning patterns are a function of both nature and nurture. Many researchers describe the importance of socialisation within the family, immediate culture, and wider culture. They agree that "cultural differences in children's learning styles develop through their early experience".

Sometimes people wonder which is more important: innate personality traits or the influence of culture? This question has no clear answer. The most accurate response is probably "it depends." Variables such as the congruence of innate traits with cultural influences; the support, or lack of it, within the environment for preferred behaviours and for taking risks; and general life successes will influence how learning patterns are shaped.

Every child of every culture, race, ethnicity, socioeconomic status, gender, age, ability, and talent deserves to have an equal opportunity to be successful in school. Knowing each student's culture is essential for providing successful learning opportunities. Understanding learning differences will help educators facilitate, structure and validate successful learning for every student.

7.10.8. Similarities and Differences

Reports about culture and learning style consistently agree that within a group, variations among individuals are as great as commonalties. Even as we acknowledge that culture affects learning styles, we know that distinct learning style patterns don't fit a specific cultural group. Researchers have clearly established that there is no single or dual learning style for the members of any cultural, national, racial, or religious group.

This important point is often verbally acknowledged, but ignored in practice.

In general, there are two sources of information about learning styles and culture. The first source includes descriptions and profiles of learners of certain cultural groups written by people familiar with these groups to sensitise those outside the culture to children's experiences within the culture. For instance, in the US; descriptions of minority students' learning patterns often are contrasted with the "majority" white Anglo students' ways of learning and with expectations in the schools designed by this majority group.

There are a variety of descriptions of typical learning patterns of African Americans which report the students'desire for oral experiences, physical activity, and strong personal relationships. These patterns would call for classroom work that includes collaboration, discussion, and active projects.

The same authors report that mainstream white male Americans value independence, analytic thinking, objectivity and accuracy. These values translate into learning experiences that focus on information, competition, tests, grades, and critical thinking. It is no surprise that these patterns are prevalent in most schools because they were established and are generally administrated by mainstream white males. The further away from this style of education a student is, the more difficulty he or she has adjusting.

Another way we know about the links between culture and learning style is research study descriptions of specific groups. In this class of inquiry, researchers administer learning/cognitive style assessments to produce a profile of a particular cultural group, to make comparisons with previously studied groups, or to validate a particular instrument for cross-cultural application. While a variety of published studies use this approach, it is important to realise that they are based on various assessment instruments that "measure" learning styles in different ways.

Many of these instruments are self-reports. In other words, the adult or student fills out a response to a series of questions, and the frequency of responses indicates certain preferences for specific approaches to learning. When a person is asked to respond to specific words and questions, the language is interpreted through personal experience. Some assessment instruments test a person's strengths, or the ability to do tasks with a certain approach. When strengths are tested and learning style inferred from the results of these instruments, a great deal of variety exists within like-cultural groups.

Thus, the information obtained from formal assessments of learning styles of specific cultural groups has been based on different ways of assessing and describing style. Yet results of different studies are often compared, ignoring or diminishing the relevance of the type of assessment instrument in the report of the findings. The variation in type of assessment instrument used often accounts for the seemingly contradictory information reported about groups of learners.

From both sources of "research" we see that culture and learning style are connected, but cautions about specific application of this information are necessary. When educators apply knowledge of culture and learning style to the classroom they face a number of unresolved areas and differences of opinion.

Even when such information exists, some teachers intentionally don't read students' files. They argue that they want to form their own impressions of each learner. Other educators feel that comprehensive background and educational history of each student is invaluable for helping the learner be successful. When these same issues are applied to knowledge relating to a specific cultural group, there is also lack of agreement.

7.10.9. Achievement Differences

The relationship of culture and learning style is also addressed in reference to student achievement. Most researchers believe that learning styles are neutral. All learning styles can be successful, but they also could become a stumbling block when overused or applied inappropriately. This concept explains the success or failure of different learning approaches with different tasks, especially as they relate to expectations in schools. There is evidence that students with specific learning style patterns underachieve in school. Regardless of their cultural background, students who have these dominant learning style patterns have limited opportunities to use their style strengths in the classroom.

While relating culture, style, and achievement requires much more examination, serious inequity results if schools undervalue behaviours that certain cultures foster. Cultural practices yield "Children and adults who are characteristic of their own culture and who may appear dysfunctional in a culture that embraces a divergent or opposing set of assumptions". This appearance of dysfunction affects the student's potential for successful achievement. Some students are caught in a no-win situation, unable to be true to their culture or meet school expectations. The cultures of students of colour or their way of life are often incongruous with the expected middle-class cultural values, beliefs, and norms of schools. These cultural differences are major contributions to the school failure of students of colour.

It is also important to be willing to confront the issue of cultural identity and self-esteem. Many large city school systems struggle with the appropriateness of ethnically identified schools such as an African American academy. Bilingual programmes continue to debate the priority of instruction in students' first languages. All- girl schools, math classes, and science classes are promoted for their affirmative action approach. The goal of encouraging positive self-esteem would lead one to argue for like-groups at certain stages of development.

7.10.10. Teachers' Cultures

Another unresolved issue is how teachers working from their own cultures and teaching styles can successfully reach the diverse populations in most schools today. What training do teachers need for this challenge? To the extent that teachers teach as they have been taught to learn, and to the extent that culture shapes learning style, students who share a teacher's ethnic background will be favoured in class. Also ignoring the effects of culture and learning style affects all students:

If classroom expectations are limited by our own cultural orientations, we impede successful learners guided by another cultural orientation. If we only teach according to the ways we ourselves learn best, we are also likely to thwart successful learners who may share our cultural background but whose learning styles deviate from our own.

Some argue that teachers play a special role in representing their own culture. However, we all have learned successfully from teachers who differed from us in learning style or culture. Often, these were masterful, caring teachers. Sometimes our own motivation helped us learn in spite of the teacher. Yet teachers of all cultural backgrounds and style will have to work conscientiously to provide equity for students as classrooms increasingly reflect the diversity of our society.

7.10.11. Applications

How should we accommodate differences in style and culture? Must schools and other institutions adapt to the diversity of the people who work and study there. With the large numbers of people who learn and work in schools, uniform approaches are justified. But when we choose a uniform curriculum program, we definitely decide that students must adapt to the demands of a particular approach. When we require all teachers be evaluated in the same way, we demand that they fulfil the style requirements of that specific evaluation process.

Although using variety in teaching methods is certainly not a new idea, most educators would agree that we have a long way to go to adequately provide for learners' diversity. Seldom is there only one way to learn. It is this understanding that should encourage us to value students' and colleagues' differences. Teachers and administrators who understand these concepts consciously attempt to respond to the diversity they regularly encounter in schools. Practical implementation of learning styles concepts and research challenges us to develop two things: understanding of individuality, and a commitment to help each individual do his or her best in the learning and teaching process.

The very first practical application is awareness of style and cultural differences. When we accept that people learn in different ways, we face daily decisions about uniformity and diversity. But, a deep awareness of diverse learning styles requires a commitment to the belief that all students can be successful learners. If a learning experience is adjusted to accommodate diverse styles, students will be able to use their strengths to achieve this success. We know that currently not all learning styles are equally valued in schools. Most schools do a more effective job with learners who are reflective, linear or analytic than those who are active, holistic, personal or practical. Learners whose styles are accommodated more frequently in school achieve more immediate success. Students who struggle to adapt to an uncomfortable way of learning often underachieve.

Awareness of learning differences results in educators working together on various programs with a learning style perspective. As new curriculum materials are selected, discipline policies formed, and staff development goals set, questions of individual diversity and style will be prominent. The concepts of learning styles will be discussed on a regular basis, and opportunities for learning more about the theories and research will grow from these discussions.

Belief in learning differences becomes a rationale for many educational decisions. It is particularly important for teachers to adapt new techniques through an understanding of learning styles. In other words, a teacher would be motivated to apply a new method with the goal of accommodating the needs of certain students in the classroom. By focusing on learning styles, teachers would understand that a specific technique is successful because it provides the opportunity for approaching a task in a way that is important for certain, though not necessarily all, learners.

For example, cooperative learning is successful not just because it is an alternative to lecture but because it allows some students the opportunity to process externally, to work with their peers, and to share responsibility for a task. Integrated curriculum is successful because it offers opportunities for connections that are made naturally in some students' minds and for the chance to study a topic in depth, which is appreciated by other students.

Teachers who understand learning and cultural differences will strive for intentional variety in instruction, curriculum, classroom management, and assessment. Administrators who believe in learning styles actively value differences in teaching styles. Curriculum specialists who practise a learning styles approach encourage diverse programs in classrooms, schools, and the district. Administrators can increase awareness of individual learning styles and cultural differences through encouraging and supporting appropriate professional development experiences for all levels of school personnel, including their own.

7.10.12. Implications

Knowledge of the child's culture and learning styles helps teachers examine their own instructional practices and become sensitive to providing diverse learning experiences. Intentional instructional diversity will benefit all students. In other words, improved instructional methodologies and practices for certain students will result in improved instruction for all.

A teacher who brings outstanding skills and competencies to his work offers students from all cultures and with varying learning styles greater opportunities for success. These teachers know that to provide effective instruction, they must accommodate both the cultural values and individual learning styles of their students. Therefore, they are continually interested in learning about their students.

A teacher who cares about and develops methodologies sensitive to the needs of the learners she works with will foster success. Too often, the accommodation of cultural differences is limited to a holiday celebration or a multicultural fair. Even the study of multicultural content often fails to consider the different ways students learn. Thus, serious consideration of culture and learning styles together will offer the opportunity for more depth for culturally sensitive teaching. While the questions of culture and style are not easy to address, they are crucial to contemplate together. Explicit, ongoing dialogue about both learning styles and culture will provide educators with valuable information to help more students be successful learners.

References

Evans, C. Exploring the relationship between cognitive style and teaching style. *Educational psychology, 24*(4), 509-530. 2004

Gardner, H. *Frames of mind: The theory of multiple intelligences.* New York: Basic Books. 1983

Loo, R. Kolb's learning styles and learning preferences: Is there a linkage? *Educational psychology,* 24(1), 99-108. 2004

Pritchard, A. *Ways of learning: Learning theories and learning styles in the classroom.* London, UK: David Fulton. 2005

Stahl, S. Different strokes for different folks? In L. Abbeduto (Ed.), *Taking sides: Clashing on controversial issues in educational psychology (pp. 98-107).* Guilford, CT: McGraw Hill. 2002.

Witkin, H., Moore, C., Goodenough, D., & Cox, R. Field-dependent and field-independent cognitive styles and their educational implications. *Review of Educational Research, 47,* 1-64. 1977.

Zhang, L. & Sternberg, R.. *The nature of intellectual styles.* Mahwah, NJ: Erlbaum. 2006.

8

Moral Development

Morality has three principal meanings. In its first, descriptive usage, morality means a code of conduct which is held to be authoritative in matters of right and wrong. Morals are created by and define society, philosophy, religion or individual conscience.

In its second, normative and universal sense, morality refers to an ideal code of conduct, one which would be espoused in preference to alternatives by all rational people, under specified conditions. In this "prescriptive" sense of morality as opposed to the above described "descriptive" sort of sense, moral value judgements are made. To deny 'morality' in this sense is a position known as moral skepticism, in which the existence of objective moral "truths" is rejected.

In its third usage, 'morality' is synonymous with ethics, the systematic philosophical study of the moral domain. Ethics seeks to address questions such as how a moral outcome can be achieved in a specific situation, how moral values should be determined, what morals people actually abide by, what the fundamental nature of ethics or morality is, including whether it has any objective justification, and how moral capacity or moral agency develops and what its nature is. In applied ethics, for example, the prohibition against taking human life is controversial with respect to capital punishment, abortion and wars of invasion. In normative ethics, a typical question might be whether a lie told for the sake of protecting someone from harm is justified. In meta-ethics, a key issue is the meaning of the terms "right" or "wrong".

Moral realism would hold that there are true moral statements which report objective moral facts, whereas moral anti-realism would hold that morality is derived from any one of the norms prevalent in society. Some thinkers hold that there is no correct definition of right behaviour, that morality can only be judged with respect to particular situations, within the standards of particular belief systems and socio-historical contexts. This position, known as moral relativism, often cites empirical evidence from anthropology as evidence to support its claims. The opposite view, that there are universal, eternal moral truths are known as moral absolutism. Moral absolutists might concede that forces of social conformity significantly shape moral decisions, but deny that cultural norms and customs define morally right behaviour.

Moral psychology is a field of study in both philosophy and psychology. Some use the term "moral psychology" relatively narrowly to refer to the study of moral development. However, others tend to use the term more broadly to include any topics at the intersection of ethics and psychology. Such topics are ones that involve the mind and are relevant to moral issues. Some of the main topics of the field are moral responsibility, moral development, moral character, altruism, psychological egoism, moral luck, and moral disagreement.

Historically, early philosophers such as Aristotle and Plato engaged in both empirical research and *a priori* conceptual analysis about the ways in which people make decisions about issues that raise moral concerns. Moral psychological issues have been central theoretical issues explored by philosophers from the early days of the profession right up until the present. With the development of psychology as a discipline separate from philosophy, it was natural for psychologists to continue pursuing work in moral psychology, and much of the empirical research of the 20th century in this area was completed by academics working in psychology departments.

Nowadays, moral psychology is a thriving area of research in both philosophy and psychology, even at an interdisciplinary level. For example, the psychologist Lawrence Kohlberg questioned boys and young men about their thought processes when they were faced with a moral dilemma, producing one of many very useful empirical studies in the area of moral psychology. As another example, the philosopher, Joshua Knobe, recently completed an empirical study on how the way in which an ethical problem is phrased dramatically affects an individual's intuitions about the proper moral response to said problem. More conceptually focused research has recently been completed by researchers such as John Doris. He discusses the way in which social psychological experiments—such as the Stanford Prison Experiments involving the idea of situationism—call into question a key component in virtue ethics: the idea that individuals have a single, environment-independent moral character.

8.1. Kohlberg's Stages of Moral Development

Lawrence Kohlberg's stages of moral development constitute an adaptation of a psychological theory originally conceived of by the Swiss psychologist Jean Piaget. The theory holds that moral reasoning, the basis for ethical behaviour, has six identifiable developmental stages, each more adequate at responding to moral dilemmas than its predecessor. Kohlberg followed the development of moral judgement far beyond the ages studied earlier by Piaget, who also claimed that logic and morality develop through constructive stages. Expanding on Piaget's work, Kohlberg determined that the process of moral development was principally concerned with justice, and that it continued throughout the individual's lifetime, a notion that spawned dialogue on the philosophical implications of such research.

There have been critiques of the theory from several perspectives. Some argue that it emphasizes justice to the exclusion of other moral values, such as caring; or that there is such an overlap between stages that they should more properly be regarded as separate domains; or that evaluations of the reasons for moral choices are mostly post hoc rationalisations of essentially intuitive decisions.

Nevertheless, an entirely new field within psychology was created as a result of Kohlberg's theory.

8.1.1. Six Stages

Kohlberg's six stages can be more generally grouped into three levels of two stages each: pre-conventional, conventional and post-conventional. Following Piaget's constructivist requirements for a stage model, as described in his theory of cognitive development, it is extremely rare to regress backward in stages. Stages cannot be skipped; each provides a new and necessary perspective, more comprehensive and differentiated than its predecessors but integrated with them.

8.1.1.1. Level 1 (Pre-Conventional)

1. Obedience and punishment orientation
   (How can I avoid punishment?)
2. Self-interest orientation
   (What's in it for me?)

8.1.1.2. Level 2 (Conventional)

3. Interpersonal accord and conformity
   (Social norms)
   (The good boy/good girl attitude)
4. Authority and social-order maintaining orientation
   (Law and order morality)

8.1.1.3. Level 3 (Post-conventional)

5. Social contract orientation
6. Universal ethical principles
   (Principled conscience)

8.1.1.4. Pre-conventional

The pre-conventional level of moral reasoning is especially common in children, although adults can also exhibit this level of reasoning. Reasoners at this level judge the morality of an action by its direct consequences. The pre-conventional level consists of the first and second stages of moral development, and is solely concerned with the self in an egocentric manner.

In stage one, individuals focus on the direct consequences of their actions on themselves. For example, an action is perceived as morally wrong if the perpetrator is punished. "The last time I did that I got spanked so I will not do it again." The worse the punishment for the act is, the more "bad" the act is perceived to be. This can give rise to an inference that even innocent victims are guilty in proportion to their suffering. It is "egocentric", lacking recognition that others' points of view are different from one's own. There is "deference to superior power or prestige".

Stage two espouses the "what's in it for me" position, in which right behaviour is defined by whatever is in the individual's best interest. Stage two reasoning shows a limited interest in the needs of others, but only to a point where it might further the individual's own interests. As a result, concern for others is not based on loyalty or intrinsic respect, but rather a "you scratch my back, and I'll scratch yours" mentality. The lack of a societal perspective in the pre-conventional level is quite different from the social contract, as all actions have the purpose of serving the individual's own needs or interests. For the stage two theorist, the world's perspective is often seen as morally relative.

8.1.1.5. Conventional

The conventional level of moral reasoning is typical of adolescents and adults. Those who reason in a conventional way judge the morality of actions by comparing them to society's views and expectations. The conventional level consists of the third and fourth stages of moral development.

In stage three, the self enters society by filling social roles. Individuals are receptive to approval or disapproval from others as it reflects society's accordance with the perceived role. They try to be a "good boy" or "good girl" to live up to these expectations, having learned that there is inherent value in doing so. Stage three reasoning may judge the morality of an action by evaluating its consequences in terms of a person's relationships, which now begin to include things like respect, gratitude and the "golden rule". "I want to be liked and thought well of; apparently, not being naughty makes people like me." Desire to maintain rules and authority exists only to further support these social roles. The intentions of actions play a more significant role in reasoning at this stage; "they mean well ...".

In stage four, it is important to obey laws, dictums and social conventions because of their importance in maintaining a functioning society. Moral reasoning in stage four is thus beyond the need for individual approval exhibited in stage three; society must learn to transcend individual needs. A central ideal or ideals often prescribe what is right and wrong, such as in the case of fundamentalism. If one person violates a law, perhaps everyone would-thus there is an obligation and a duty to uphold laws and rules. When someone does violate a law, it is morally wrong; culpability is thus a significant factor in this stage as it separates the bad domains from the good ones. Most active members of society remain at stage four, where morality is still predominantly dictated by an outside force.

8.1.1.6. Post-conventional

The post-conventional level, also known as the principled level, consists of stages five and six of moral development. There is a growing realisation that individuals are separate entities from society, and that the individual's own perspective should have precedence over society's view. Because of this level's "nature of self before others", the behaviour of post-conventional individuals, especially those at stage six, can be confused with that of those at the pre-conventional level.

In stage five, individuals are viewed as holding different opinions and values. Similarly, laws are regarded as social contracts rather than rigid dictums. Those which do not promote the general welfare should be changed when necessary to meet "the greatest good for the greatest number of people". This is achieved through majority decision and inevitable compromise. Thus democratic government is ostensibly based on stage five reasoning.

In stage six, moral reasoning is based on abstract reasoning using universal ethical principles. Laws are valid only insofar as they are grounded in justice, and a commitment to justice carries with it an obligation to disobey unjust laws. Rights are unnecessary, as social contracts are not essential for deontic moral action. Decisions are not reached hypothetically in a conditional way but rather categorically in an absolute way, as in the philosophy of Immanuel Kant. This involves an individual imagining what they would do in another's shoes, if they believed what that other person imagines to be true. The resulting consensus is the action taken. In this way action is never a means but always an end in itself; the individual acts because it is right, and not because it is instrumental, expected, legal, or previously agreed upon.

Although Kohlberg insisted that stage six exists, he found it difficult to identify individuals who consistently operated at that level.

8.1.2. Theoretical Assumptions

The picture of human nature which Kohlberg begins with is that humans are inherently communicative and capable of reason; they also possess a desire to understand others and the world around them. The stages of Kohlberg's model relate to the qualitative moral reasonings adopted by individuals, and so do not translate directly into praise or blame of any individual's actions or character. In order to argue that his theory measures moral reasoning and not particular moral conclusions, Kohlberg insists that the form and structure of moral arguments is independent of the content of those arguments, a position he calls "formalism".

Kohlberg's theory centres on the notion that justice is the essential characteristic of moral reasoning. Justice itself relies heavily upon the notion of sound reasoning based on principles. Despite being a justice-centred theory of morality, Kohlberg considered it to be compatible with plausible formulations of deontology and eudaimonia.

Kohlberg's theory understands values as a critical component of the right. Whatever the right is, for him, it must be universally valid across societies: there can be no relativism. Moreover, morals are not natural features of the world; they are prescriptive. Nevertheless, moral judgements can be evaluated in logical terms of truth and falsity.

According to Kohlberg, someone progressing to a higher stage of moral reasoning cannot skip stages. For example, an individual cannot jump from being concerned mostly with peer judgements to being a proponent of social contracts. On encountering a moral dilemma and finding their current level of moral reasoning unsatisfactory, however, an individual will look to the next level. Realising the limitations of the current stage of thinking is the driving force behind moral development, as each progressive stage is more adequate than the last. The process is therefore considered to be constructive, as it is initiated by the conscious construction of the individual, and is not in any meaningful sense a component of the individual's innate dispositions, or a result of past inductions.

8.1.3. Formal Elements

Progress through Kohlberg's stages happens as a result of the individual's increasing competence, both psychologically and in balancing conflicting social-value claims. The process of resolving conflicting claims to reach an equilibrium is called "justice operation". Kohlberg identifies two of these justice operations: "equality" which involves an impartial regard for persons; and "reciprocity", which means a regard for the role of personal merit. For Kohlberg, the most adequate result of both operations is "reversibility", in which a moral or dutiful act within a particular situation is evaluated in terms of whether or not the act would be satisfactory even if particular persons were to switch roles within that situation.

Knowledge and learning contribute to moral development. Specifically important are the individual's "view of persons" and their "social perspective level", each of which becomes more complex and mature with each advancing stage. The "view of persons" can be understood as the individual's grasp of the psychology of other persons; it may be pictured as a spectrum, with stage one having no view of other persons at all, and stage six being entirely sociocentric. Similarly, the social perspective level involves the understanding of the social universe, differing from the view of persons in that it involves an appreciation of social norms.

8.1.4. Examples of Applied Moral Dilemmas

Kohlberg established the Moral Judgement Interview in his original 1958 dissertation. During the roughly 45-minute tape recorded semi-structured interview, the interviewer uses moral dilemmas to determine which stage of moral reasoning a person uses. The dilemmas are fictional short stories that describe situations in which a person has to make a moral decision. The participant is asked a systemic series of open-ended questions, like what they think the right course of action is, as well as justifications as to why certain actions are right or wrong. The form and structure of these replies are scored and not the content; over a set of multiple moral dilemmas an overall score is derived.

A dilemma that Kohlberg used in his original research was the druggist's dilemma: Heinz Steals the Drug In Europe.

Kohlberg's theory holds that the justification the participant offers is what is significant, the form of their response. Below are some of many examples of possible arguments that belong to the six stages:

Stage one (obedience): Heinz should not steal the medicine because he will consequently be put in prison which will mean he is a bad person. Or: Heinz should steal the medicine because it is only worth $200 and not how much the druggist wanted for it; Heinz had even offered to pay for it and was not stealing anything else.

Stage two (self-interest): Heinz should steal the medicine because he will be much happier if he saves his wife, even if he will have to serve a prison sentence. Or: Heinz should not steal the medicine because prison is an awful place, and he would probably languish over a jail cell more than his wife's death.

Stage three (conformity): Heinz should steal the medicine because his wife expects it; he wants to be a good husband. Or: Heinz should not steal the drug because stealing is bad and he is not a criminal; he tried to do everything he could without breaking the law, you cannot blame him.

Stage four (law-and-order): Heinz should not steal the medicine because the law prohibits stealing, making it illegal. Or: Heinz should steal the drug for his wife but also take the prescribed punishment for the crime as well as paying the druggist what he is owed. Criminals cannot just run around without regard for the law; actions have consequences.

Stage five (human rights): Heinz should steal the medicine because everyone has a right to choose life, regardless of the law. Or: Heinz should not steal the medicine because the scientist has a right to fair compensation. Even if his wife is sick, it does not make his actions right.

Stage six (universal human ethics): Heinz should steal the medicine, because saving a human life is a more fundamental value than the property rights of another person. Or: Heinz should not steal the medicine, because others may need the medicine just as badly, and their lives are equally significant.

8.2. Moral Development

Morals are systems of social rules that shape our interactions and guide our behaviour. Our sense or right and wrong can influence our feelings of altruism or prejudice, can affect in our daily lives and relationships with friends or at work, and can even (although perhaps not often enough) have a bearing on social policy. One important social question is how we come to behave in moral (or immoral) ways. Obviously, part of this question depends on how attitudes or reasoning connect with moral behaviour and action. But another part, which is at least as important, concerns how we come to understand or reason about these rules themselves.

The child's moral development involves a gradual immersion into the world of adults' rules and principles. Social learning theorists argue that it is, and that it is the mechanics of that learning which need to be understood by theorists.

8.2.1. Social Learning Theories

Aronfeed suggested that children gain an understanding of morality through a form of social conditioning. When a child behaves in a particular way they may receive feedback on their actions from others. Parents or caregivers occupy a very important role for the child's development since support or encouragement for any particular form of behaviour will increase the chances of a child repeating that behaviour later. Conversely criticism or punishment will decrease the chances of that behaviour being repeated since it entails negative consequences for the child. According to this social conditioning model it is through adults' reinforcement of certain forms of behaviour that the child comes to behave in a way which is deemed morally appropriate or inappropriate. For Aronfeed moral thought is therefore the consequence of a process of association: the child associates its behaviour and the feedback to that behaviour with the thoughts that preceded it.

A further social learning approach has been suggested by Bandura who argued that children's moral development comes about through the more indirect process of observational learning or vicarious conditioning. Bandura and McDonald found that children who observed an adult 'model' making moral judgments tended to give more mature responses themselves in a subsequent post-test. On the other hand children who had seen no adult model, but whose own responses had been reinforced whenever they reflected more mature forms of reasoning, showed no such improvement. Bandura concluded that an important mechanism for the child's moral development is the mimicking or imitation of adult behaviour.

According to Bandura the child observes, internalises and then replicates the moral judgment and behaviour of adults. As these observations increase in both depth and scope the child comes to grasp some of the complexities (and perhaps vagueries) of more mature moral thought. Both Aronfeed's and Bandura's theories share a sense in which the child absorbs a sense of morality from those around them. Yet whilst Aronfeed sees the adult as the direct conditioning agent in the child's moral development, Bandura views development of the child's judgment as rather more detached from immediate features of the relationship between adult and child.

Although social learning accounts appear empirically robust, the theoretical simplicity of the approach is not without its difficulties. For a start there is an abiding concern that social learning theories tend to relegate children's lived experiences to a behaviouristic plane, where the personal significance of social relationships is of little importance. There is also an ethical worry for Aronfeed's social conditioning model. If punishment is a key to preventing immoral behaviour and thought then it would seem that the greater the degree of punishment the more effective the moral 'education'. This, in turn, leads to a rather odd conception of morality since the rightness or wrongness of an action is determined by the strength, perhaps physical, of reactions to it.

A further difficulty for Aronfeed's theory is that children may learn to exhibit 'moral' behaviour only in the presence of those who are able to enforce punishments. Away from the watchful gaze of an adult the child might feel no constraints to producing behaviour that would not be sanctioned if an adult were present. Indeed, children can be well aware of the differences between interaction with peers and with adults and can act differently in each separate context.

Aspects of Bandura's approach also need clarification. If moral development is a product of the child's modelling of others' judgments it needs to be established whether all 'models' are equally effective in promoting development. For example, is one parent more influential than the other as a model for the child's behaviour and judgment?

Lastly, it is certainly debatable whether all children grow up simply reproducing the moral rules and norms of adults. In this sense, it would appear that the notion of the 'socialising agent' requires rather more elaboration than either Aronfeed or Bandura give it.

8.3. Parents and Moral Development

Perhaps the most prominent influence a child receives is that of the parents or caregivers. Parents not only provide the child with protection, support and basic material needs. In most cases parents also act as the principal figures who enforce moral and other rules.

Freud proposed that our sense of moral duty arises from our relationships with our parents. The importance of this relationship is a result of the parents' role as principal caregivers and as sources of comfort, support and security – or, as Freud puts it, as love objects. However, when a child does something that his or her parents disapprove of, the child is punished. This punishment leads to feelings of frustration and anger in the child and parents become objects of hate.

In the early years punishment acts as an external form of control exercised by parents. Over time this external form of control becomes internalised. However, the child does not usually enforce this internal form of control by means of self-punishment. Rather, when a child does something wrong he or she feels guilt which acts as the principal mechanism for internalised self-control. To avoid guilt, or self-punishment, the child is motivated to act morally and in accordance with the mother's or father's moral standards. Identification with the punitive parent therefore leads the child to adopt the moral standards and principles of that parent - the parent's superego. Thus moral rules move from external to internal forms of control, and a child adopts the moral standards of his or her parents.

The psychoanalytic approach, like social learning theories, places an emphasis on punishment as the principal motivator of moral development. Freud, however, presents us with a more sophisticated account of the means by which external processes of control become translated into internal processes of self-regulation. Also, by introducing the notion of identification Freud's theory allows us to conceptualise how different individuals may have a qualitatively different influence upon the child's development.

However, Freud's theory has, generally, been criticised not only for the lack of empirical evidence but also because many aspects of the theory are difficult to test. For example, Freud claims that external control leads to feelings of guilt which, in turn, motivate the child to act morally. Yet it would seem difficult to distinguish a child who refrains from certain behaviour because of guilt or, to adopt a social conditioning theory explanation, through fear. Thus whilst evidence has generally supported the proposition that children reflect the moral values of their parents it is difficult to determine whether Freud's account, or other socialisation accounts, are the best for explaining this process.

Hoffman has described how different forms of parenting might influence a child's moral reasoning. Hoffman & Saltzstein identified three different styles of parenting through interviews with parents, and then observed how others rated the behaviour of these parents' children in real life situations. The first parenting style, love-oriented discipline, involves the parent withholding affection or approval when a child behaves badly. According to Freudian theory this would be an effective form of moral education. However, the children of parents who used predominantly love-oriented forms of discipline did not show benefits (over and above other children) in their rate of moral development.

Parents who employed predominently power-assertive discipliniary techniques used a variety of punitive measures to enforce their rules, or simply gave their position of power or authority over the child as a justification for preventing the child from acting in a certain way. Results indicated that a consequence of this parenting technique is that children tended to respond only to the threat of sanction. Thus, away from adult supervision children showed little sense of how to behave appropriately. With the third parenting style, inductive discipline, parents explained to their children the reasons behind a particular moral prohibition. Pointing out the consequences of certain forms of behaviour and the reasons for not acting in a particular way was the most effective in ensuring a child developed a moral sense for themselves.

Hoffman's work suggests that moral development is promoted when children are given rationales for their moral behaviour and judgments. Similar work by Baumrind has also indicated that combining parental authority with justifications for the rules that parents enforce is the most effective form of helping children to attain social competence and avoid deviance up to adolescence.

There are however problems establishing a link between parenting styles and development. The relationship between a child and his or her parent is something that researchers can only ever hope to capture briefly, or second-hand from either self-reports or reports from others involved with the child and parents. Such reports may be subject to some inaccuracies if not all participants in the research judge by the same criteria when reporting behaviour, or fail to present themselves to researchers in an entirely candid fashion. Moreover, the work of Baumrind and Hoffman provides evidence of only a correlation between parenting styles and children's reasoning or behaviour. For example, it may be that authoritative or inductive disciplinary techniques are more prevalent amongst parents from middle class backgrounds and so there is at least a possibility that different, over-arching social factors might also have a causal role in the positive outcomes associated with inductive or authoritative parenting styles.

8.4. Society and Morality

A child's parents have an important influence upon a their moral development. Yet an emphasis upon parents and other adults as the principal socialisers of a child runs the risk of neglecting the role of the wider social context in a child's development. Durkheim suggested that a sense of moral duty arises from a feeling of connectedness to society; "we are moral beings only to the extent that we are social beings". What binds individuals together is the recognition that "society" is something more than the sum of the individual's who make it up. It is the source of all moral knowledge and the authority by which morality can be held to be legitimate.

For Durkheim morals possess power because they regulate behaviour between people as a sort of social bond or contract. Mature moral reasoning therefore reflects an awareness of the importance of maintaining our social relationships. In spite of the sociological basis of Durkheim's theory, the consequences of his theory for moral education are rather similar to traditional social learning accounts. In order to understand morality, Durkheim argued, the child must come to understand the rules which preserve social relations. Moral development can therefore only come about through the imposition of these rules by the adult upon the child.

Moral education, according to Durkheim, requires that the child forms a 'spirit of discipline' in respect to his or her moral thought and conduct. The spirit of discipline is principally instilled when the child goes to school. At home family feelings of altruism and solidarity can obscure the need for hard and fast rules. At school, on the other hand, the child has his or her first experience of a more formal, social institution which, in turn, demands a more rigorous adherence to collective rules. The teacher possesses social authority and acts as an intermediary between society and the child.

A strength of Durkheim's theory is that it allows a conceptualisation of morality as a social process: moral judgments possess a power because they locate an individual in a society or social group which shares certain practices and rules. However, an (at least tacit) implication of Durkheim's theory is that to act morally is nothing more than to conform to the rules of society. Thus there is little room for any meaningful development in social morality beyond the status quo.

A second difficulty lies in Durkheim's claim that all morality is imposed upon the child by the group or (in the case of the teacher) a representative of society. It is important to remember that this imposition of morality does not function in quite the same way as it does for social learning theories. Durkheim's conception of 'society' allows us to invoke an idea of morality as something more than, in its strictest sense, self-interest.

8.5. Piaget's Theory

Piaget complained that Durkheim too readily equated adult morality with the morality and neglected the ways in which children develop for themselves a sense in which moral rules are legitimate. In his book, *The Moral Judgment of the Child,* Piaget outlined his own theory of moral development.

8.5.1. Rules of the Game

Piaget's investigations began by exploring how children from Geneva and Neuchâtel in Switzerland understood the rules of a game. The rules of these games, argued Piaget, were handed down from one generation of children to the next, a little like the ways in which moral standards are handed down from adults to children. Piaget employed a structured, clinical interview to gauge the underlying form of a child's thought.

Piaget found that children's reasoning about rules could be summarised in three stages through which the child's thinking progressed. For the very young child (up until around 3 years) motor rules allow the child to understand the concept of regularity. The notion of regularity can come about either through the rituals imposed by parents (e.g. going to bed or eating at a certain time and place), or through the habits that the child develops for itself by manipulating the marbles.

The beginnings of a sense of obligation come about with an appreciation of rules as coercive. Of course, in one sense, the rituals imposed upon the child by parents in the early years are also coercive. But what distinguishes the second stage is that the child can begin to appreciate the social nature of a rule. With this unilateral respect rules are sacred and cannot be changed; they possess their power precisely because they are seen as things which are imposed upon the child from without. Coercive rules are similar in origin and function to the rules of society that Durkheim envisaged since both the rule and the reasons for following it come from an authority figure.

Amongst the older children (from roughly 10 years) Piaget noted that rules were still seen as binding because they allowed children to play with one another in a meaningful and regulated way. However, changing the rule to make a new game or improved version of the game was acceptable so long as everyone else playing appreciated and agreed with the change. Piaget claimed that this more mature understanding reflected an awareness of rational rules. Rational rules were not imposed by an authority figure. Instead, a mutual respect for one another allowed children to change rules until they found the best (or most 'rational') ones.

After establishing changes in children's understanding of the rules of games Piaget proceeded to explore how children came to understand more specifically moral problems. Piaget asked children some general questions about morality - for example, what a lie is, or what purpose punishment fulfils. To compliment his findings from more general questions Piaget presented children with moral stories or vignettes. These vignettes typically contrasted the behaviour of two children in a range of situations. Piaget's interviewees were usually asked to judge whether one of the two protagonists was naughtier than the other, and then to justify their selection. Younger children tended to regard the material consequences of action as the crucial determinants of right and wrong. Thus, for these younger children the greater the amount of material damage done, or the greater the threat of sanction from an adult authority figure, the more morally reprehensible the action was. Older children, on the other hand, tended to base their judgments more concretely on the characters' motivations and intentions. Thus, an illintentioned act was judged to be morally worse than one that was the result of clumsiness.

Piaget then explored the judgments of children in another area of morality - lying. Once again Piaget found two broadly distinguishable forms of thinking. In general, younger children's judgments as to the severity of a lie were not based upon the intention of the liar to deceive. Rather, for these younger children, to tell a lie was "to commit a moral fault by means of language". Moreover, the further the departure from the truth the worse a lie was deemed to be regardless of whether it was intended or not. Once again, for the older children the severity of a lie was judged according to the liar's intention to deceive.

— A little boy called John is in his room. He is called to dinner. He goes into the dining room. But behind the door there was a chair, and on the chair there was a tray with fifteen cups on it. John couldn't have known that there was all this behind the door. He goes in, the door knocks against the tray, bang go the fifteen cups and they all get broken!

— Once there was a little boy whose name was Henry. One day when his mother was out he tried to get some jam out of the cupboard. He climbed up on to a chair and stretched out his arm. But the jam was too high and he couldn't reach it and have any. But while he was trying to get it he knocked over a cup. The cup fell down and broke.

8.5.2. Heteronomy and Autonomy

For Piaget, the two types of moral reasoning were indicative of two fundamentally different ways of thinking about the source of morality. Younger children, in general, reasoned in a way which Piaget described as heteronomous. Not only did younger children's moral judgments focus on the material features of a situation. They were also strongly influenced by the potential responses of an authority figure, invariably an adult or an older child, who determined what was right or wrong for these younger children. And, importantly, it was not that the younger children were unable to understand an actor's intentions.

Piaget argued that heteronomous reasoning is egocentric; in making moral judgments the egocentric reasoner cannot appreciate that others may see the situation differently, or from a different perspective from their own. As a consequence authority figures possess an almost magical quality for the child since they have the ability to impose punishments and to enforce the moral law by virtue of their position of relative power. So the greater the amount of material damage the greater the child perceives the adverse reaction of the authority figure will be and hence the worse the consequences (in terms of punishment) for the child.

Amongst the older children, however, Piaget noted that reasoning was more autonomous in character. The older children's moral thought was based on notions of intention and motivation. For older children morality was not something that was seen to be determined by authority figures.

As with the rules of the game (where, for the older children, rules could be changed if everyone agreed) moral rules are not determined by an authority figure but through an appreciation of others' perspectives. Autonomous thought allows the child to understand that others have different moral perspectives from their own. The child's thought is no longer egocentric and this allows the child to construct an understanding of morality with others. With autonomy, moral rules can only be changed through mutual consent. Autonomy allows, more than anything, a method for the construction of new moral values and for the improvement of existing ones through rational processes.

Clearly the shift from heteronomy to autonomy – what has been called the "two moral worlds" view is of developmental significance. But although most children under 8 years of age reason with heteronomy and the majority over 10 years can reason with autonomy, strict age limits to the different forms of reasoning should be regarded with caution for at least two reasons. Firstly, the progress from heteronomous to autonomous forms of thought is not a global shift in the child's thinking and may occur in different domains of a child's thinking at different times. Secondly, the shift in moral thought correlates with a change in the child's orientation to morality - specifically in the child's conception of the social relation or social bond which morals regulate. Thus it is perfectly possible for an adult to reason with heteronomy under relevant conditions.

Finally Piaget turned to examine how children thought about justice. Younger reasoners equated justice with retribution which served an expiatory function and a punishment was just precisely because it was severe. Older children, and more autonomous reasoners, viewed justice as more a question of reciprocity - putting right what had been wrong. With distributive justice (for example, the share each child received of a cake), whilst the younger children thought that a fair (or just) share was whatever an adult authority figure decided, older children (roughly 8-10 years) tended to prefer a more equalitarian distribution.

Children who were over 10 years tended to prefer equitarian forms of distribution - to give more to those whose need was greatest. Piaget also noted how the notion of collective responsibility developed as children matured. Whilst the younger ones had little willingness to accept that all members of a group should take a share of the blame if one of them did something wrong, older children felt that in certain circumstances members of a group should share some of the responsibility.

8.5.3. Social Relations

Heteronomous and autonomous forms of reasoning relate to the ways in which we think about social relations. With heteronomy, authority figures give the relations between individuals a unidirectional or asymmetric flavour. With autonomy, on the other hand, morality is seen as more consensual and the product of a symmetric relation which is based upon equality.

Piaget argued that this change in the way a child thinks about social relations correlated with a growing recognition of the social and interpersonal nature of moral duties and obligations. And by imposing their authority over children adults actually maintain the child's egocentricity, moral heteronomy and a morality of constraint.

For the child to develop an understanding of the true function of morality children had to engage in relationships which were not governed by the pressure of authority and the need to conform to an authority figure's wishes. Such an understanding could only come about through interaction with peers, in a context in which the child's moral thought was not constrained. With peers children could cooperate to develop a sense in which moral duty was a social contract made on an equal (or equitable) and rational basis. Thus it was through peer relations of cooperation that children could learn a sense of right and wrong for themselves.

A number of researchers have explored whether social interaction (and in particular peer and adult-child interaction) influences development. Youniss suggested that parents and peers have a qualitatively different role in the child's moral development. Parents, as authority figures, tended to act as a source of moral knowledge for heteronomous reasoners. Peers, on the other hand, provided the possibility of the construction of new knowledge for more autonomous reasoners.

Kruger explored, more explicitly, the differential effects of adult-child and peer relations on children's moral development. Kruger paired 8 year old children with either a peer or an adult. These children were then asked to discuss a moral dilemma together with their conversation partner. During the conversation, those children who were paired with a peer were more active participants in the conversation than those who were paired with an adult. Moreover, in a subsequent post-test children who had been paired with a peer demonstrated higher 'levels' of moral reasoning.

However, in adult-child interaction many different aspects of authority (e.g. physical power, knowledge and the ability to impose punishment) are compounded. Leman and Duveen studied children's (8 to 10 years) discussions amongst their own peer group about one of Piaget's moral stories. Whilst children using autonomous forms of justification were better able to persuade their peers, conversations were profoundly influenced by the gender of the two children interacting. Leman and Duveen suggested that, depending upon the context or task, gender could act as a source of authority deriving from the social roles and attributes associated with different gender groups.

A number of researchers have argued that Piaget's claim that heteronomous reasoners see adults as infallible authority figures is simply incorrect. Laupa and Turiel argue that young children do not show unilateral respect for adult authority figures. For example, when asked whether an immoral action would be acceptable if an adult condoned it, young children often said that it would not. However, Laupa's results did show some of the features of heteronomy and in particular the non-differentiation of adult authority attributes, amongst the younger children in her studies.

A further criticism of Piaget's theory is that it is based in an ethnocentric and gender-specific conception of morality. For example, Weinreich-Haste argues that Piaget bases his conception of morality too much around concepts of rules and rationality and that these, in turn, were more in keeping with a "male" notion of morality. In a similar vein, Buck-Morss argues that Piaget's emphasis on questions of epistemology and the developmental process runs the risk of neglecting the importance of social and cultural influences in development. Given the importance of authority and social relations in Piaget's theory, these social aspects of moral development do indeed deserve a degree of scrutiny that Piaget did not give them.

REFERENCES

Cole, M, et al., *The Development of Children*, New York: Worth Publishers, 2005.

Crain, William C., *Theories of Development,* 2Rev Ed, Prentice-Hall, 1985.

Kohlberg, Lawrence, *Essays on Moral Development, Vol. I: The Philosophy of Moral Development*, Harper & Row, 1981.

McShane, John, *Cognitive development: An information-processing approach*, Cambridge, MA: Basil Blackwell. 1991.

Woolfolk, A. E., Winne, P. H., & Perry, N. E., *Educational Psychology,* Toronto, Canada: Pearson, 2006.

9

Character Development

There are three major issues in the education of young people today. The first is the development of a vision for one's life that includes the discovery and/or defining of one's life mission and desired lifestyle. The second is the development of one's character, dealing with concerns of direction and quality of life. The third deals with the development of competence that deals with concerns of how well one is able to do something.

In general, character, good or bad, is considered to be observable in one's conduct. Thus, character is different from values in that values are orientations or dispositions whereas character involves action or activation of knowledge and values. From this perspective, values are seen as one of the foundations for character. In the context of the model of human behaviour presented at this site, values includes both cognitive and affective components, but not necessarily conative or behavioural components. Character includes all four components.

Scholarly debate on moral development and character formation extends at least as far back as Aristotle's Nichomacean Ethics and Socrates's *Meno* and continues through to modern times. In the last several hundred years, character education has been seen as a primary function of educational institutions. For example, John Locke, 17th century English philosopher, advocated education as education for character development. This theme was continued in the 19th century by English philosophers John Stuart Mill and Herbert Spencer. The American philosopher, John Dewey, an influential philosopher and educator of the early 20th century, saw moral education as central to the school's mission.

Spears's survey of members of Phi Delta Kappa on goals of education showed the following ranking of the goals of public schools:

1. develop skills in reading, writing, speaking, and listening;
2. develop pride in work and feeling of self-worth; and
3. develop good character and self-respect.

In terms of defining good character, educators stated that this should include developing:

1. moral responsibility and sound ethical and moral behaviour;
2. capacity for discipline;
3. a moral and ethical sense of the values, goals, and processes of a free society;
4. standards of personal character and ideas.

In two more recent Gallup surveys of public attitudes toward public schools, 79 percent of respondents indicated they favour "instruction in schools that would deal with morals and moral behaviour."

9.1. Pillars of Character Education

Whether at work, at home, or at play, there are basic values that define ethical behaviour. These values are not political, religious or culturally biased. Josephson Institute calls them the Six Pillars of Character, and they form the basis of all programmes and materials.

9.1.1. Trustworthiness

This pillar encompasses a variety of qualities: honesty, integrity, reliability, and loyalty. Being trustworthy means keeping promises and doing one's best not to deceive, even with white lies or statements that one might defend as "technically true."

9.1.2. Respect

The Golden Rule is the most useful guide here: Treat others as you wish to be treated. That means being courteous, listening to others, and accepting individual differences.

9.1.3. Responsibility

This pillar includes accountability, self-control, and the pursuit of excellence. Being responsible also requires that we carefully consider the consequences of our choices before we make them.

9.1.4. Fairness

Being fair means playing by the rules and not taking advantage of others. A fair person makes informed judgements without favoritism or prejudice and does not blame others carelessly.

9.1.5. Caring

Kindness, compassion, altruism - these are the heart of ethics. Of course, some ethical decisions inevitably cause pain, but the caring person acts to minimise hardship and to help others whenever possible.

9.1.6. Citizenship

Good citizens work to make their community better. They are committed to protecting our environment and to making our democratic institutions work. They know the law, and they often do more than it requires and less than it allows.

9.2. Trends in Character Education

Since the 1960's teacher education has downplayed the teacher's role as a transmitter of social and personal values and emphasized other areas such teaching techniques, strategies, models and skills. Educational psychology, rather than philosophy and religion, has become the basis of teacher training. In most cases, educational psychology focuses on the individual, separated from the social context. Additionally, modern education has been heavily influenced by the behavioural approach, which has proved adept at developing instructional methods that impact achievement as measured by standardised tests. In the opinion of most researchers in the area of character and moral development, additional emphasis must be placed on the philosophical "why" of education in addition to the technical "how."

The two educational goals most desired by both the public and educators—academic competence and character development—are not mutually exclusive, but complementary. Competence allows character to be manifested in highest forms and vice versa.

There are four major questions to be addressed when focusing on character development:

1. What is good character?
2. What causes or prevents it?
3. How can it be measured so that efforts at improvement can have corrective feedback? and
4. How can it best be developed?

As previously discussed, good character is defined in terms of one's actions. Character development traditionally has focused on those traits or values appropriate for the industrial age such as obedience to authority, work ethic, working in group under supervision, etc. Modern education must promote character based on values appropriate for the information age: truthfulness, honesty, integrity, individual responsibility, humility, wisdom, justice, steadfastness, dependability, etc.

In terms of what influences character development, the following are major factors in the moral development and behaviour of youth:

1. heredity
2. early childhood experience
3. modeling by important adults and older youth
4. peer influence
5. the general physical and social environment
6. the communications media
7. what is taught in the schools and other institutions
8. specific situations and roles that elicit corresponding behaviour.

These sources of influence are listed in approximate order of least tractable to most tractable in order to suggest why we often seek solutions to social problems through schools. It is important to realise that while schools do and should play a role in the development of character, families, communities, and society in general also have an important influence.

The measurement of character has proven difficult since character, by definition, involves behaviour, but character is often defined in terms of traits (i.e., honesty, integrity, etc.). Some possible measures that are suggested are:

1. student discipline;
2. student suicide rates;
3. crimes: assault, burglary, homicides;
4. pregnancy rates of teenage girls; and
5. prosocial activities.

Even a cursory glance would indicate that our society is changing in ways that produce discomfort for most of us. While Gross Domestic Product has risen dramatically relative to the growth in population, with a corresponding increase in spending on social programmes, data on indicators that might be used as a measure of the nation's character show movement in the opposite direction. This type of analysis is quite beneficial because it is at a level that includes the influence of all of the major social institutions that influence character development in our young people, not just schools. However, schools do have an important influence and we should use that influence judiciously.

There are a variety of alternatives to dealing with moral and character education in the schools. First, we can ignore it completely which assumes the issue is outside the bounds of proper curriculum. The interest by professional organisations and the public suggests that this view is inappropriate. Second, we can take a "values neutral" stance and provide opportunities for students to clarify and defend their own values without making recommendations or advocating a particular viewpoint. This is the position taken by the advocates of the values clarification movement and assumes that in important ways no values or character traits are more valid than others. However, to the extent that certain values or character traits are more likely to lead to socially desired outcomes, it would seem inappropriate to not identify these as "better" values. This is not to say that the techniques used in values clarification have no merit, but that when educators and the public have developed a consensus about the worth of certain values, it seems entirely appropriate to teach those to students.

A third approach is to teach students a specific process to follow when making decisions and putting these into action. This is the approach of the analysis view used in values education and assumes moral and character decisions are made rationally.

Another cognitively-oriented approach is to engage students in discussions of relevant moral issues with the expectation that students who hear their peers discuss the issue from a higher level will gravitate to that position. This position is expounded in the moral development approach of Lawrence Kohlberg whose theory was based on the cognitive development theory of Jean Piaget. While the techniques used in both of these approaches have been shown to be effective in changing thinking, there is scant evidence to support the belief that changing thinking will automatically lead to a change in behaviour. And it is impact on behaviour that distinguishes values education from character education.

A fifth approach is to teach students a given set of values and accompanying appropriate actions. This is the position taken by the inculcation approach to values clarification. This approach assumes a set of absolute values agreed upon by society that are unchanging and that be applied equally appropriately in all situations.

A final approach is to use the inculcation, values education, analysis, and moral development approaches described above when and where appropriate and then to have students put their thoughts and feelings into action in a variety of social actions as suggested in the action learning or service learning approaches. This combination of approaches is much more likely to impact the two important aspects of character not included in values education—volition and action.

From the perspective of a systems view, which is most compatible with the action learning and service learning approaches to character education, we need to define character development in terms of the three components of mind: and the component of behaviour as depicted in the systems model of human behaviour. The cognitive component of character consists of both a knowledge base of right and wrong as well as the rational and creative processes necessary to work with that knowledge base to make sound moral decisions. There is a related value system that defines what the individual holds in high esteem or to which he or she is attached. These are the criteria that students use to make moral or ethical judgements. Students learn to value what is in their knowledge base; they will also more deeply esteem what they critically and creatively think about. These two components influence what students are willing to commit to, what they are willing to set goals for, what they are willing to plan for and put energy towards accomplishing. As students make these commitments and plans, it adds to their knowledge base and strengthens their thinking skills and values. These three components then influence the final component, overt behaviour. This behaviour has two aspects: personal virtues such as being courageous and self-disciplined and social virtues such as being compassionate, courteous, and trustworthy. As students reflect on their behaviour, it adds to the knowledge base, strengthens their thinking skills, and impacts their values. Of course, behaviour can also be directly influenced through the application of consequences as described by operant conditioning theory and through observation and modelling as described by social learning theory.

The basic principle of this model is that much of the knowledge and values that students hold are implicit and have been obtained though observation, modelling, and the application of consequences. As important as it is to impact overt moral behaviour, it is equally important to help students make explicit one's own knowledge base, value system, and the process of committing and planning so as to make that behaviour more intentional. This multifaceted view of character development is more similar to Bandura's social cognition theory with its emphasis on reciprocal determinism than it is to a behavioural, cognitive, or humanistic view, each of which is more likely to focus on one component to the detriment of the others.

In assisting students to develop their morals and character, we should acknowledge that these components come into play within a rapidly changing context and therefore, we cannot teach our students all the specific knowledge, values, or behaviours that will lead to success in all aspects of their lives. We must therefore acknowledge that some values are relative and teach students to develop their own views accordingly. At the same time, we must acknowledge that there are some absolutes with respect to morality and character as accepted by commonalties among members of specific communities, major world religions, and moral philosophers. We, therefore, have an obligation to teach these in the family, in our religious organisations, and to support this effort in our communities.

Moral and character development is integral to the development of self, and is as much the responsibility of early caregivers as it is of later educators.

In sum, as parents, educators, affiliates of religious organisations, and community members, we have an obligation to provide young people with training appropriate to their age level that would assist them in holding to the absolutes that are common across philosophies and the scriptures of the major religious traditions, while at the same time helping them clarify and defend their own acquired values.

Any framework for impacting moral and character development is arbitrary unless it is based on some philosophical foundation. Since no current approach to moral education is consistent with all philosophies and meta-ethical theories, educators must first decide these and then develop curriculum. An atmosphere of adult harmony is vitally important. Schools effectively assisting pupil character development are:

1. directed by adults who exercise their authority toward faculty and students in a firm, sensitive, and imaginative manner, and who are committed to both academics and pupil character development;
2. staffed by dedicated faculty who make vigourous demands on pupils and each other;
3. structured so that pupils are surrounded by a variety of opportunities for them to practise helping conduct;
4. managed to provide pupils—both individually and collectively—with many forms of recognition for good conduct;
5. oriented toward maintaining systems of symbols, slogans, ceremonies, and songs that heighten pupils' collective identities;
6. dedicated to maintaining pupil discipline, via clear, widely disseminated discipline codes that are vigourously enforced and backed up with vital consequences;
7. committed to academic instruction and assigned pupils significant homework and otherwise stressed appropriate academic rigour;
8. sensitive to the need to develop collective pupil loyalties to particular classes, clubs, athletic groups, and other subentities in the school;

9. sympathetic to the values of the external adult society, and perceive it as largely supportive and concerned with the problems of the young;
10. always able to use more money to improve their programs, but rarely regard lack of money as an excuse for serious programme deficiencies;
11. open to enlisting the help, counsel, and support of parents and other external adults, but willing to propose important constructive changes in the face of (sometimes) ill-informed parent resistance;
12. disposed to define "good character" in relatively immediate and traditional terms.

9.3. Domain Approach to Values Education

One of the most significant advances made during the past 15 years of research and theory on social development has been the discovery that children's conceptions of morality and social convention are not aspects of single developmental system of morality, but constitute distinct conceptual and developmental domains. More recently we have begun to make progress in applying these findings from developmental psychology to what we call "domain appropriate" values education.

The domain approach to values education emerges from the discovery that children's social concepts do not form a single conceptual system, but are structured within discrete areas of social knowledge that account for qualitatively differing aspects of societal and interpersonal regulation. Within this framework, morality pertains to the set of interpersonal actions such as hitting and hurting that have non arbitrary consequences for the rights or welfare of persons. Moral issues, then, are treated as categorical, and universalisable; specific moral concepts (i.e., it is wrong to hit and hurt another) are structured by underlying conceptions of justice, rights, and welfare (beneficence).

Whereas morality deals with issues inherent in interpersonal relations, social conventions such as modes of dress, forms of address, sex roles, manners, and aspects of mores regarding sexuality are the arbitrary and agreed-upon uniformities in social behaviour determined by the social system in which they are formed. Thus, conventions are seen as alterable, and context dependent. Through accepted usage, however, these standards serve to coordinate the interactions of individuals within systems by providing them with a set of expectations regarding appropriate behaviour. In turn, the matrix of social conventions and customs serves as one element in the structuring and maintenance of the general social order. Judgements about social convention are structured by underlying conceptions of social organisation.

Three forms of evidence are offered in support of the moral-conventional distinction. First, interview studies with children as young as 2 1/2 years-of-age have reported that subjects distinguish between matters of morality and social convention. In these studies it has been found that subjects view moral transgressions as wrong irrespective of the presence of governing rules, while conventional acts are viewed as wrong only if they are in violation of an existing standard. Interview studies have also found that individuals view conventional standards as alterable, while moral prescriptions are viewed as universal and unchangeable.

The second form of evidence comes from observational studies of children's and adolescents' social interactions in family, school, and playground contexts. These studies have reported that the forms of social interactions in the context of moral events differ qualitatively from interactions in the context of conventions. It was found that children's and adults' responses to events in the moral domain focus on features intrinsic to the acts, while responses in the context of conventions focus on aspects of social order. The general pattern of results reported in the interview and observational studies have been replicated with subjects in other cultures indicating that the distinction between morality and convention is not confined to subjects reared in Western societies.

The third piece of evidence comes from developmental studies examining age-related changes in children's moral and conventional judgements. These studies have reported that concepts in the moral and conventional domains follow distinct developmental patterns. The sequence of changes observed in the moral domain indicates that as children develop, they form increased understandings of benevolence, equality, and reciprocity. In the conventional domain development entails transformation in the child's underlying conceptions of social organisation and moves toward an understanding of convention as constitutive of social systems and as important for the coordination of social interactions.

9.3.1. Morality and Convention in Interaction

Often social situations will contain elements from both domains. For example, conventions sometimes result in injustices, as in the case of sex conventions that discriminate against women. In other cases, conventions, such as waiting in line to purchase theatre tickets, act in the service of fairness. When people reason about such issues they tend to do one of three things:

1. Emphasize on one domain and subordinate the other: For example, people worried about, or committed to maintaining the existing social order may not even recognise the potential injustice in existing sex role conventions that give greater privileges to men than women. Others, on the other hand, focusing on such injustices may not take into account the impact on social organisation in such contexts as family structure, that might result from a single-minded focus on rights and equality.
2. Experience conflict between the two, and engage in inconsistencies and vacillation with an absence of resolution or reconciliation of the components
3. Coordination of the two components, so that the two are taken into account in consideration of the issue. For example, concerns for fairness and equality are coupled with changes in the conventions regarding household tasks, child care, etc., that allow for family life to go forward in an organised and functional way.

This view of social reasoning is consistent with a reinterpretation of earlier, global theories of social development, such as Kohlberg's stages of moral development, as an approximation of the age-related changes in domain coordinations. From the distinct domains perspective, however, one would not interpret such interdomain coordinations as representing a stable context-independent cognitive structure. From this perspective one would predict a great deal more intraindividual, and cross-cultural variation in social reasoning than is permitted by Kohlbergian stages of moral judgement, since morality is but one element to be interrelated in the process of generating actions in multifaceted social contexts.

9.3.2. Basic Principles of Domain Appropriate Education

One educational implication of these psychological findings is that values instruction be coordinated with domain of the issues addressed in a given lesson. The first step in such an approach, would entail the teacher's analysis and identification of the moral or conventional nature of social issues employed in values lessons. Such an analysis would be necessary to ensure that the issues discussed are concordant with the domain of the values dimension they are intended to affect. A related function of the teacher would be to focus student activity on the underlying features concordant with the domain of the issue. Thus, students dealing with a moral issue would be directed to focus on the underlying justice or human welfare considerations of the episode.

With respect to conventions, the focus of the student activity would be on the role of social expectations and the social organisational function of such social norms. As we noted earlier, not all issues of social right and wrong fall simply into one domain or the other. Cases of domain overlap would involve both the domain concordant practices just outlined as well as activities that would involve students in reasoning that necessitates the coordination of knowledge from more than one social dimension.

The second general principle is that the activities and questions posed to students be appropriate for their developmental level. Students in the 8th grade and 9th grades are approximately 13 to 15 years-old. In terms of their conceptions of convention, the majority of such young adolescents are either at Level 4 negation, in which conventions are viewed as the arbitrary and unimportant dictates of authority, or are in the process of shifting toward Level 5 affirmation, in which conventions are understood to be constitutive of social systems. At Level 4, students' lack of understanding of the role conventions play in organising and structuring social systems, coupled with their knowledge that the specific conventions of society are arbitrary leads them to either downplay or discount the importance of convention,

"What's the difference if I eat my peas with a fork or a butter knife?", or conform to convention out of fear of peer or adult sanctions, "Sure, I refer to my teachers by Mr. and Mrs. instead of first names. I have enough trouble being in school; who needs more?"

Sometimes, as in the case of teacher names, Level 4 adolescents will go along with conventions in order not to cause moral harm in the form of perceived hurt feelings or disrespect that may come from violating someone else's strongly held convention. These Level 4 adolescents, however, do not understand why anyone's feelings should be hurt, and simply conform in order not to be gratuitously hurtful.

It is at Level 5 that the person's conceptions of convention can first be described as reflecting an understanding of society as a system. For the first time, students clearly perceive that while individual conventions are arbitrary, they form the set of norms that structures society in particular ways.

People who are members of a society are obligated to adhere to conventions in order for society to function. History teachers are probably familiar with the kinds of difficulties that arise when students are not at a point where they have achieved this Level 5 understanding of social systems and their relations to conventions and customs. Many school districts respond to this developmental transition by delaying the teaching of world history until the sophomore year of high school when most students are 15 to 16 years of age and generally at Level 5 in their conventional understandings. In doing so, schools wait for development, rather than contributing to it. The materials and practices described below are based on a different premise, namely that the transition point from Level 4 and 5 presents a great opportunity to link the teaching of particular school subject matter with the dynamics of development. Done well, such a link carries with it payoffs in the form of student motivation, and interest in the subject matter as well as increased sophistication in their understanding of the academic content.

In the moral domain adolescents are generally beyond childhood conceptions of fairness as "raw justice", and are beginning to apply their moral understandings to issues that require an integration of concerns for equal treatment with concerns for equity. Fairness is understood as requiring more than a simple tit-for-tat approach to social interactions. At this age, adolescents are also beginning to couple their moral understandings with a broadening sense of their moral community. By engaging students at this age in coordinating their concerns for morality with their emerging conceptions of society, teachers can begin to contribute to the ability of students to take a moral perspective in relation to society as a whole.

9.4. Emotional Development

According to Erik Erikson, the socialisation process consists of eight phases - the "eight stages of man." His eight stages of man were formulated, not through experimental work, but through wide - ranging experience in psychotherapy, including extensive experience with children and adolescents from low - as well as upper - and middle - social classes. Each stage is regarded by Erikson as a "psychosocial crisis," which arises and demands resolution before the next stage can be satisfactorily negotiated. These stages are conceived in an almost architectural sense: satisfactory learning and resolution of each crisis is necessary if the child is to manage the next and subsequent ones satisfactorily, just as the foundation of a house is essential to the first floor, which in turn must be structurally sound to support and the second story, and so on.

9.4.1. Learning Basic Trust Versus Basic Mistrust (Hope)

Chronologically, this is the period of infancy through the first one or two years of life. The child, well - handled, nurtured, and loved, develops trust and security and a basic optimism. Badly handled, he becomes insecure and mistrustful.

9.4.2. Learning Autonomy Versus Shame (Will)

The second psychosocial crisis, Erikson believes, occurs during early childhood, probably between about 18 months or 2 years and 3½ to 4 years of age. The "well - parented" child emerges from this stage sure of himself, elated with his new found control, and proud rather than ashamed. Autonomy is not, however, entirely synonymous with assured self - possession, initiative, and independence but, at least for children in the early part of this psychosocial crisis, includes stormy self - will, tantrums, stubbornness, and negativism. For example, one sees may 2 year olds resolutely folding their arms to prevent their mothers from holding their hands as they cross the street. Also, the sound of "NO" rings through the house or the grocery store.

9.4.3. Learning Initiative Versus Guilt (Purpose)

Erikson believes that this third psychosocial crisis occurs during what he calls the "play age," or the later preschool years (from about 3½ to, in the United States culture, entry into formal school). During it, the healthily developing child learns: (1) to imagine, to broaden his skills through active play of all sorts, including fantasy (2) to cooperate with others (3) to lead as well as to follow. Immobilised by guilt, he is: (1) fearful (2) hangs on the fringes of groups (3) continues to depend unduly on adults and (4) is restricted both in the development of play skills and in imagination.

9.4.4. Industry Versus Inferiority (Competence)

Erikson believes that the fourth psychosocial crisis is handled, for better or worse, during what he calls the "school age," presumably up to and possibly including some of junior high school. Here the child learns to master the more formal skills of life: (1) relating with peers according to rules (2) progressing from free play to play that may be elaborately structured by rules and may demand formal teamwork, such as baseball and (3) mastering social studies, reading, arithmetic. Homework is a necessity, and the need for self-discipline increases yearly. The child who, because of his successive and successful resolutions of earlier psychosocial crisis, is trusting, autonomous, and full of initiative will learn easily enough to be industrious. However, the mistrusting child will doubt the future. The shame - and guilt-filled child will experience defeat and inferiority.

9.4.5. Learning Identity Versus Identity Diffusion (Fidelity)

During the fifth psychosocial crisis (adolescence, from about 13 or 14 to about 20) the child, now an adolescent, learns how to answer satisfactorily and happily the question of "Who am I?" But even the best - adjusted of adolescents experiences some role identity diffusion: most boys and probably most girls experiment with minor delinquency; rebellion flourishes; self - doubts flood the youngster, and so on.

Erikson believes that during successful early adolescence, mature time perspective is developed; the young person acquires self-certainty as opposed to self-consciousness and self-doubt. He comes to experiment with different - usually constructive - roles rather than adopting a "negative identity" (such as delinquency). He actually anticipates achievement, and achieves, rather than being "paralysed" by feelings of inferiority or by an inadequate time perspective.

In later adolescence, clear sexual identity - manhood or womanhood - is established. The adolescent seeks leadership (someone to inspire him), and gradually develops a set of ideals (socially congruent and desirable, in the case of the successful adolescent). Erikson believes that, in our culture, adolescence affords a "psychosocial moratorium," particularly for middle - and upper-class American children. They do not yet have to "play for keeps," but can experiment, trying various roles, and thus hopefully find the one most suitable for them.

9.4.6. Learning Intimacy Versus Isolation (Love)

The successful young adult, for the first time, can experience true intimacy - the sort of intimacy that makes possible good marriage or a genuine and enduring friendship.

9.4.7. Learning Generativity Versus Self-Absorption (Care)

In adulthood, the psychosocial crisis demands generativity, both in the sense of marriage and parenthood, and in the sense of working productively and creatively.

9.4.8. Integrity Versus Despair (Wisdom)

If the other seven psychosocial crisis have been successfully resolved, the mature adult develops the peak of adjustment; integrity. He trusts, he is independent and dares the new. He works hard, has found a well - defined role in life, and has developed a selfconcept with which he is happy. He can be intimate without strain, guilt, regret, or lack of realism; and he is proud of what he creates - his children, his work, or his hobbies. If one or more of the earlier psychosocial crises have not been resolved, he may view himself and his life with disgust and despair.

These eight stages of man, or the psychosocial crises, are plausible and insightful descriptions of how personality develops but at present they are descriptions only. The best rudimentary and tentative knowledge of just what sort of environment will result, for example, in traits of trust versus distrust, or clear personal identity versus diffusion. Helping the child through the various stages and the positive learning that should accompany them is a complex and difficult task, as any worried parent or teacher knows. Search for the best ways of accomplishing this task accounts for much of the research in the field of child development.

Socialisation, then is a learning - teaching process that, when successful, results in the human organism's moving from its infant state of helpless but total egocentricity to its ideal adult state of sensible conformity coupled with independent creativity.

9.4.9. Factors Affecting Emotional Development

9.4.9.1. Temperament

Temperament is a set of in-born traits that organize the child's approach to the world. They are instrumental in the development of the child's distinct personality. These traits also determine how the child goes about learning about the world around him. These traits appear to be relatively stable from birth. They are enduring characteristics that are actually never "good" or "bad." How they are received determines whether they are perceived by the child as being a bad or good thing.

When parents understand the temperament of their children, they can avoid blaming themselves for issues that are normal for their child's temperament. Some children are noisier than other. Some are more cuddly than others. Some have more regular sleep patterns that others. When parents understand how their child responds to certain situations, they an learn to anticipate issues that might present difficulties for their child. They can prepare the child for the situation or in other cases they may avoid a potentially difficult situation all together.

Parents can tailor their parenting strategies to the particular temperamental characteristics of the child. They can also avoid thinking that a behaviour that reflects a temperament trait represents a pathological condition that requires treatment. Parents feel more effective as they more fully understand and appreciate their child's unique personality.

When the demands and expectations of people and the environment are compatible with the child's temperament there is said to be a "goodness-of-fit." When incompatibility exists, you have what is known as a "personality conflict." Early on parents can work with the child's temperamental traits rather than in opposition to them. Later as the child matures the parents can help the child to adapt to their world by accommodating to their temperamental traits.

The 9 temperamental traits are;

1. *Activity Level*: This is the child's "idle speed or how active the child is generally. Does the infant always wiggle, more squirm? Is the infant difficult to diaper because of this? Is the infant content to sit and quietly watch? Does the child have difficulty sitting still? Is the child always on the go? Or, does the child prefer sedentary quiet activities? Highly active children may channel such extra energy into success in sports; may perform well in high-energy careers and may be able to keep up with many different responsibilities.
2. *Distractibility*: The degree of concentration and paying attention displayed when a child is not particularly interested in an activity. This trait refers to the ease with which external stimuli interfere with ongoing behaviour. Is the infant easily distracted by sounds or sights while drinking a bottle? Is the infant easily soothed when upset by being offered alternate activity? Does the child become sidetracked easily when attempting to follow routine or working on some activity? High distractibility is seen as positive when it is easy to divert a child from an undesirable behaviour but seen as negative when it prevents the child from finishing school work.
3. *Intensity*: The energy level of a response whether positive or negative. Does the infant react strongly and loudly to everything, even relatively minor events? Does the child show pleasure or upset strongly and dramatically? Or does the child just get quiet

when upset? Intense children are more likely to have their needs met and may have depth and delight of emotion rarely experienced by others. These children may be gifted in dramatic arts. Intense children tend to be exhausting to live with.

4. *Regularity*: The trait refers to the predictability of biological functions like appetite and sleep. Does the child get hungry or tired at predictable times? Or, is the child unpredictable in terms of hunger and tiredness? As grown-ups irregular individuals may do better than others with traveling as well as be likely to adapt to careers with unusual working hours.
5. *Sensory Threshold*: Related to how sensitive this child is to physical stimuli. It is the amount of stimulation (sounds, tastes, touch, temperature changes) needed to produce a response in the child. Does the child react positively or negatively to particular sounds? Does the child startle easily to sounds? Is the child a picky eater or will he eat almost anything? Does the child respond positively or negatively to the feel of clothing? Highly sensitive individuals are more likely to be artistic and creative.
6. *Approach/Withdrawal*: Refers to the child's characteristic response to a new situation or strangers. Does the child eagerly approach new situations or people? Or does the child seem hesitant and resistant when faced with new situations, people or things? Slow-to-warm up children tend to think before they act. They are less likely to act impulsively during adolescence.
7. *Adaptability*: Related to how easily the child adapts to transitions and changes, like switching to a new activity. Does the child have difficulty with changes in routines, or with transitions from one activity to another? Does the child take a long time to become comfortable to new situations? A slow-to-adapt child is less likely to rush into dangerous situations, and may be less influenced by peer pressure.
8. *Persistence*: This is the length of time a child continues in activities in the face of obstacles. Does the child continue to work on a puzzle when he has difficulty with it or does he just move on to another activity? Is the child able to wait to have his needs met? Does the child react strongly when interrupted in an activity? When a child persists in an activity he is asked to stop, he is

labeled as stubborn. When a child stays with a tough puzzle he is seen a being patient. The highly persistent child is more likely to succeed in reaching goals. A child with low persistence may develop strong social skills because he realizes other people can help.

9. *Mood*: This is the tendency to react to the world primarily in a positive or negative way. Does the child see the glass as half full? Does he focus on the positive aspects of life? Is the child generally in a happy mood? Or, does the child see the gall as half empty and tend to focus on the negative aspects of life? Is the child generally serious? Serious children tend to be analytical and evaluate situations carefully.

Temperament is the innate behaviour style of an individual that seems to be biologically determined. Although some experts feel that labeling a child too quickly as "difficult" may create a self-fulfilling prophecy of problematic parent-child interaction, knowing what kind of temperament your child has may make the difference between a happy and a troubled child - and between an accepting and frustrated parent.

9.4.9.2. Adolescent Stages of Development

Children must pass through several stages, or take specific steps, on their road to becoming adults. For most people, there are four or five such stages of growth where they learn certain things: infancy (birth to age two), early childhood (ages 3 to 8 years), later childhood (ages 9 to 12) and adolescence (ages 13 to 18). Persons 18 and over are considered adults in our society. Of course, there are some who will try to act older than their years. But, for the most part, most everybody grows in this same pattern. Parents learn much about taking care of their babies and young children. At the hospital or with the doctor, you might pick up information about what to feed them or how long they should sleep.

Later, school staff may remind you about the importance of talking and reading to your young children. You can also see how your friends or relatives treat their kids. You cannot say the same thing about learning to talk with teenagers (adolescents). It seems like everyone, even teachers and neighbors, have problems understanding them.

Giving up, you might turn to doing and saying the same things your parents did with you. But those were other times! You can begin to understand this age group if you look at its place on the growth sequence. Notice how it's right next to the adult stage, the last step before being an adult. This is a time for adolescents to decide about their future line of work and think about starting their own families in a few years.

One of the first things they must do is to start making their own decisions. For example adolescents can begin to decide what to buy with their own money or who will be their friend. To do this they must put a little distance between themselves and their parents. This does not mean that you can't continue to "look after them" or help them when needed. You should, as much as possible, let them learn from the results of their actions. Adolescents also need to be around other adults, both male and female. These can be relatives, neighbors, or teachers. Of course, they should be positive role models. Your teenagers can learn from them about things like how to fix the car, getting along with others, or ideas for future jobs. Finally, don't worry if they want to spend time alone. Adolescents can "spend hours" day dreaming about their future life. They might be planning the things they can do or will buy "when they grow up." Remember, to travel far, one begins with the first few steps!

9.4.9.3. Chronic Health Conditions

Children with chronic health conditions and disabilities should not be excluded from fitness activities; they receive the same positive benefits from exercise. Some activities may need to be modified or adapted to your child's disability. Certain activities are dangerous for some health conditions. Consult your child's doctor about the safety of fitness activities for your child with a disability.

As children develop, so do their physical skills. Children ages 4 and 5 play in an increasingly coordinated manner and can participate in organized games. Four- and 5-year-olds can roll large balls, play catch and may be able to navigate a bike with training wheels. However, children this age cannot safely maneuver a bicycle in areas where there is traffic because they lack judgment and safety awareness as well as coordination skills. Swimming is an excellent fitness activity and teaches a valuable skill. Other fitness activities they may enjoy include dance, skiing or skating.

No matter what the sport or activity, parents should remember that events should always be fun. If your child isn't having fun, ask why and try to resolve what is bothering your child or find some other fitness activity. This is particularly true of organized sports. Kids who are pressured to compete may develop a negative attitude toward fitness or injure themselves while trying to please others with their performance. Make sure your child's time is not overscheduled; this may cause stress. Unstructured time allows your child to learn important skills and time to wind down.

If your child refuses to participate in any fitness activity, it can be an indication of a physical or psychological problem. Children who complain of pain when they play or consistently refuse to join other children in outdoor play may need to be seen by a doctor. Even a shy child needs to play with other kids.

9.4.9.4. Physical Fitness

As a parent, you need to encourage healthy habits - including exercise - in your youngsters. Physical activity should become as routine a part of their lives as eating and sleeping. Reassure them that sports such as cycling (always with a helmet), swimming, basketball, jogging, walking briskly, cross-country skiing, dancing, aerobics and soccer, played regularly, are not only fun but can promote health. Some sports, like baseball, that require only sporadic activity are beneficial in a number of ways, but they do not promote fitness. Physical activity can be healthful in the following ways:

- Increase cardiovascular endurance
- Improve large muscle strength and endurance
- Increase flexibility
- Maintain proper weight
- Reduce stress
- Increase Cardiovascular Endurance

More Americans die from heart disease than any other ailment; regular physical activity can help protect against heart problems. Exercise can improve your child's fitness, make him feel better and strengthen his cardiovascular system. Aerobic activity can make the heart pump more efficiently, thus reducing the incidence of high blood pressure. It can also raise blood levels of HDL (high-density lipoprotein) cholesterol, the "good" form of cholesterol that removes excess fats from the bloodstream. Even though most cardiovascular diseases are thought to be illnesses of adulthood, fatty deposits have been detected in the arteries of children as young as age 3, and high blood pressure exists in about 5 percent of youngsters.

At least three times a week, your middle-years child needs to exercise continuously for 20 minutes to 30 minutes at a heart rate above his resting level. As a guideline, the effort involved in continuous brisk walking is adequate to maintain fitness. Each exercise session should be preceded and followed by a gradual warm-up and cool-down period, allowing muscles, joints and the cardiovascular system to ease into and out of vigorous activity, thus helping to guarantee a safe workout. This can be accomplished by stretching for a few minutes before and after exercise.

9.4.9.5. Improve large muscle strength and endurance

As your child's muscles become stronger, he will be able to exercise for longer periods of time, as well as protect himself from injuries - strong muscles provide better support for the joints. Modified sit-ups (knees bent, feet on the ground) can build up abdominal muscles, increase lung capacity and protect against back injuries. For upper body strength, he can perform modified pull-ups (keeping the arms flexed while hanging from a horizontal bar) and modified push-ups (positioning the knees on the ground while extending the arms at the elbow).

9.4.9.6. Increase flexibility

For complete physical fitness, children need to be able to twist and bend their bodies through the full range of normal motions without overexerting themselves or causing injury. When children are flexible like this, they are more agile. Although most people lose flexibility as they age, this process can be retarded by stretching to maintain suppleness throughout life, beginning in childhood. Stretching exercises are the best way to maintain or improve flexibility, and they can be incorporated into your child's warm-up and cool-down routines. In most stretching exercises, your child should stretch to a position where he begins to feel tightness but not pain, then hold steady for 20 seconds to 30 seconds before relaxing. He should not bounce as he stretches, since this can cause injury to the muscles or tendons.

9.4.9.7. Maintain proper weight

Twelve percent of children in the prepuberty years are overweight, but few of these youngsters are physically active. Exercise can effectively burn calories and fat and reduce appetite. Ask your pediatrician to help you determine whether your youngster has a healthy percentage of body fat for his or her age and sex.

9.4.9.8. Reduce stress

Unmanaged stress can cause muscle tightness, which can contribute to headaches, stomachaches and other types of discomfort. Your child needs to learn not only to recognize stress in his body but also to diffuse it effectively. Exercise is one of the best ways to control stress. A physically active child is less likely to experience stress-related symptoms than his more sedentary peers.

Perhaps the best way to get children to enjoy exercise is to make it a family affair, with parents setting a good example and encouraging the youngsters to join the fun. The entire family can participate together in many physical activities, from swimming to cycling to hiking. Not only will everyone's fitness improve, but the unity of the family can be strengthened too. If you can get your child interested in fitness at a young age, you will improve the chances that physical activity will become a lifetime habit.

9.5. Personality Development

To study successful personality development one must first have a way of thinking about the course of lives and a way of assessing how adaptational processes are patterned over time. There are three general approaches to this conceptual problem: growth models, lifespan models, and life-course models. Each of these social-developmental approaches provides a framework for understanding adaptational processes and the coherence of personality development by focusing on the distinctive ways individuals organise their behaviour to meet new environmental demands and developmental challenges.

9.5.1. Growth Models of Personality Development

Growth models of personality development are not homogeneous in their orientation, but are based on different traditions and conceptual backgrounds. For example, humanistic theories of personality development are best known for emphasising the potential for positive development. People can take charge of their lives and direct them toward creativity and self-actualisation which involves self-fulfilment and the realisation of one's potential. In contrast, psychoanalytically oriented models tend to emphasise the growth of ego through age stages.

Integrity is the goal of successful development in Erikson's theory, as well as in Loevinger's model of ego development and in the model of Labouvie-Vief which integrates Piaget's theory of cognitive development with emotions and social relations. Erikson's theory covers eight stages across the lifespan. Each stage involves a crisis or an age-specific challenge that should be satisfactorily resolved for optimal development.

The theory states that a successful resolution of each crisis results in the refinement of a predominantly positive quality, such as trust in infancy. The psychosocial crises to be solved in adulthood concern intimacy versus isolation, generativity versus stagnation, and integrity versus despair. Common virtues or ego skills such as hope, will, purpose, and skill in childhood, fidelity in adolescence, and love, care, and wisdom in adulthood emerge as successful outcomes of the crises. Development is based on successful resolution of psychological crises leading finally to integrity in old age.

The passage from one developmental stage to another is also central to Levinson's work, who has studied what he calls "life structures": things that a person finds important in work and love, as well as the values and emotions that make these important. Life structures are subjected to change during transitional periods when people reappraise and restructure important things in their lives. According to Levinson, people spend about half their adult lives in transitional periods.

Sanford, another psychodynamically influenced theorist, described a fully developed person as one characterised by high degrees of both differentiation and integration. Specifically, the fully developed person has a rich and varied impulse life, a broad and refined conscience, a strong sense of individuality, and a balance of control and expression of needs. As for when people reach this stage, Sanford placed the development of impulse control in adolescence and the development of ego, or the controlling function of personality, in adulthood. In both cases, Sanford did not presuppose that personality ever stopped changing: "The highly developed person is always open to new experience, and capable of further learning."

9.5.1.1. Lifespan Models

Research on lifespan personality development is concerned with three major influence systems:

— agegraded influences (e.g., education) which shape individual development in relatively normative ways;

— history-graded influences (e.g., wars) which make development different across historical periods; and

— nonnormative influences (e.g., accidents) which may have powerful effects on an individual's development.

Lifespan development theories hold that psychological functioning is not fixed at a certain age. Rather, "during development, and at all stages of the life span, both continuous (cumulative) and discontinuous (innovative) processes are at work". Development is defined as "selective age-related change in adaptive capacity" and special attention is given to the developing person's contribution to the creation of his or her own development. Individuals steer their physical, cognitive, social, and personality development by constructing strategies for coping with various developmental challenges, by setting goals, and by making choices.

According to Brandtst¨adter, such intentional self development over the life span is geared to the realisation and maintenance of normative representations that individuals construct of themselves and their future. Pulkkinen, Nurmi, and Kokko discuss how individuals steer their development by setting goals and making choices as responses to developmental challenges. On the one hand, personal goals reflect major agegraded transitions and normative demands. On the other hand, individual differences in personal goals reflect motivational orientations, such as security seeking or aiming at personal growth, which result in intraindividual coherence in goal patterns.

An agentic conception of human nature is also central in Heckhausen's work on control. Heckhausen proposes that humans strive to maximise primary control of their environment throughout life. However, control capacities undergo radical changes and losses and individuals have to disengage from unattainable goals and manage their own emotional responses to such loss experiences. This type of control that is directed at the internal world of the individual is referred to as secondary control.

Heckhausen shows how the age-normative structure of life-course transitions allows individuals to anticipate decremental changes in the opportunities to attain developmental goals. For example, an individual can increase primary control striving when approaching "developmental deadlines" (e.g., union formation, health-maintenance in old age) and use secondary control to compensate for potential negative affect and self-evaluation associated with failure to meet or resolve developmental deadlines successfully.

Brandtst adter's work on intentional self-development is also striking in its appreciation of the tension between gains and losses in lifespan development. Although lifespan models do not articulate what is success, some commentators have noted that developmental models that emphasise freedom of individual decision and action are plagued by a Western bias associated with an individualistic cultural base. There is a clear need for cultural psychologists to engage lifespan researchers in testing the limits of the developmental models that have been advanced. Still, the models that have been put forth are exciting because they articulate hypotheses about how individuals at different junctures in their lives struggle to derive meaning from and make sense of life events, and of their part in these events.

9.5.1.2. Life-course Models

Especially beyond childhood the study of successful adaptation becomes more complicated, and it may be that a purely psychological approach is insufficient for the study of personality development as the individual increasingly negotiates social roles defined by the culture. Whereas lifespan theories specify the temporal order of life stages, such as childhood, adolescence, and adulthood, life-course researchers tend to emphasise social-role demands at different ages. Social trajectories are influenced by four factors. First, they are influenced by human agency, the choices that persons make about their own lives.

Second, they are influenced by the timing of life-course events in relation to other events in an individual's life. Third, they are influenced by linked lives, because social changes are expressed in an individual's life through the experiences of related others. Finally, they are influenced by historical changes. Lifespan and life-course models are complementary. Biological changes across the life span and social demands across the life course define typical life events and social roles in people's lives. Indeed, some psychological researchers have found it useful to adopt a sociocultural perspective and to conceive of the life course as a sequence of culturally-defined, agegraded roles that the individual enacts over time.

Helson introduced the concept of a "social clock project" as a framework for studying lifespan development. The concept of a social clock focuses attention on the age-related life schedules of individuals in particular cultures and cohorts, and organises the study of lives in terms of patterned movements into, along, and out of multiple role-paths such as education, work, marriage, and parenthood. In this fashion, the life course can be charted as a sequence of social roles that are enacted over time, and adaptational processes can be explored by investigating the ways different persons select and perform different social-cultural roles.

In her 30-year longitudinal study of female college seniors, who were first studied in 1958-60, Helson examined the personality antecedents and consequences of adherence to a Feminine Social Clock (FSC) and a Masculine Occupational Clock (MOC). For example, women who adhered to the FSC were earlier in life characterised by a desire to do well and by a need for structure; women in this birth cohort who adhered to a MOC were earlier in life more rebellious and less sensitive to social norms. Helson et al. were thus able to identify "culturally salient need-press configurations through time" and to show predictable and meaningful relations between personality and behaviour in different social settings at different ages.

Laursen and Williams explore the role of ethnic identity, a personally and politically-charged topic that is also a profound source of strength. The authors conceive of ethnic identity as a personality variable that shapes the nature and course of successful adolescent adjustment, and describe how ethnic identity offers an important mechanism through which minority adolescents cope with the tension between the inner self and the psychological environment of the majority culture. Silbereisen and his colleagues have capitalised on a "natural experiment" - the unification of Germany during the 1990s - to examine how historical changes shape the nature of adolescent transitions.

Bouchard correctly argued that a purely sociocultural perspective on the life course "ignores the fact that lifehistories themselves are complex evolved adaptations," and suggests that an evolutionary perspective may complement the sociocultural perspective by exploring how personality variation is related to those adaptively-important problems with which human beings have had to repeatedly contend. Evolutionary psychology thus focuses attention on the coherence of behavioural strategies that people use in, for example, mate selection, mate retention, reproduction, parental care, kin investment, status attainment, and coalition building.

It focuses research on the genetically-influenced strategies and tactics that individuals use for survival and reproduction. An evolutionary perspective on successful life-course development could thus offer a fusion of concerns in evolutionary theory, behaviour genetics, and demography. For example, using the evolutionary perspective, Draper and Belsky and Gangestad and Simpson have offered intriguing hypotheses about personality characteristics and reproductive strategies that facilitate adaptations in different environments at different ages.

Ormel tackles this problem from a somewhat different perspective and introduces social production function (SPF) theory as a heuristic for studying successful development. The theory attempts to integrate the various strengths of psychological theories and economic consumer/household production theories. It identifies two ultimate goals that all humans seek to optimise (physical well-being and social wellbeing) and five instrumental goals by which they are achieved (stimulation, comfort, status, behavioural confirmation, affection). The core notion of SPF theory is that people choose and substitute instrumental goals so as to optimise the production of their well-being, subject to constraints in available means of production.

9.5.2. Personality Differences

The starting point for such work should be a system for describing individual differences in personality dispositions and temperamental traits. This is not to suggest that these psychological constructs are the only way to study the contribution of personality differences to successful development. Indeed, motivational concepts in personality are better represented in much of the research on adult development. Over the past 15 years, the intensity and productivity of psychological research on the dimensionality of adult personality has been phenomenal, and has influenced research in diverse fields such as organisational behaviour, psychiatry, and genetics. An emerging consensus points to the existence of five important factors: Extraversion (active, assertive, enthusiastic, outgoing), Agreeableness (generous, kind, sympathetic, trusting), Conscientiousness (organised, planful, reliable, responsible), Neuroticism (anxious, self-pitying, tense, worrying), and Openness to Experience (artistic, curious, imaginative, having wide interests). Each superfactor covers a broad domain of individual differences and includes a number of more specific personality dimensions or facets.

Some developmental researchers have noted that this Five-Factor Model of personality does not provide a theory of personality, which is correct to the extent that most personality taxonomies are focused on describing regularities in behaviour rather than examining dynamic and developmental processes. Other critics have noted that researchers interested in the Five-Factor Model have not paid attention to issues of personality development. Indeed, whereas the study of personality structure in adulthood has influenced research on adult development and aging, the study of personality structure in childhood has been all but neglected. But these are criticisms of what has been done, not of what can be accomplished.

An especially important area of integration involves efforts to connect existing models of infant and child temperament with studies of adult personality structure. What are normally understood as personality traits may be aspects of temperament differentiated in the course of life experience. But, surprisingly, there has been virtually no contact between child psychologists who study temperament and personality psychologists who are concerned with personality differences. Halverson and colleagues have made a strong case that research on lifespan personality development will remain unintegrated unless child psychologists begin to study the structure of personality. Research linking temperament to the development of personality will be facilitated by two parallel achievements: the development of a consensual system for describing the structure of personality differences in adulthood, as noted earlier, and the development of such a system for temperamental traits.

In the domain of temperament, conceptual reviews and factor-analytic studies have identified several "consensus" dimensions of infant and childhood temperament that might show influences on later developmental outcomes. For example, some researchers cling to the notion that temperament can only be assessed in the young infant and that temperament cannot be shaped by experience.

Rothbart and Putnam define temperament as "constitutionally based individual differences in reactivity and self-regulation, influenced over time by heredity and experience." Reactivity refers to the excitability, responsivity, or arousability of the behavioural and physiological systems of the individual, and self-regulation refers to the behavioural processes that modulate this reactivity. Importantly, Rothbart and Putnam note that such temperament differences develop and they are not immune to experience. Recent research shows that infants' temperament is shaped by experience even before birth (e.g., fetal nutrition, fetal substance exposure, daylight during pregnancy).

Moreover, behavioural genetic studies have established that individual differences in temperament, measured even during the first year of life, are only partially heritable and are influenced significantly by unique environmental events, suggesting that younger age of measurement does not guarantee that temperament is purely "constitutional."

9.5.3. Stages of Personality Development

According to Indian philosophy, five dimensions are involved in forming the human personality. These are:

1. Physical self,
2. Energy self,
3. Intellectual self,
4. Mental self, and
5. Blissful self.

Well-integrated personality is the sum total of harmonious expression of these five dimensions.

Physical self: relates to our senses. Proper nourishment and growth of physical faculties is essential by way of balanced diet, recreation, music, and care and concern from near and dear ones. A simple pat on the back for any achievement in life goes a long way to build up confidence. However, discretion and discrimination are the key words in this regard. Otherwise, there is every chance that senses would create havoc by way of infatuation and attachment to the sense objects.

Energy self: is somewhat subtler than the first. It relates to metabolism and the gross manifestations of energy (Prana), for instance the act of breathing. The control of Prana is achieved by control of anger, anxiety, and restlessness.

Intellectual self: concerns with discriminative power and knowledge, what we call "*buddhi*"

Mental self: is related to stress and psychology. Here selflessness, control, concentration, and calmness of mind plays essential role.

Blissful self: is the function of state of being. It calls for remaining calm and unaffected, nay to remain happy, in all the frivolities of world, in neck break competition and struggle, in calamities and disasters, in suffering and loss, in failure and success.

9.5.4. Theoretical Perspectives

In psychology, personality is a collection of emotion, thought and behaviour patterns unique to a person. There are several theoretical perspectives on personality in psychology, which involve different ideas about the relationship between personality and other psychological constructs, as well as different theories about the way personality develops.

9.5.4.1. Personality models

Modern personality models may generally be broken into three types: factorial models, typologies and circumplexes.

Factorial models: posit that there are dimensions along which human personality differs. The main purpose of a personality model is thus to define the dimensions of personality. Factor analysis is a primary tool of theorists composing factorial models. Such models arise directly from a classical individual differences approach to the study of human personality. Goldberg's Big Five models described below may be the best-known example of this type of theory.

Typologies or type models: arise naturally from some theories that posit types of people. For example, astrological signs represented a well-known, pre-scientific typological model. Typological models posit a relatively small number of model types and possibly some interaction between the types.

Circumplex models: may resemble factorial or type models but further specify a relationship between the different types or factors. Typically, some types or factors are more related than others and can be presented on a polygon.

9.5.5. Personality Theories

Most personality theories can be grouped into one of the following classes.

9.5.5.1. Trait theories

Personality traits are prominent aspects of personality that are exhibited in a wide range of important social and personal contexts. In other words, persons have certain characteristics which partly determine their behaviour. According to the theory, a friendly person is likely to act friendly in any situation because of the traits in his personality. One criticism of trait models of personality as a whole is that they lead professionals in clinical psychology and lay-people alike to accept classifications, or worse offer advice, based on superficial analysis of one's profile.

The most common models of traits incorporate five broad dimensions or factors. These are:

— extraversion,

— neuroticism,

— agreeableness,

— conscientiousness and

— openness to experience

Gordon Allport, Raymond Cattell, Lewis Goldberg, John L. Holland and Carl Jung are some of the major proponents of this theory.

9.5.5.2. Psychodynamic theories

Psychodynamic theories explain human behaviour in terms of interaction between the various components of personality. Sigmund Freud was the founder of this school. Freud drew on the physics of his day to coin the term psychodynamics: based on the popular ideas of conversion of heat into mechanical energy and vice versa, he proposed the conversion of psychic energy into behaviour. He broke the human personality down to three significant components: the ego, superego, and id. According to Freud, personality is shaped by the interactions of these three components.

9.5.5.3. Behaviourist theories

Behaviourists explain personality in terms of reactions to external stimuli. This school of thought was initiated by B. F. Skinner. According to these theories, people's behaviour is formed by processes such as operant conditioning.

9.5.5.4. Cognitive and social-cognitive theories

In cognitivism behaviour is explained as guided by cognitions about the world, and especially those about other people. Albert Bandura, a social learning theorist suggested that the forces of memory and emotions worked in conjunction with environmental influences.

9.5.5.5. Humanistic theories

In humanistic psychology it is emphasised that people have free will and that they play an active role in determining, how they behave. Accordingly, humanistic psychology focuses on subjective experiences of persons instead of factors that determine behaviour. Abraham Maslow and Carl Rogers were proponents of this view.

9.5.6. Shaping Factors in a Personality

There are many potential factors that are involved in shaping a personality. These factors are usually seen as coming from heredity and the environment. Research by psychologists over the last several decades has increasingly pointed to hereditary factors being more important, especially for basic personality traits such as emotional tone. However, the acquisition of values, beliefs, and expectations seem to be due more to socialisation and unique experiences, especially during childhood. Some hereditary factors that contribute to personality development do so as a result of interactions with the particular social environment in which people live. For instance, your genetically inherited physical and mental capabilities have an impact on how others see you and, subsequently, how you see yourself. If you have poor motor skills that prevent you from throwing a ball straight and if you regularly get bad grades in school, you will very likely be labelled by your teachers, friends, and relatives as someone who is inadequate or a failure to some degree. This can become a self-fulfilling prophesy as you increasingly perceive yourself in this way and become more pessimistic about your capabilities and your future.

Likewise, your health and physical appearance are likely to be very important in your personality development. You may be frail or robust. You may have a learning disability. You may be slender in a culture that considers obesity attractive or vice-versa. These largely hereditary factors are likely to cause you to feel that you are nice-looking, ugly, or just adequate. Likewise, skin colour, gender, and sexual orientation are likely to have a major impact on how you perceive yourself. Whether you are accepted by others as being normal or abnormal can lead you to think and act in a socially acceptable or marginal and even deviant way.

There are many potential environmental influences that help to shape personality. Child rearing practices are especially critical. In North America, children are usually raised in ways that encourage them to become self-reliant and independent. Children are often allowed to act somewhat like equals to their parents. For instance, they are included in making decisions about what type of food and entertainment the family will have on a night out. Children are given allowances and small jobs around the house to teach them how to be responsible for themselves. In contrast, children in China are usually encouraged to think and act as a member of their family and to suppress their own wishes when they are in conflict with the needs of the family. Independence and self-reliance are viewed as an indication of family failure and are discouraged. It is not surprising that Chinese children traditionally have not been allowed to act as equals to their parents.

Despite significant differences in child rearing practices around the world, there are some similarities. Boys and girls are socialised differently to some extent in all societies. They receive different messages from their parents and other adults as to what is appropriate for them to do in life. They are encouraged to prepare for their future in jobs fitting their gender. Boys are more often allowed freedom to experiment and to participate in physically risky activities. Girls are encouraged to learn how to do domestic chores and to participate in child rearing by baby-sitting. If children do not follow these traditional paths, they are often labelled as marginal or even deviant—girls may be called "tomboys" and boys may be ridiculed for being "effeminate."

There are always unique situations and interpersonal events that help to shape our personalities. Such things as having alcoholic parents, being seriously injured in a car accident, or being raped can leave mental scars that make us fearful and less trusting. If you are an only child, you don't have to learn how to compromise as much as children who have several siblings. Chance meetings and actions may have a major impact on the rest of our lives and affect our personalities. For instance, being accepted for admission to a prestigious university or being in the right place at the right time to meet the person who will become your spouse or life partner can significantly alter the course of the rest of your life.

Personality development is the development of the organised pattern of behaviours and attitudes that makes a person distinctive. It occurs by the ongoing interaction of temperament, character, and environment.

All most all normal human beings always like to develop into something better. There are some ways to achieve this metamorphosis in one's personality. If one were to understand these basic rules, one can develop him into anything he aspires for. The first step to this is planning. Make a clear plan of what you want to be and how you want to go about achieving it. A plan should be clear, focused and practical. Then put your plan into imagination. Here you would find it strange why you first plan and they're after image.

You might have noticed that people sometimes come with solutions to grave problems in deep sleep. It so happens that they have gone through the same situation over and over again in their imagination, to reach the stage when the subconscious minds itself comes up with the solutions. To bring any planning into reality it has to be propelled by the energy of imagination. Sound planning and imagination coupled with determination and perseverance can turn any dream into reality.

Personality development is the developing a personality cult so as to create a strong positive impression about self with the targeted group, or in general; and more pertinent aspect of such personality is to maintain and prove in a long run. The ten important points for a complete personality are given below.

1. Appearance.
2. Intelligence.
3. Smartness.
4. Trustworthy, High Integrity and Responsible.
5. Knowledge, in depth.
6. Management.
7. Efficiency.
8. Economic Independence.
9. Morality/Character.
10. Being beneficial/Advantageous.

The strong negative aspects to which spoil a personality are:

1. Unhygienic.
2. Hurting attitude.
3. Useless approach.
4. Non-beneficial communication.
5. Untrustworthy, Irresponsible, Lack of integrity.
6. Below average performance.
7. Powerless egoism.
8. Financial in-discipline.
9. Mismanagements.
10. Uncontrolled burst of negative emotions.

It is true that the external appearances of a person can make its personality. However the proper functioning of the nervous and the glands are even more important in the development of a complete personality. The proper functioning of the thyroid glands are very important to personality development. A person whose thyroid glands produce less than sufficient thyroxin will become easily irritable his capacity to memorise decreases and so does his capacity to make decisions. If on the other hand thyroxin is produced in greater quantity then anxiety and anger will become more prominent. If a person or a child becomes violent for trivial matters then it could be suspected that the sympathetic nervous system is not functioning well.

Determination and willpower alone can make an ordinary person a giant personality. Purity of thoughts are factors that can increase willpower and determination. If the will power has to be increased, then it is essential to be away from feelings such as jealousy, false allegations, small talks etc.

The main factors for developing a strong personality in social environment include:

1. Pleasing appearance.
2. Beneficial communication.
3. Adapting and adhering to social values in interactions.
4. Developing confidence of:
   (a) Sincerity, integrity and trust.

(b) Completing duties, fulfilling responsibilities in time.

(c) Economic independent, but not being miser.

5. Additional spices for the best impression:

(a) Awareness and alertness.

(b) Useful application of: knowledge in depth, positive intelligence and defensive smartness.

(c) Self-Confidence, Initiative, dynamism, leadership qualities, will-power and self-discipline.

(d) Adaptive to moral values.

The main factors for developing a strong personality in working field:

1. Sincerity, integrity and trust.
2. Awareness, alertness and grasping capacity.
3. Beneficial communication skill.
4. Useful application of required knowledge in depth, positive intelligence and defensive smartness.
5. Non dependence of economic condition other than for rightful privileges.
6. Completing duties and fulfilling responsibilities in time and absolute accountability.
7. Pleasing appearance with good health.
8. Social interactions in tune with institutional decorum.
9. Sensible thinking in-spite of emotionally charged, or embarrassing, circumstances.
10. Dynamism in positive approaches, initiative in new skills and adaptive to institutional policies.
11. Being in tune with changing times; especially so with changing technologies in the respective line.
12. Not to be with:

(a) Creating helplessness, self-satisfaction at others' cost, egoism, sadism, criticism, putting blame on others to escape, irritating communication, untrustworthiness.

(b) Laziness, lethargic attitude, falling into helplessness, unusual attitude, useless/boom-ranging approaches, irresponsibility, ignorance, borrowings, unhygienic/ disliking appearance.

9.5.7. Role of Relationship

During infancy, childhood, adolescence, and young adulthood, new needs and tensions arise in the individual. In attempt to seek ways of adapting to these new found stresses, people develop different kinds of intimate relationships that ultimately form their personality. Relationships formed during each stage of life serve as a prototype for interactions in later stages. For this reason, there exists a continuum of relationships formed throughout a lifetime that shape and mold specific personality traits.

Neither intimacy nor individual development can exist alone. The birth of a child initiates a human being into a life-long process of mutual adaptation between the child, his or her intimate relationship partners and the broader social environment. Intimate interactions and relationships affect adaptations to the changing needs and stresses that evolve with each stage of development throughout one's lifetime.

Intimate interactions from early life serve as the basis upon which relationships later in life are formed. Environmental contingencies to which individuals must adapt are rooted in these relationships. In an attempt to adapt to other people's styles of relating, one must adjust his or her own behaviours. Based on the fact that human development is a product of complex interplay of forces that reside within the individual human being and the environment by which he or she is surrounded, it can be proposed that interpersonal interactions and relationships shape individual personality and coping styles. Psychological maturity involves integrating intimacy into a life framework that encompasses all parts of the self.

From the time of birth, every individual is biologically predisposed to approach the world with his or her own personal style. Studies of infants suggest that some variability in human behaviour may result directly or indirectly from genetic differences. Developmental psychologists term these differences as dimensions of temperament. Based on chemical, biological, experiential, interpersonal, and social factors, different dimensions of temperament manifest themselves over time and across different situations.

Psychologists Buss and Plomin have proposed the existence of four basic temperament dimensions present in human beings:

— *Emotionality:* is the tendency to express negative emotions such as anger and fear frequently and vigorously.
— *Activity:* is the degree of physical movement that a person characteristically shows.
— *Impulsivity:* is the degree to which a person acts quickly without deliberation, moves from one activity to the next, and finds it difficult to practice self-control.
— *Sociability:* is the tendency to be outgoing and friendly and to enjoy the company of others.

According to this theory, persons are inherently born with tendencies to develop these four temperaments to different levels. These dimensions are present in infancy and continue to grow throughout childhood and adulthood. The social environment reacts to these tendencies, modifying and shaping them in different ways. Such modifications are the results of interpersonal relationships that begin to form during early life. The development of a unique interpersonal style is a function of temperament.

References

Bunch, Wilton H. "Changing moral judgement in divinity students". *Journal of Moral Education* 34 (3): 363–370. 2005

Crain, William C. *Theories of Development* (2Rev ed.). Prentice-Hall. 1985

Hedl, John J.; Glazer, H. and Chan, F. "Improving the Moral Reasoning of Allied Health Students". *Journal of Allied Health* 34 (2): 121–1. 2005.

Kohlberg, Lawrence *From* Is *to* Ought*: How to Commit the Naturalistic Fallacy and Get Away with It in the Study of Moral Development*. New York: Academic Press. 1971.

Rest, James. *Development in Judging Moral Issues*. University of Minnesota Press. 1979.

10

Classroom Management

Classroom management is a term used by teachers to describe the process of ensuring that classroom lessons run smoothly despite disruptive behaviour by students. The term also implies the prevention of disruptive behaviour. It is possibly the most difficult aspect of teaching for many teachers and indeed experiencing problems in this area causes some to leave teaching altogether.

Once a teacher loses control of their classroom, it becomes increasingly more difficult for them to regain that control. Also, the time that teacher has to take to correct misbehaviour caused by poor classroom management skills results in a lower rate of academic engagement in the classroom.

Classroom management is closely linked to issues of motivation, discipline and respect. Methodologies remain a matter of passionate debate amongst teachers; approaches vary depending on the beliefs a teacher holds regarding educational psychology. A large part of traditional classroom management involves behaviour modification, although many teachers see using behavioural approaches alone as overly simplistic. Many teachers establish rules and procedures at the beginning of the school year. They also try to be consistent in enforcing these rules and procedures. Many would also argue for positive consequences when rules are followed, and negative consequences when rules are broken.

There are newer perspectives on classroom management that attempt to be holistic. One example is affirmation teaching, which attempts to guide students toward success by helping them see how their effort pays off in the classroom. It relies upon creating an environment where students are successful as a result of their own efforts.

10.1. Techniques of Management

10.1.1. Corporal Punishment

Until recently, corporal punishment was widely used as a means of controlling disruptive behaviour but it is now no longer fashionable, though it is still advocated in some contexts.

10.1.2. Rote Discipline

Also known as 'lines', Rote Discipline is a negative sanction used for behaviour management. It involves assigning a disorderly student sentences or the classroom rules to write repeatedly. Among the many types of classroom management approaches, it is very commonly used.

10.1.3. Preventative Techniques

Preventative approaches to classroom management involve creating a positive classroom community with mutual respect between teacher and student. Teachers using the preventative approach offer warmth, acceptance and support unconditionally - not based on a student's behaviour. Fair rules and consequences are established and students are given frequent and consistent feedback regarding their behaviour.

Preventative techniques also involve the strategic use of praise and rewards to inform students about their behaviour rather than as a means of controlling student behaviour. In order to use rewards to inform students about their behaviour, teachers must emphasize the value of the behaviour that is rewarded and also explain to students the specific skills they demonstrated to earn the reward. Teachers should also encourage student collaboration in selecting rewards and defining appropriate behaviours that will earn rewards.

10.1.4. Discipline with Dignity

According to its founders, Discipline with Dignity is one of the most widely practised behaviour management philosophies in the world.

The program is utilised in more than 12 different countries. Discipline with Dignity, provides an indepth flexible approach for effective school and classroom management. With a strong focus on developing responsibility, it is a comprehensive, practical programme that leads to improved student behaviour through responsible thinking, cooperation, mutual respect and shared decisionmaking.

Positive Classrooms sees positive classroom management as the result of four factors: how teachers regard their students (spiritual dimension), how they set up the classroom environment (physical dimension), how skilfully they teach content (instructional dimension), and how well they address student behaviour (managerial dimension).

10.2. Importance of Classroom Management

Classroom management is about "orchestrating" or coordinating entire sets or sequences of learning activities so that everyone, misbehaving or not, learns as easily and productively as possible. Educators sometimes therefore describe good classroom management as the creation of a positive learning environment, because a term calls attention to the totality of activities and people in a classroom, as well as to their goals and expectations about learning.

Managing the learning environment is both a major responsibility and an on-going concern for every teacher, even those with years of experience. There are several reasons. In the first place, a lot goes on in classrooms simultaneously, even when students seem to be doing only "one" task together. Twenty-five students may all be working on a sheet of math problems. But look more closely: several may be stuck on a particular problem, but each for different reasons. A few others have worked only the first problem or two and are now chatting quietly with each other instead of continuing. Still others have finished and are wondering what to do next. At any one moment each student needs something different-different information, different hints, different kinds of encouragement. The diversity increases even more if the teacher deliberately assigns multiple activities to different groups or individuals.

Another reason that managing the environment is challenging is because a teacher can never predict everything that will happen in a class. A well-planned lesson may fall flat on its face, or take less time than you expect, and you find yourself improvising to fill class time. On the other hand an unplanned moment may become a wonderful, sustained exchange among students; so you have to drop previous plans and "go with the flow" of their discussion. Interruptions happen continually: a quick drop-in visit from another teacher or from the principal, a call on the intercom from the office. An activity may turn out well, but also end up rather differently than you intended; you therefore have to decide how, if at all, to adjust the next day to allow for this surprise.

A third reason for the importance of management is that students form opinions and perceptions about your teaching that may coincide neither with your own nor with other students'. What seems to you like encouragement of a shy student may seem to the student herself like "forced participation." A more eager, outgoing classmate watching your special effort to encourage the shy student, however, may not see you as either encouraging or coercing, but as overlooking or ignoring other students who are already more willing to participate. The variety of perceptions can lead to surprises in students' responses to you—most often small ones, but occasionally more major.

At the broadest, society-wide level, management challenges teachers because public schooling is not voluntary, and students' presence in a classroom is therefore not a sign, in and of itself, that they wish to learn. Students' presence is instead just a sign that an opportunity exists for teachers to motivate students to learn. Many students, of course, do enjoy learning and being in school-but not all. Others do enjoy school, but primarily because teachers have worked hard to make classroom life pleasant and interesting. They become motivated because you have successfully created a positive learning environment and have sustained it through skilful management.

Fortunately it is possible to earn this sort of commitment from students, and this chapter describes some ways of doing so. We begin with some ways of preventing management problems in the first place by increasing students' focus on learning. The methods include the arrangement of classroom space, the establishment of procedures, routines and rules, and communicating the importance of learning both to students and to parents. After these prevention oriented discussions, we look at ways of refocusing students when and if their minds or actions do stray from the tasks at hand. As you probably know from your own experience as a student, bringing students back on task can happen in many ways, ways that vary widely in the energy and persistence required of the teacher. We try to indicate some of this diversity, but because of space limitations and because of the richness of classroom life, we cannot describe them all.

10.3. Tackling Management Problems

The easiest management problems to solve are ones that do not happen in the first place! You can help to prevent problems even before the first day of school by.

One of the best ways to prevent management problems is by pacing and structuring lessons or activities as smoothly and continuously as possible.

So far we have focused on preventing behaviours that are off-task, or inappropriate, or annoying. Our advice has all been proactive or forward-looking: plan the classroom space thoughtfully, create reasonable procedures and rules, pace lessons and activities appropriately, and communicate the importance of learning clearly. Although we consider these ideas to be important, it would be naïve to imply they are enough to prevent all behaviour problems.

There are two messages that are important. One is that management issues are important, complex, and deserve any teacher's serious attention. The other is that management strategies exist and can reduce, if not eliminate, management problems when and if they occur. We have explained what some of those strategies are, including some intended to prevent problems from happening and others intended to remedy problems if they do occur.

But there is a third message that this chapter cannot convey by itself: that good classroom management is not an end in itself, but a means for creating a climate where learning happens as fully as possible. During the stress of handling problem behaviours, there is sometimes a risk of losing sight of this idea. Quiet listening is never a goal in itself, for example; it is desirable only because it allows students to hear the teacher's instructions or classmates' spoken comments, or because it allows students to concentrate on their work or assignments better.

There may therefore actually be moments when quiet listening is not important to achieve, such as during a "free choice" time in an elementary classroom or during a period of group work in a middle school classroom. As teachers, we need to keep this perspective firmly in mind. Classroom management should serve students' learning, and not the other way around.

References

Allen, J.D. Classroom management: students' perspectives, goals, and strategies. *American Educational Research Journal,* 23, 437-459. 1986.

Bear, G.G., Cavalier, A., & Manning, M. *Developing self-discipline and preventing and correcting misbehaviour*. Boston: Allyn & Bacon.2005.

Jones, V. & Jones, L. *Comprehensive classroom management: Creating communities of support and solving problems, 6th edition.* Boston: Allyn & Bacon. 2006.

Good, T. & Brophy, J. *Looking in classrooms, 9th edition.* Boston: Allyn & Bacon. 2002.

Kauchak, D., and Eggen, P. *Introduction to teaching: Becoming a professional* (3rd ed.). Upper Saddle River, NJ: Pearson Education, Inc.2008.

11

Psychology of Online Learning

There is ongoing debate about whether it is the use of a particular delivery technology or the design of the instruction that improves learning. It has long been recognised that specialised delivery technologies can provide efficient and timely access to learning materials; however, technologies are merely vehicles that deliver instruction, but do not themselves influence student achievement. Meta-analysis studies on media research have shown that students gain significant learning benefits when learning from audio-visual or computer media, as opposed to conventional instruction; however, the same studies suggest that the reason for those benefits is not the medium of instruction, but the instructional strategies built into the learning materials. Similarly, learning is influenced more by the content and instructional strategy in the learning materials than by the type of technology used to deliver instruction.

To promote higher-order thinking on the Web, online learning must create challenging activities that enable learners to link new information to old, acquire meaningful knowledge, and use their metacognitive abilities; hence, it is the instructional strategy and not the technology that influences the quality of learning. The particular attributes of the computer are needed to bring real-life models and simulations to the learner; thus, the medium does influence learning. However, it is not the computer *per se* that makes students learn, but the design of the real-life models and simulations, and the students' interaction with those models and simulations. The computer is merely the vehicle that provides the processing capability and delivers the instruction to learners.

Online learning allows for flexibility of access, from anywhere and usually at anytime-essentially, it allows participants to collapse time and space — however, the learning materials must be designed properly to engage the learner and promote learning. Online learning has many promises, but it takes commitment and resources, and it must be done right. "Doing it right" means that online learning materials must be designed properly, with the learners and learning in focus, and that adequate support must be provided. Online learning should have high authenticity, high interactivity, and high collaboration.

Different terminologies have been used for online learning, a fact that makes it difficult to develop a generic definition. Terms that are commonly used include e-learning, Internet learning, distributed learning, networked learning, tele-learning, virtual learning, computer-assisted learning, Web-based learning, and distance learning. All of these terms imply that the learner is at a distance from the tutor or instructor, that the learner uses some form of technology to access the learning materials, that the learner uses technology to interact with the tutor or instructor and other learners, and that some form of support is provided to learners.

There are many definitions of online learning in the literature, definitions that reflect the diversity of practice and associated technologies. Online learning can be defined as educational material that is presented on a computer or as an innovative approach for delivering instruction to a remote audience, using the Web as the medium. However, online learning involves more than just the presentation and delivery of the materials using the Web: the learner and the learning process should be the focus of online learning.

11.1. Benefits of Online Learning

Increasingly, organisations are adopting online learning as the main delivery method to train employees. At the same time, educational institutions are moving toward the use of the Internet for delivery, both on campus and at a distance. However, for organisations and institutions to make this often expensive move, there must be a perception that using online learning provides major benefits. Some of the benefits for learners and instructors are outlined below.

For learners, online learning knows no time zones, and location and distance are not an issue. In asynchronous online learning, students can access the online materials at anytime, while synchronous online learning allows for real time interaction between students and the instructor. Learners can use the Internet to access up-to-date and relevant learning materials, and can communicate with experts in the field in which they are studying. Situated learning is facilitated, since learners can complete online courses while working on the job or in their own space, and can contextualise the learning.

For the instructor, tutoring can be done at anytime and from anywhere. Online materials can be updated, and learners are able to see the changes at once. When learners are able to access materials on the Internet, it is easier for instructors to direct them to appropriate information based on their needs. If designed properly, online learning systems can be used to determine learners' needs and current level of expertise, and to assign appropriate materials for learners to select from to achieve the desired learning outcomes.

11.2. Designing Online Learning Materials

The goal of any instructional system is to promote learning. Therefore, before any learning materials are developed, educators must, tacitly or explicitly, know the principles of learning and how students learn. This is especially true for online learning, where the instructor and the learner are separated. The development of effective online learning materials should be based on proven and sound learning theories. The delivery medium is not the determining factor in the quality of learning; rather, the design of the course determines the effectiveness of the learning.

There are many schools of thought on learning, and no one school is used exclusively to design online learning materials. As there is no single learning theory to follow, one can use a combination of theories to develop online learning materials. In addition, as research progresses, new theories are evolving that should be used in developing online materials. The online developer must know the different approaches to learning in order to select the most appropriate instructional strategies. Learning strategies should be selected to motivate learners, facilitate deep processing, build the whole person, cater for individual differences, promote meaningful learning, encourage interaction, provide feedback, facilitate contextual learning, and provide support during the learning process.

11.3. Schools of Learning

Early computer learning systems were designed based on a behaviourist approach to learning. The behaviourist school of thought, influenced by Thorndyke, Pavlov and Skinner, postulates that learning is a change in observable behaviour caused by external stimuli in the environment. Behaviourists claim that it is the observable behaviour that indicates whether or not the learner has learned something, and not what is going on in the learner's head. In response, some educators claimed that not all learning is observable and that there is more to learning than a change in behaviour. As a result, there was a shift away from behaviourist to cognitive learning theories.

Cognitive psychology claims that learning involves the use of memory, motivation, and thinking, and that reflection plays an important part in learning. They see learning as an internal process, and contend that the amount learned depends on the processing capacity of the learner, the amount of effort expended during the learning process, the depth of the processing, and the learner's existing knowledge structure.

Recently, there has been a move to constructivism. Constructivist theorists claim that learners interpret information and the world according to their personal reality, and that they learn by observation, processing, and interpretation, and then personalise the information into personal knowledge. Learners learn best when they can contextualise what they learn for immediate application and to acquire personal meaning.

When the behaviourist, cognitivist, and constructivist schools of thought are analysed closely, many overlaps in the ideas and principles become apparent. The design of online learning materials can include principles from all three. The three schools of thought can in fact be used as a taxonomy for learning. Behaviourists' strategies can be used to teach the "what", cognitive strategies can be used to teach the "how", and constructivist strategies can be used to teach the "why".

11.3.1. Behaviourist School of Learning

The behaviourist school sees the mind as a "blackbox," in the sense that a response to a stimulus can be observed quantitatively, totally ignoring the effect of thought processes occurring in the mind. The school, therefore, looks at overt behaviours that can be observed and measured as indicators of learning.

11.3.1.1. Implications for Online Learning

1. Learners should be told the explicit outcomes of the learning so that they can set expectations and can judge for themselves whether or not they have achieved the outcome of the online lesson.
2. Learners must be tested to determine whether or not they have achieved the learning outcome. Online testing or other forms of testing and assessment should be integrated into the learning sequence to check the learner's achievement level and to provide appropriate feedback.
3. Learning materials must be sequenced appropriately to promote learning. The sequencing could take the form of simple to complex, known to unknown, and knowledge to application.
4. Learners must be provided with feedback so that they can monitor how they are doing and take corrective action if required.

11.3.2. Cognitivist School of Learning

Cognitivists see learning as an internal process that involves memory, thinking, reflection, abstraction, motivation and meta-cognition. Cognitive psychology looks at learning from an information processing point of view, where the learner uses different types of memory during learning. Sensations are received through the senses into the sensory store before processing occurs. The information persists in the sensory store for less than one second; if it is not transferred to working memory immediately, it is lost.

Online instruction must use strategies to allow learners to attend to the learning materials so that they can be transferred from the senses to the sensory store and then to working memory. The amount of information transferred to working memory depends on the amount of attention that was paid to the incoming information, and on whether cognitive structures are in place to make sense of the information. So, designers must check to see if the appropriate existing cognitive structure is present to enable the learner to process the information. If the relevant cognitive structure is not present, pre-instructional strategies, such as advance organisers, should be included as part of the learning process.

The duration in working memory is approximately 20 seconds, and if information in working memory is not processed efficiently, it is not transferred to long-term memory for storage.

Online learning strategies must present the materials and use strategies to enable students to process the materials efficiently. Since working memory has limited capacity, information should be organised or chunked in pieces of appropriate size to facilitate processing. Because humans have limited short-term memory capacity, information should be grouped into meaningful sequences. Information should be chunked into five to nine (i.e., 7 ± 2) meaningful units to compensate for the limited capacity of short-term memory.

After the information is processed in working memory, it is stored in long-term memory. The amount transferred to long-term memory is determined by the quality and depth of processing in working memory. The deeper the processing, the more associations the acquired new information forms in memory. Information transferred from short-term memory to long-term memory is either assimilated or accommodated in long-term memory. During assimilation, the information is changed to fit into existing cognitive structures. Accommodation occurs when an existing cognitive structure is changed to incorporate the new information.

Cognitive psychology postulates that information is stored in long-term memory in the form of nodes which connect to form relationships; that is, in networks. Information maps that show the major concepts in a topic and the relationships between those concepts should be included in the online learning materials. Information map generation requires critical reflection and is a method for externalising the cognitive structure of learners. To facilitate deeper processing, learners should be encouraged to generate their own information maps.

summary activity after the lesson. In addition to facilitating deep processing, information maps can provide the "big picture" to learners, to help them comprehend the details of a lesson. Online learning can capitalise on the processing and visual capabilities of the computer to present information maps to learners or to ask learners to generate information maps using mapmaking software.

Other strategies that promote deep processing should be used to help transfer information to long-term storage. Strategies that require learners to apply, analyse, synthesise, and evaluate promote higher-level learning, which makes the transfer to long-term memory more effective. Online strategies to allow learners to apply the information in real life should also be included, to contextualise the learning and to facilitate deep processing.

11.3.2.4. Inclusion of Activities for Different Learning Styles

Online learning materials should include activities for the different learning styles, so that learners can select appropriate activities based on their preferred style. Concrete-experience learners prefer specific examples in which they can be involved, and they relate to peers and not to people in authority. They like group work and peer feedback, and they see the instructor as coach or helper. These learners prefer support methods that allow them to interact with peers and obtain coaching from the instructor. Reflective-observation learners like to observe carefully before taking any action. They prefer that all the information be available for learning, and see the instructor as the expert. They tend to avoid interaction with others. Abstract-conceptualisation learners like to work more with things and symbols and less with people. They like to work with theory and to conduct systematic analyses. Active-experimentation learners prefer to learn by doing practical projects and through group discussions. They prefer active learning methods and interacting with peers for feedback and information. They tend to establish their own criteria for evaluating situations.

In addition to activities, adequate supports should be provided for students with different learning styles. Ally and Fahy found that students with different learning styles have different preferences for support. For example, assimilators prefer high instructor presence, while accommodators prefer low instructor presence.

11.3.2.5. Presentation of Information

Information should be presented in different modes to accommodate individual differences in processing and to facilitate transfer to long-term memory. Where possible, textual, verbal, and visual information should be presented to encourage encoding. According to dual-coding theory, information received in different modes will be processed better than that presented in a single mode. Dual-coded information is processed in different parts of the brain, resulting in more encoding.

11.3.2.6. Importance of Motivation to Learn

Learners should be motivated to learn. It does not matter how effective the online materials are, if learners are not motivated, they will not learn. The issue is whether to use intrinsic motivation or extrinsic motivation. Designers of online learning materials should use intrinsic motivation strategies; however, extrinsic motivation should also be used since some learners are motivated by externally driven methods.

11.3.2.7. Individual Differences

The cognitive school recognises the importance of individual differences, and of including a variety of learning strategies in online instruction to accommodate those differences. Learning style refers to how a learner perceives, interacts with, and responds to the learning environment; it is a measure of individual differences. Different learning style instruments are used to determine students' learning styles. The Kolb Learning Style Inventory (LSI) looks at how learners perceive and process information, whereas the Myers-Briggs Type Indicator uses dichotomous scales to measure extroversion versus introversion, sensing versus intuition, thinking versus feeling, and judging versus perception.

11.3.2.8. Kolb Learning Style Inventory

Kolb suggests that two components make up our learning experience: perceiving and processing. Perceiving refers to the way learners sense and absorb the information around them, from concrete experience to reflective observation. Concrete experience relates to students' desire to learn things that have personal meaning in life. During reflective observation, students like to take the time to think about and reflect on the learning materials. The second component, processing, is related to how learners understand and process the information that is absorbed after perceiving. Processing ranges from abstract conceptualisation to active experimentation. Learners who have a preference for abstract conceptualisation like to learn facts and figures, and to research new information on different topics. Those who have a preference for active experimentation prefer to apply what they learn to real-life situations and to go beyond what was presented. They like to try things and learn from their experience. Online learning can cater for individual differences by determining the learner's preference and providing appropriate learning activities based on the learner's style.

Cognitive style refers to a learner's preferred way of processing information; that is, the person's typical mode of thinking, remembering, or problem solving. Thus, cognitive style is another individual difference indicator.

Cognitive style is considered to be a personality dimension that influences attitudes, values, and social interaction. One of the dimensions of cognitive style that has implications for online learning is the distinction between field-dependent and field-independent personalities. Field-independent personalities approach the environment in an analytical manner; for example, they are able to distinguish figures as discrete from their backgrounds. Field-dependent individuals experience events in a more global, less differentiated way. Field-dependent individuals have a greater social orientation compared with field-independent personalities. Field-independent individuals are likely to learn more effectively under conditions of intrinsic motivation, and are influenced less by social reinforcement.

11.3.2.9. Strategies for Online Learning

Attention: Capture the learners' attention at the start of the lesson and maintain it throughout the lesson. The online learning materials must include an activity at the start of the learning session to connect with the learners.

Relevance: Inform learners of the importance of the lesson and how taking the lesson could benefit them. Strategies could include describing how learners will benefit from taking the lesson, and how they can use what they learn in real-life situations. This strategy helps to contextualise the learning and make it more meaningful, thereby maintaining interest throughout the learning session.

Confidence: Use strategies such as designing for success and informing learners of the lesson expectations. Design for success by sequencing from simple to complex, or known to unknown, and use a competency-based approach where learners are given the opportunity to use different strategies to complete the lesson. Inform learners of the lesson outcome and provide ongoing encouragement to complete the lesson.

Satisfaction: Provide feedback on performance and allow learners to apply what they learn in real-life situations. Learners like to know how they are doing, and they like to contextualise what they are learning by applying the information in real life.

11.3.2.10. Metacognition

Encourage learners to use their metacognitive skills to help in the learning process. Metacognition is a learner's ability to be aware of his or her cognitive capabilities and use these capabilities to learn. When learning online, learners should be given the opportunity to reflect on what they are learning, collaborate with other learners, and check their progress. Self-check questions and exercises with feedback throughout a lesson are good strategies to allow learners to check how they are doing, so that they can use their metacognitive skills to adjust their learning approach if necessary.

11.3.2.11. Real-life Applications and Information

Online strategies that facilitate the transfer of learning should be used to encourage application in different and real-life situations. Simulation of the real situation, using real-life cases, should be part of the lesson. Also, learners should be given the opportunity to complete assignments and projects that use real-life applications and information. Transfer to real-life situations could assist the learners to develop personal meaning and contextualise the information.

Cognitive psychology suggests that learners receive and process information to be transferred into long-term memory for storage. The amount of information processed depends on the amount that is perceived, and the amount stored in long-term memory depends on the quality of the processing in working memory. Effective online lessons must use techniques to allow learners to sense and perceive the information, and must include strategies to facilitate high-level processing for transfer of information to long-term memory. After learners acquire the information, they create personal knowledge to make the materials meaningful.

11.3.3. Constructivist School of Learning

Constructivists see learners as being active rather than passive. Knowledge is not received from the outside or from someone else; rather, it is the individual learner's interpretation and processing of what is received through the senses that creates knowledge. The learner is the center of the learning, with the instructor playing an advising and facilitating role. Learners should be allowed to construct knowledge rather than being given knowledge through instruction.

A major emphasis of constructivists is situated learning, which sees learning as contextual. Learning activities that allow learners to contextualise the information should be used in online instruction. If the information has to be applied in many contexts, then learning strategies that promote multi-contextual learning should be used to make sure that learners can indeed apply the information broadly. Learning is moving away from one-way instruction to construction and discovery of knowledge.

Transformative learning involves reflectively transforming the beliefs, attitudes, opinions, and emotional reactions that constitute our meaning schemes or transforming our meaning perspectives. Learning involves five interacting contexts: the frame of reference or meaning perspective in which the learning is embedded, the conditions of communication, the line of action in which the learning occurs, the self-image of the learner, and the situation encountered during the learning process.

11.3.3.1. Implications for Online Learning

1. *Learning should be an active process.* Keeping learners active doing meaningful activities results in high-level processing,

which facilitates the creation of personalised meaning. Asking learners to apply the information in a practical situation is an active process, and facilitates personal interpretation and relevance.

2. *Learners should construct their own knowledge rather than accepting that given by the instructor*. Knowledge construction is facilitated by good interactive online instruction, since the students have to take the initiative to learn and to interact with other students and the instructor, and because the learning agenda is controlled by the student. In the online environment, students experience the information at first-hand, rather than receiving filtered information from an instructor whose style or background may differ from theirs. In a traditional lecture, the instructor contextualises and personalises the information to meet their own needs, which may not be appropriate for all learners. In online instruction, learners experience the information first-hand, which gives them the opportunity to contextualise and personalise the information themselves.
3. Collaborative and cooperative learning should be encouraged to facilitate constructivist learning. Working with other learners gives learners real-life experience of working in a group, and allows them to use their metacognitive skills. Learners will also be able to use the strengths of other learners, and to learn from others.
4. Learners should be given control of the learning process. There should be a form of guided discovery where learners are allowed to make decision on learning goals, but with some guidance from the instructor.
5. Learners should be given time and opportunity to reflect. When learning online, students need the time to reflect and internalise the information. Embedded questions on the content can be used throughout the lesson to encourage learners to reflect on and process the information in a relevant and meaningful manner; or learners can be asked to generate a learning journal during the learning process to encourage reflection and processing.
6. Learning should be made meaningful for learners. The learning materials should include examples that relate to students, so that

they can make sense of the information. Assignments and projects should allow learners to choose meaningful activities to help them apply and personalise the information.

7. Learning should be interactive to promote higher-level learning and social presence, and to help develop personal meaning. Learning is the development of new knowledge, skills, and attitudes as the learner interacts with information and the environment. Interaction is also critical to creating a sense of presence and a sense of community for online learners, and to promoting transformational learning. Learners receive the learning materials through the technology, process the information, and then personalise and contextualise the information. In the transformation process, learners interact with the content, with other learners, and with the instructors to test and confirm ideas and to apply what they learn. It is the design of the educational experience that includes the transactional nature of the relationship between instructor, learners, and content that is of significance to the learning experience.

Different kinds of interaction will promote learning at different levels. A framework of interaction in online learning that consists of three levels is proposed. Level one is learner-self interaction, which occurs within the learner to help the learner monitor and regulate their own learning. Level two interaction is learner-human and learner-non-human interactions, where the learner interacts with human and non-human resources. Level three is learner-instruction interaction, which consists of activities to achieve a learning outcome.

At the lowest level of interaction, there must be learner-interface interaction to allow the learner to access and sense the information. The interface is where learners use the senses to register the information in sensory storage. In online learning, the interface is with the computer to access the content and to interact with others. Once learners access the online materials, there must be learner-content interaction to process the information. Learners navigate through the content to access the components of the lesson, which could take the form of pre-learning, learning, and post-learning activities. These activities could access reusable learning objects from a repository, or they could use content that has been custom created by the designer or instructor.

Students should be given the ability to choose their own sequence of learning, or should be given one or more suggested sequences. As online learners interact with the content, they should be encouraged to apply, assess, analyse, synthesize, evaluate, and reflect on what they learn. It is during the learner-content interaction that learners process the information to transform it from short-term to long-term memory. The higher the level of processing, the more associations are made in long-term memory, which results in higher-level learning.

As learners work through the content, they will find the need for learner support, which could take the form of learner-to-learner, learner-to-instructor, instructor-to-learner, and learner-to-expert interactions. There should be strategies to promote learner-context interaction to allow learners to apply what they learn in real life so that they can contextualise the information. Learner-context interaction allows learners to develop personal knowledge and construct personal meaning from the information.

11.4. Learner Preparation

A variety of pre-learning activities can be used to prepare learners for the details of the lesson, and to get them connected and motivated to learn the online lesson. A rationale should be provided to inform learners of the importance of taking the online lesson and to show how it will benefit them. A concept map should be provided to establish the existing cognitive structure, to incorporate the details of the online lesson, and to activate learners' existing structures to help them learn the details in the lesson. The lesson concept map also gives learners the "big picture".

Learners should be informed of the learning outcomes of the lesson, so that they know what is expected of them and will be able to gauge when they have achieved the lesson outcomes. An advance organiser should be provided to establish a structure to organise the details in the online lesson or to bridge what learners already know and what they need to know.

Learners must be told the prerequisite requirements so that they can check whether they are ready for the lesson. Providing the prerequisites to learners also activates the required cognitive structure to help them learn the materials. A self-assessment should be provided at the start of the lesson to allow learners to check whether they already have the knowledge and skills taught in the online lesson. If learners think they have the knowledge and skills, they should be allowed to take the lesson final test. The self-assessment also helps learners to organise the lesson materials and to recognise the important materials in the lesson. Once learners are prepared for the details of the lesson, they can go on to complete the online learning activities to learn the details of the lesson.

11.4.1. Learner Activities

Online learners should be provided with a variety of learning activities to achieve the lesson learning outcome and to accommodate learners' individual needs. Examples of learning activities include reading textual materials, listening to audio materials, or viewing visuals or video materials. Learners can conduct research on the Internet and link to online information and libraries to acquire further information. The preparation of a learning journal will allow learners to reflect on what they learn and provide personal meaning to the information. Appropriate application exercises should be embedded throughout the online lesson to establish the relevance of the materials. Practice activities, with feedback, should be included to allow learners to monitor how they are performing, so that they can adjust their learning method if necessary. A summary should be provided, or learners should be required to generate a lesson summary, to promote higher-level processing and to bring closure to the lesson.

11.4.2. Learner Interaction

As learners complete the learning activities, they will be involved with a variety of interactions. Learners need to interact with the interface to access the online materials. The interface should not overload learners, and should make it as easy as possible for learners to sense the information for transfer to sensory store and then into short-term memory for processing. Learners must interact with the content to acquire the information needed to form the knowledge base. There should be interaction between the learner and other learners, between the learner and the instructor, and between the learner and experts to collaborate, participate in shared cognition, form social networks, and establish social presence. Learners should be able to interact within their context to personalise information and construct their own meaning.

11.4.3. Learner Transfer

Opportunities should be provided for learners to transfer what they learn to real-life applications, so that they can be creative and go beyond what was presented in the online lesson.

References

Chandler, P., & Sweller, J. Cognitive load theory and format of instruction. *Cognition and Instruction*, 8, 293-332. 1991.

Clark, G., Horan, J. J., Tompkins Bjorkman, A., Kovalski, T., & Hackett, G. Interactive career counseling on the Internet. *Journal of Career Assessment*, 8, 85-93. 2000.

Harasim, L., Hiltz, S. R., Teles, L., & Turoff, M. *Learning network.* Cambridge, MA: The MIT Press. 1995.

Kazdin, A. E. (Ed.) *Encyclopedia of psychology*. New York: Oxford University. 2002.

Khan, B. H. *Web-Based Instruction*, Englewood Cliffs, NJ: Educational Technology Publications. 1997.

Bibliography

Allen, J.D. Classroom management: students' perspectives, goals, and strategies. *American Educational Research Journal,* 23, 437-459. 1986.

Ames, Carole A., "Motivation: What Teachers Need to Know", Teachers College Record 91, 3, Spring 1990.

Ausubel, D. P., "A cognitive structure view of word and concept meaning", In R. C. Anderson & D. P. Ausubel (Eds.), *Readings in the psychology of cognition,* New York: Holt, Rinehart and Winston, Inc., 1965.

Bates, John, and Theodore Wachs, eds., *Temperament: Individual Differences at the Interface of Biology and Behaviour,* Washington, DC: American Psychological Association, 1994.

Bear, G.G., Cavalier, A., & Manning, M. *Developing self-discipline and preventing and correcting misbehaviour.* Boston: Allyn & Bacon.2005.

Binet A; Simon T *The development of intelligence in children.* Baltimore: Williams & Wilkins (original); Kessinger Publishing. 2007.

Black, P., & Wiliam, D. (1998). *Inside the black box: Raising standards through classroom assessment.* London: King's College London.

Blakeslee, Sandra; Hawkins, Jeff. *On intelligence.* New York: Times Books. 2004

Brophy, Jere, "On Motivating Students", *Occasional Paper* No. 101, East Lansing, Michigan: Institute for Research on Teaching, Michigan State University, October 1986.

Bourke, Sid, "How smaller is better: Some relationships between class size, teaching practices, and student achievement", *American Educational Research Journal,* 1986.

Bowlby, John, *Attachment and Loss,* Vol. 1:*Attachment,* New York:Basic, 1969..

Bunch, Wilton H. "Changing moral judgement in divinity students". *Journal of Moral Education* 34 (3): 363–370. 2005

Cameron, J., Pierce, W. D., Banko, K. M., & Gear, A., "Achievement-based rewards and intrinsic motivation: A test of cognitive mediators", *Journal of Educational Psychology,* 2005.

Chandler, P., & Sweller, J. Cognitive load theory and format of instruction. *Cognition and Instruction*, 8, 293-332. 1991.

Clark, G., Horan, J. J., Tompkins Bjorkman, A., Kovalski, T., & Hackett, G. Interactive career counseling on the Internet. *Journal of Career Assessment*, 8, 85-93. 2000.

Cohen, S. & Trostle, S.L., "Young children's preferences for school-related physical-environmental setting characteristics", *Environment and Behaviour,* 1990.

Cole, M, et al., *The Development of Children*, New York: Worth Publishers, 2005.

Crain, William C. *Theories of Development* (2Rev ed.). Prentice-Hall. 1985

Dunn, R. Krimsky, J.S., Murray, J.B. & Quinn, P.J., "Light up their lives: A research on the effects of lighting on children's achievement and behaviour", *The Reading Teacher*, 1985.

Evans, C. Exploring the relationship between cognitive style and teaching style. *Educational psychology, 24*(4), 509-530. 2004

Gardner, H. *Frames of mind: The theory of multiple intelligences.* New York: Basic Books. 1983

Geary, D. C., "Evolution and cognitive development", In R. Burgess & K. MacDonald (Eds.), *Evolutionary perspectives on human development* (pp. 99-133). Thousand Oaks, CA: Sage Publications, 2004.

Good, T. & Brophy, J. *Looking in classrooms, 9th edition.* Boston: Allyn & Bacon. 2002.

Harasim, L., Hiltz, S. R., Teles, L., & Turoff, M. *Learning network.* Cambridge, MA: The MIT Press. 1995.

Hedl, John J.; Glazer, H. and Chan, F. "Improving the Moral Reasoning of Allied Health Students". *Journal of Allied Health* 34 (2): 121–1. 2005.

Jones, V. & Jones, L. *Comprehensive classroom management: Creating communities of support and solving problems, 6th edition.* Boston: Allyn & Bacon. 2006.

Kauchak, D., and Eggen, P. *Introduction to teaching: Becoming a professional* (3rd ed.). Upper Saddle River, NJ: Pearson Education, Inc.2008.

Kazdin, A. E. (Ed.) *Encyclopedia of psychology*. New York: Oxford University. 2002.

Khan, B. H. *Web-Based Instruction*, Englewood Cliffs, NJ: Educational Technology Publications. 1997.

Kohlberg, Lawrence *From* Is *to* Ought*: How to Commit the Naturalistic Fallacy and Get Away with It in the Study of Moral Development.* New York: Academic Press. 1971.

Kohlberg, Lawrence, *Essays on Moral Development, Vol. I: The Philosophy of Moral Development*, Harper & Row, 1981.

Kuhn, D., *A developmental model of critical thinking*, Educational Researcher, 1999.

Lave, J. and Wenger, E. *Situated Learning, Legitimate peripheral participation*, Cambridge: University of Cambridge Press, 1991.

Loo, R. Kolb's learning styles and learning preferences: Is there a linkage? *Educational psychology,* 24(1), 99-108. 2004

Maehr, Martin L., and Carol Midgley, "Enhancing Student Motivation: A Schoolwide Approach", *Educational Psychologist*, 1991.

McShane, John, *Cognitive development: An information-processing approach*, Cambridge, MA: Basil Blackwell. 1991.

Mezirow, J., *Transformative Dimensions of Learning,* San Francisco: Jossey-Bass, 1991.

Neisser, U., *Cognitive psychology*, New York: Appleton-Century Crofts, 1967.

Newman, F. and Holzman, L., *"The End of Knowing", A new developmental way of learning*, London: Routledge, 1997.

Pritchard, A. *Ways of learning: Learning theories and learning styles in the classroom.* London, UK: David Fulton. 2005

Rest, James. *Development in Judging Moral Issues*. University of Minnesota Press. 1979.

Retallick, J., Cocklin, B. and Coombe, K., *Learning Communities in Education, London: Cassell,* 1998.

Seamus Hegarty and Mithu Alur, *Education and Children with Special Needs: From Segregation to Inclusion*, New Delhi, Sage, 2002.

Sheehy, Gail, *Passages: Predictable Crises of Adult Life*, New York: E. P. Dutton, 1976.

Stahl, S. Different strokes for different folks? In L. Abbeduto (Ed.), *Taking sides: Clashing on controversial issues in educational psychology (pp. 98-107)*. Guilford, CT: McGraw Hill. 2002.

Terman, L. *The measurement of intelligence*. Boston: Houghton Mifflin. 1916.

Vygotskii, L. S, *Educational psychology*, Trans. Robert Silverman. Boca Raton, FL: St. Lucie Press. 1997.

Wake, Warren K.; Gardner, Howard; Kornhaber, Mindy L. *Intelligence: Multiple perspectives*. Fort Worth, TX: Harcourt Brace College Publishers. 1996

Weiner, B., "Interpersonal and intrapersonal theories of motivation from an attributional perspective", *Educational Psychology Review,* 2000.

Wenger, E., "Communities of Practice", *Learning, meaning and identity,* Cambridge: Cambridge University Press, 1999.

Wertsch, J.V. (ed), *Culture, communication and cognition*, Cambridge: Cambridge University Press, 1985.

Witkin, H., Moore, C., Goodenough, D., & Cox, R. Field-dependent and field-independent cognitive styles and their educational implications. *Review of Educational Research, 47,* 1-64. 1977.

Woolfolk, A. E., Winne, P. H., & Perry, N. E., *Educational Psychology,* Toronto, Canada: Pearson, 2006.

Zhang, L. & Sternberg, R.. *The nature of intellectual styles.* Mahwah, NJ: Erlbaum. 2006.

Index